# THE EASTER OFFENSIVE

## VIETNAM, 1972

### COL. G.H. TURLEY, USMCR (RET.)

**WARNER BOOKS**

A Warner Communications Company

WARNER BOOKS EDITION

This Warner Books Edition is published by arrangement with the author.

Cover photo by Magnum Photos, Inc.

Warner Books, Inc.
666 Fifth Avenue
New York, N.Y. 10103

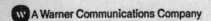 A Warner Communications Company

Printed in the United States of America

First Warner Books Printing: October, 1989

10  9  8  7  6  5  4  3  2  1

# CONTENTS

# FOREWORD

Many Americans forget that the South Vietnamese repelled two massive Communist offensives before the antiwar movement in this country prevailed on the Congress to cut off the funds which would have made it possible for them to defend themselves.

The first offensive, which occurred during the Tet holiday of 1968, has become known as the watershed event of the war from the American perspective, since public support fell steadily from that point forward. Nonetheless, Tet 1968 was a clear military victory. American and South Vietnamese forces, at a cost of 4,000 and 5,000 lives respectively, killed 58,000 enemy soldiers, turned back the communists at every point, and effectively destroyed the South Vietnamese communist military (NLF). In Vietnamese terms Tet 1968 was a political victory as well. Contrary to the predictions of General Giap and others, the South Vietnamese people declined to support the communists who temporarily gained control of their towns and villages.

The second major offensive occurred four years later, during Easter, 1972. The North Vietnamese launched a full-scale invasion across the DMZ and elsewhere, replete with tanks and heavy artillery. In a series of bloody battles more reminiscent of Passchendaele in World War I, or the Battle of the Bulge in World War II than any previous fights in Vietnam, the South Vietnamese successfully stopped this assault.

But by then the American people had grown weary of the

war, and the South Vietnamese were fighting for the most part alone. For both of those reasons, most Americans have little appreciation for the true ferocity of the Easter Invasion, or for the indication it gave us of the South Vietnamese willingness to fight and die for their independence. *The Easter Offensive: Vietnam, 1972* is an important book because it helps resolve those inadequacies in our understanding, and therefore makes an essential contribution to the history of the Vietnam War.

There are two stories in this book, both told with painstaking honesty by a man known throughout the U.S. Marine Corps for his integrity and his military expertise. The first is a chronology of the offensive itself, from the perspective of one who played a crucial, and even spectacular role in stopping the invasion. The other is the author's own story.

Days after Gerald Turley, then a Lieutenant Colonel, reported aboard for a tour as an advisor to the Vietnamese Marine Corps, he travelled from Saigon to the DMZ to visit the units and to meet their leaders. Through a series of events which he most charitably describes as happenstance, Gerald Turley inherited responsibility for coordinating the overall defense of northern Military Region One, the region hit hardest by North Vietnamese tank attacks, even though he had no official military responsibilities in the area at all. Ordered by a U.S. Army general to take charge of all military actions in I Corps, Lieutenant Colonel Turley was thrust into a leadership role perhaps unprecedented in the history of U.S. military operations. While attempting to halt a massive enemy invasion, Turley ended up having also to fight the U.S. military command in Saigon, 350 miles away, which on the one hand refused to believe a major attack was in progress, and on the other refused to believe anyone named Lieutenant Colonel Gerald Turley possessed the authority to coordinate major defensive moves and offshore combined arms support. The reader, upon finishing this book, will agree that it was a lucky thing for those South Vietnamese and Americans involved that Gerald Turley happened on the scene when he did.

But this is a book devoid of the narcissism and histrionics one so often finds in war memoirs. In the best tradition of the U.S. Marine Corps, Gerald Turley was an officer who looked after his men, and this book carefully tells their story also. The U.S. advisors to the Vietnamese Marine Corps, and the U.S. Army field advisors, known as COVANS (friends) by their counterparts, performed heroically under conditions seldom faced by Americans in that war. In five historic days, often under a cloud cover that prevented any sort of American air support, combat bases were overrun and abandoned, Vietnamese units ceased to exist, the largest bridge in the northern part of South Vietnam was destroyed against higher orders in order to halt a tank assault, B-52s were diverted seconds before they erroneously bombed the besieged U.S. advisors. And, most importantly, despite the chaos the South Vietnamese not only stopped the attack, but were able to counterattack a short time later.

One notes a direct relationship between the strength of leadership in the American advisors and the willingness of the South Vietnamese to fight and die. This was, in a way, the Vietnam war in microcosm: the advisors were symbols of our national willingness to stay with the South. Where there was trust and leadership, the South Vietnamese did very well. It is a tribute to Gerald Turley and his fellow COVANS that not one U.S. Marine advisor abandoned his unit. And, not coincidentally, not one major Vietnamese Marine Corps unit surrendered.

For those who might not believe that individuals make the difference in war, this book will surely change their minds.

James H. Webb, Jr.
Author of *Fields of Fire,*
*Sense of Honor,* and
*A Country Such as This*

# ACKNOWLEDGMENTS

In writing this book I have been fortunate to receive advice and assistance from many different people. They all contributed their most precious possession—their time. My wife, Bunny, has been a constant companion and tireless assistant without whose reassurances, particularly on those days or nights when the pen ran dry and the mind went blank, the full story might never have been told.

I have received special encouragements from two eminently known editors, namely Peter Braestrup (editor of the *Wilson Quarterly*, Woodrow Wilson International Center for Scholars at the Smithsonian Institution), who has been my principal mentor, (Mr. Braestrup was the first to hear this unusual story and publish on the destruction of the Dong Ha Bridge); and Col. John Greenwood (editor of the *Marine Corps Gazette*). The patience and craftsmanship of these individuals will always be appreciated. Col. H. Roger McPike, USMCR, a long-time friend and counselor, also played a key role as he gave so freely of his time, exceptional insights and organizational skills.

Those who were kind enough to "stay the course" and comment upon the various chapters included Col. James R. Davis, USMC, and John Ripley, USMC, Lt. Cols. William Wischmeyer and W. Richard Higgins, USMC.

The Historical Center of the U.S. Marine Corps provided unlimited access to its volumes and rare materials on the Vietnam War, while Maj. Edward F. Wells, USMC, provided resources and his scholarly counsel over a two-year period involved in the gestation of this story.

Four secretaries combined their word processing skills to achieve the final draft: Mrs. Carlota Castillo, Marcia Wing, Ms. Karen Wagner and Theresa Orlando, while the illustrations are by Les L. Amen.

Finally, a debt of gratitude most certainly is owed to the 600 U.S. Marines and U.S. Navy medical personnel (the COVANs) who had served earlier advisory tours with the Vietnamese Marines. While no fighting force suddenly solidifies as a viable military organization, the superb combat performance of the Vietnamese Marine Corps during the Easter invasion of 1972 did not just happen overnight. Rather, as a new Corps of Marines, it had been nurtured and matured in more than eighteen years of nearly endless combat, evolving over this period of time into one of the two elite South Vietnamese armed forces, the other being the ARVN airborne units.

The early labors of so many COVANs who had served in the earlier years was of immeasurable assistance when the Marine division deployed into Military Region One (MR-1) to contest and defeat the North Vietnamese invaders. Those of us who served as COVANs in the Marine advisory unit during the Easter Offensive itself probably survived because of the achievements of our predecessors in instilling in their counterparts the concepts of esprit de corps, duty, country and resolve to fight on against all odds.

To them all I say "Thank you."

# PROLOGUE

But for an accident in time and place, someone else would have written this story. It happened to be my fate to be in the northernmost provinces of South Vietnam when the North Vietnamese Army launched its 1972 Easter Offensive; an invasion designed to reunite the Viet peoples and to test President Nixon's Vietnamization program.

Fate also placed other Americans under the enemy's artillery and armored attacks. Most wanted to leave the rapidly deteriorating battle scene. Several did, abandoning their South Vietnamese counterparts in reckless haste. A few, intimately aware of the imminent dangers, stayed to meet the challenge—to do their duty.

In telling this unusual story I have tried not to hurt anyone. I have changed the names of several individuals to protect them and their families' privacy. Where I disagreed with certain individuals, my dissension is confined to time and place. These disputes did not flow into personal hard feelings, at least not from my standpoint.

In recording these events I have relied upon my memory, buttressed by several hundred letters and documents. Many of the documents have never been referenced before. The materials have been acquired from a wide variety of sources: operational journals, official records, unit histories and newspapers. The primal historical documentation has come from oral history interviews and personal narratives of the U.S. Army, Air

Force, and Marine Corps personnel who were entrapped by the invading North Vietnamese Army.

Where quotations are included, they have been taken literally from the source. References to South Vietnamese general officers and their Joint General Staff (JGS), which present command and leadership difficulties, were obtained from an assortment of monographs written by a select group of these officers after the final collapse of their country in 1975. These Indo-China monographs have been published by the U.S. Army's Center of Military History.

There is a saying about military men to the effect that during a service career, "one must prepare himself for a moment that may never come; to thrust himself into the uncharted arena of battle should the need arise." Most military men faithfully prepare for this eventuality. However, neither time nor circumstances may arise to create for them that special period of challenge, yet their careers are deemed successful because they were prepared for their potential challenge.

Every peacetime soldier with any imagination at all surely wonders if, when the shells and bullets become real, he will be found wanting. Of a thousand officers who stand underway watches on the bridge of Navy ships, perhaps only one will experience a true test of professional seamanship or personal resolve. So it is with aviators and submariners as their uncounted operational sorties are skillfully planned and executed. They have fulfilled their responsibilities, but fate never presented that special challenge.

This is the story of a group of young Americans who were brought together at an unusual time and under unusual circumstances. Strangers to each other, as members of the U.S. Army, Navy, Air Force and Marine Corps, they welded together as a team to assist the South Vietnamese forces in halting a massive enemy invasion.

For many, unknowingly, their moment of personal challenge was at hand. This would be the time and place where circumstances would reveal the true mettle of their worth. As history recorded, some Americans quickly left the battle areas. A few stuck to their jobs and, though exposed to the gravest of combat conditions, performed admirably. Individually challenged, the circumstances brought out the extraordinary qualities which separate them from ordinary people. They became heroes in a war often described as one war without heroes. Their individual valor should not go unrecorded.

As a senior officer it was my privilege, indeed fate, to be on the scene to observe and record the acts of heroism of these soldiers, airmen, and marines who saw their duty and did it as each "climbed his mountain." They rose to the heights many aspire to climb, but only a few ever experience the view.

This is our story . . .

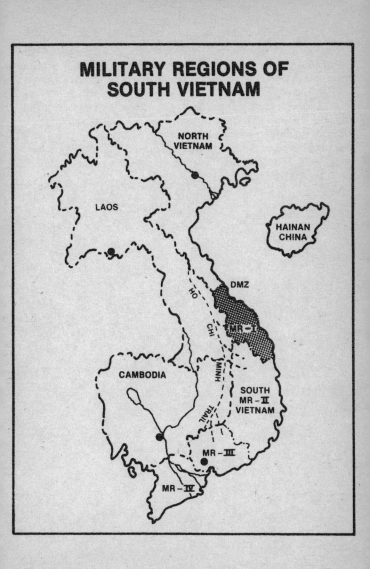

# MILITARY REGIONS OF SOUTH VIETNAM

NORTH VIETNAM

LAOS

HAINAN CHINA

DMZ

HO CHI MINH TRAIL

MR-I

CAMBODIA

SOUTH VIETNAM

MR-II

MR-III

MR-IV

# CHAPTER ONE

# COVANS: WHY WE STAYED

The passenger terminal was near to overflowing with servicemen. Marines, sailors and airmen were spilling out of every available lounge chair. Seabags, carry-ons and packages wrapped in oriental paper had reduced the aisles to narrow patches of space.

A few men in mixed uniforms had gathered near the glass doors leading to the parked aircraft. Other groups held strategic positions near the entrance to the snack bar and at the concession stand. A fleeting camaraderie was imposed by small talk, which centered on getting home, family, "my car" and "my girl."

Since the beginning of the Vietnam War, Okinawa had become one of the busiest personnel processing centers in the Far East.

The sprawling Kadena Air Force Base had become the staging center for all U.S. military personnel traveling to or from Asia. Soldiers and sailors traded magazines, paperbacks and *Stars and Stripes*. One young Marine, standing close by, folded his newspaper and offered it to me. "Here, Colonel, no sense in buying one, I'm finished," he said. I nodded my thanks. He told me he was rotating home and then on to a basic school assignment at Quantico. He seemed surprised to learn that I was not flying to the States, but rather south to Vietnam.

The headline of the *Stars and Stripes* was the announcement that President Nixon was accelerating the scheduled withdrawal of U.S. troops from South Vietnam beyond the pace that had withdrawn over 400,000 men since his Vietnamization program had begun. With less than 150,000 U.S. servicemen still serving in Nam, the article stated that the last U.S. Army infantry brigade would stand down. By 1 April 1972, only 6,000 ground combat troops would still be in-country.

When the air terminal's scratchy paging system echoed that Military Airlift Flight 814 to Travis Air Force Base in California would begin boarding in thirty minutes, the terminal erupted into a roar. The second flight announcement that Flight 79B would depart for Saigon, Vietnam, in twenty minutes brought an even louder series of cheers, and a hundred voices yelling "No Nam, no Nam, no V.C., no more, hell no." Out of the excited shouts a black Marine could be heard telling his buddies, "Hey man, you've got to be kidding. Ain't nobody going back there. They've got to be crazy."

When Flight 79B was announced ready for boarding only two of us moved toward the glass doors. Curious eyes turned to watch as we showed our boarding passes and moved toward the waiting 737 commercial jet. As the terminal doors closed, they shut off the laughing chants of "You'll be sorry." I wondered if they were right.

I felt I fully understood the outburst of voices scoffing our flight to South Vietnam. Most of the men in the passenger terminal wore combat ribbons from Vietnam. Some had obviously served several tours in the war zone, but like millions of other Americans back home, didn't really understand what the second Indo-China war was all about. I'm not sure I knew either, although here I was returning for another year.

All I really knew was that for almost a decade a violent insurgent war had been brought into millions of homes by the electronic media. Initially, the conflict was a distant Asian war that had no meaning to Americans. Hundreds of battles, helicopter flights, skirmishes and events were televised and reported during the six years of heavy U.S. involvement. Each new battle or push melted into the next in a seemingly pointless and confusing war against the black pajama-clad Viet Cong and their North Vietnamese Army allies.

Although there were frequent optimistic predictions by our national leaders declaring that the corner had been turned, or there was a light at the end of the tunnel, these predictions were never realized and the war of petty skirmishes continued until U.S. casualties surpassed 57,000 killed and four times that number maimed or wounded.

After we strapped in, the aircraft moved toward the main runway. I remember thinking if the pilot took off and flew due west, in two hours we would be over China. As programmed, the aircraft banked south shortly after take-off. Out of the port-side windows we could see the city of Naha and the ships in the harbor. A light wind put a fine spray on the rolling green waves below and rain clouds were holding over the southern tip of the island. It was a beautiful day over an island which had been almost completely rebuilt since World War II.

The war was over, while here I was headed back to Vietnam. The four-hour flight passed slowly. I glanced through a variety of magazines, but my mind was on the war and the Vietnamese Marine Corps. Before departing the States I had sought out fellow Marine officers who had completed tours of advisory duty. Almost to the man they counseled me to "be patient, forget your American ways and try to think like an Asian." Maj. George Rivers' summation of the philosophical difference between westerners and Asians proved to be accurate.

To understand the Oriental philosophy a person must first appreciate the contrast between the concepts of time. The western world thinks of time in the short term (e.g., time is money), and when applied to the military, its leadership favors the concept of "lightning wars and speedy victories." In contrast, the Orientals believe they have all the time in the world to achieve their goals. Perseverance is the key to success and only the final goal is meaningful.

As an example, George's article reminded me that General Vo Nguyen Giap had written:

The War of Liberation is a protracted war and a hard war in which we must rely upon ourselves—for we are strong politically but weak materially while the enemy is weak politically but stronger materially.[1]

This approach is almost incomprehensible to Western political, as well as military leaders, who almost daily need to deliver some evidence of tangible results to a political constituency, the media or their superiors.

During the struggle to overrun South Vietnam, the communists had repeatedly given up space to gain time. Their fundamental strategic approach was to conduct a protracted war. Despite the massive efforts of President Nixon's administration and Secretary of State Dr. Henry Kissinger, the North Vietnamese never wavered from their ultimate goal to reunify Vietnam.[2]

As a warrior returning to the battlefields it was difficult to visualize what my contribution would be to the resolution of the overall conflict. It had all the aspects of a completely different tour from my previous Vietnamese experiences in an infantry regiment. The South Vietnamese government was actively pursuing a national strategy of pacification and development to coincide with President Nixon's Vietnamization program, so I fully expected endless hours of planning reconstruction projects and no combat assignments.

At Tan Son Nhut Airport two Marine officers, Maj. Stan Pratt and Capt. Bill Wischmeyer, met us. They were well acquainted with the in-processing routine and all the key reception personnel, which resulted in my being processed into Vietnam in record time. Major Pratt was the epitome of Marine efficiency.

During the jeep ride through Saigon I learned that I would be replacing Lt. Col. Bill Swigert and, until he rotated home, would share his quarters, a second-floor suite of rooms in the Brinks Hotel, just off Tu Do Street near the presidential palace. Dropping my luggage in the room, we drove four blocks to the Bo Tu Linh Compound, headquarters of the Vietnamese Marine Corps. The American advisors' building was on the right.

Waiting to greet me was Bill Swigert and Lt. Col. Jim Poland. Jim, tall and slender, never seemed to age. We had been acquainted for ten years and had been comrades in arms together on an earlier combat tour in Vietnam. When I was wounded in July 1967, Jim, then a major, relieved me as operations officer for the 3d Battalion, 7th Marines. He was now the G-3 operations and training advisor.

Bill Swigert was new to me. He was eager to serve as my guide and led me through the eight small offices of the advisory headquarters introducing me to the remaining members of the unit. After we had visited all the staff sections we returned to his office where he began his overview briefing on the Marine Advisory Unit (MAU). The strength of MAU was fifty-eight officers and nine enlisted Marines, in addition to one U.S. Navy doctor and two corpsmen. These latter three medical specialists remained very active in the treatment of Vietnamese combat casualties. Bill looked up from his notes to say, "The Vietnamese Marines have their own hospital at Tu Duc, ten miles northeast of Saigon. We'll visit the VNMC's basic training camp and their hospital later this week."

"Gerry, your G-3 operations and intelligence briefings will begin this afternoon. There has not been much enemy activity so these will go quickly. Capts. Frank Izenour and Tom O'Toole will be briefing you. They're both convinced the North Vietnamese are about to launch a major offensive. It's a doubtful prophecy, but you should be prepared for their ominous predictions.

"Our major advisory efforts are to develop a sound logistical posture for the VNMC. Majs. Stan Pratt and Jeff Root will acquaint you with the military assistance funding programs. They are now in the process of developing next year's assistance budget which you'll have to complete after I've rotated home. There are several other projects I want to brief you on."

He then asked, "Gerry, have you ever heard of the Senior Advisor's Journal?"

I nodded. "I understand it's a logbook recording the major events of the Vietnamese Marine Corps."

"It's far more than that. It's like a ship captain's log in which each senior U.S. Marine advisor has meticulously recorded the history of the VNMC and our own advisory efforts since 1954. It was created by the first U.S. Marine advisor, Lt. Col. Vic

Croizat, and has been passed along to his thirteen successors.

"Colonel Dorsey has the Senior Advisor's Journal in his office. You'll see it tomorrow when you meet with him."

As I left, Bill handed me an informational packet to review, which included brief histories of the Vietnamese Marine Corps, the U.S. Marine advisory effort and a lengthy Order on Standing Operating Procedures (SOPs) of the Marine Advisory Unit. This obviously was to be my evening's reading in preparation for tomorrow's 0900 meeting with Colonel Dorsey.

I later had a further opportunity to learn more about the advisory unit's past before meeting with Colonel Dorsey. After the evening meal, I walked back to the MAU headquarters where the office administrators were still busily at work. They directed me to the large file room where over fifteen years of records and correspondence were stored and left me to myself. In the file drawers rows of manila folders marked off the personal history of a relationship that had begun almost as soon as the guns fell silent at Dien Bien Phu; one that had been cemented by what the poet, Robert Graves, once called "the wet bond of blood." American Marines had stood alongside their South Vietnamese counterparts in every battle of the war, sharing the same food, the same dangers and the same discomforts. The long years had created a unique bond between the Marines of the two countries. In more than two decades of fighting, no U.S. Marine advisor had ever left his Vietnamese counterpart, no matter how critical the battle.

Their name for us was COVAN. It was a title with great meaning. Although the U.S. Army, Navy and Air Force would eventually have thousands of advisors, only 600 Marines had earned this title since 1954.

I searched the files in an attempt to understand the depth and flow of this special bond. I spent a great part of that first night reading of the Vietnamese Marines and their advisors' exploits, beginning from the creation of this bond by Lt. Col. Victor Croizat in 1954. He was the first advisor, and, by the force of his personality and foresight, had helped advance the establishment of a Vietnamese Marine Corps through the direct working relationships he had developed with then Premier Diem. Croizat spoke fluent French and, after attending the French War College in 1949, had maintained a close and long association with many French officers.

When the French were beaten by the Viet Minh communists in 1954, Vic Croizat was sent to Haiphong to assist Vietnamese refugees in their "passage to freedom." Over 800,000 had chosen to relocate rather than live under a communist government. Croizat was designated to head the U.S. military advisory groups' detachment that was responsible for coordinating the evacuation conducted by the French and U.S. navies from North Vietnam.

While Colonel Croizat was in the North, Premier Diem had acted on a long-standing legislative proposal to create a small Vietnamese Marine Corps. The few French officers still in Saigon strongly endorsed the idea, but the proposal remained dormant until Croizat's return to Saigon in February 1955.

Croizat's untiring efforts at first to rescue, and then resettle the war-ravaged refugees had made him nearly a national hero in South Vietnam. He was instrumental in the construction of refugee reception centers in the North and the selection and development of resettlement areas in South Vietnam.

On returning to Saigon, Croizat was designated as the Senior U.S. Advisor to the newly created Vietnamese Marine Corps. He quickly discovered it was a hodgepodge of dissimilar units with no real identity. This new Corps of Marines, 1,150 strong, was dispersed from Hue to the Mekong Delta area. It was still dependent upon the French Expeditionary Force for logistical support and a French captain still commanded the 1st Battalion of the new unit.

Thus, the Vietnamese had a Corps of Marines in name only. However, from Croizat's view it was a beginning; and his skilled and articulate planning thereafter did much to solidify and then nurture its progressive development into a creditable fighting force.

The VNMC continued to expand. More U.S. Marines arrived to assist in building this newest Corps. The U.S. Marine advisory efforts permeated every facet of VNMC training, expansion of forces, logistic planning and field operations.

This, then, was the background I brought with me to my meeting the following morning.

Meeting with Colonel Dorsey was indeed a memorable experience. In 1966 he served as the battalion commander of 3d Battalion, 3d Marine Regiment and acquired high credentials as a combat leader and also as a fine staff officer. He spoke softly and slowly, welcoming me to the MAU and acquainting me with my forthcoming duties.

"COVAN," said Colonel Dorsey, "means trusted advisor. The word COVAN has become as meaningful to every U.S. Marine advisor as 'Semper Fidelis.' "

He searched for a cigarette and lit up. "As the assistant senior advisor, your Vietnamese counterparts are the assistant commandant and the chief of staff. Both colonels, Bui Thee Lan and Le Dinh Que speak excellent English. Both have attended our officer's schools in Quantico. You'll find them easy to work with.

"Colonel Swigert keeps a folder of dossiers on the more senior Vietnamese officers. Please review it before I introduce you to your counterparts. Bill will also brief you on the various building projects on which we are jointly working. During this next week make it a point to visit every construction project where we are providing U.S. assistance funding."

On a tablet I began to copy down my new assignments. He continued, "Later this month I want you to fly up to the northern Provinces and visit our battalion advisors deployed with Vietnamese Marine Brigades 147 and 258. Both brigades are attached to the 3d ARVN Division which is positioned along the southern edge of the Demilitarized Zone."

Moving his eyes down his checklist, the colonel looked up to say, "I've written Maj. Jim Joy. He's our senior brigade advisor to Brigade 147. He will make arrangements for you to meet all the advisors and also set up courtesy calls with the U.S. Army Advisory Team 155 supporting the 3d ARVN Division.

"As you move through the two Marine brigades take a good look at their communications and motor transport equipment. They are saying it's mostly inoperative and should be replaced. As you get acquainted with our Material Assistance Programs you'll see these two commodities represent about 70 percent of the VNMC's FY-73 budget."

A chain smoker, Colonel Dorsey reached for another cigarette, so I waited silently as he lit up and then looked out the window overlooking the Bo Tu Linh compound.

"Our advisory mission is nearing completion," he said. "The Vietnamese Marine Corps has evolved from a few naval commando and French riverine force units to one of the truly elite military organizations in the Republic of Vietnam. President Nixon's Vietnamization program is working; the Vietnam War is fast drawing to a close. It's just a matter of time before the word COVAN will become a footnote in the annals of U.S. Marine Corps history.

"Turley," he went on, "you and I will probably close up this advisory headquarters. Our real task now is to make the VNMC as logistically ready as money will allow. They've been in combat for almost twenty years. You, I and the other advisors have had only two or three years of combat experience. These people have been in heavy combat over fifteen years. There is little we can teach them except, perhaps, how to better utilize their supporting arms. Our job, which Vic Croizat began, is almost finished. The VNMC can now go it alone on any battlefield."

As Dorsey talked, it became clear that as advisors our tasks would be much easier and more clearly defined than when Lieutenant Colonel Croizat became the first U.S. Marine advisor.

Colonel Dorsey continued, "Historically, the Vietnamese Marine Corps has performed the broad mission of 'fire brigade' in South Vietnam. It is routinely committed on short notice by their Joint General Staff (JGS) to independent or joint ground operations. The VNMC has proven its capability by executing major troop movements by land, sea and air. As part of the Republic of Vietnam's general reserve, these Marines have been repeatedly employed from the 17th Parallel in the north to the offshore islands of the extreme south. Their officers and noncommissioned officers have become a band of brothers with an intense loyalty to each other. They exhibit great pride in their corps. Their missions have covered every phase of conventional combined armed warfare, civic action, search and clear, reaction to contact, helicopter assaults, riverine and static defense of a tactical area.

"They're good, Gerry. They've been in some hellish fights

and never buckled. Their front lines have been bent by the Viet Cong but never, never broken."

The colonel summarized several significant operations to emphasize his point. Included was the operation in July 1967. The VNMC's 3d and 4th battalions were combined with the U.S. 9th Infantry Division in Operation Coronado II in the Mekong Delta. These two battalions landed directly on top of a Viet Cong battalion base camp. Eight heavy machine guns peppered the landing zone, forcing the Marines to land 600 meters away and then fight their way back. Fire from the VC position was so heavy that resupply helicopter crewmen had to push ammunition out through their doors while in flight rather than land and unload.

During the course of this intense battle, Lt. Gen. Fred Weyand, the U.S. field commander, flew into the battle area to talk with the Vietnamese Marine commanders. Weyand suggested that the Marines pull back because their being in such tight contact prohibited the use of tactical air support. Both battalion commanders refused on the grounds that breaking contact would allow the Viet Cong to get away. Instead, the Marines charged the enemy base camp, killing 145 Viet Cong.

The long ashes on Colonel Dorsey's cigarette bent, hung precariously, then fell on his desk top. He brushed them away, stood up, and reached for a large, leather-covered book that was prominently displayed behind his desk. It was the size of a photograph album and about three inches thick. He picked it up carefully, placing it on the center of his desk.

"This is the senior Marine advisor's journal. In this journal is the chronological history of the world's newest Marine Corps. As the assistant senior advisor you must learn from this before you meet your primary counterpart, the chief of staff, Colonel Que. You should be fully acquainted with the progressive growth of the Vietnamese Marine Corps from a single landing battalion to their division-sized force of today; as their corps has expanded, so has our advisory unit.

It was obvious that the colonel thoroughly believed in the responsibility and challenge of the assignment. He continued, "You have an important role to play here. I believe the best way I can better acquaint you with the VNMC and the Marine

Advisory Unit is to share with you some of the key milestones entered in this journal." He folded back its leather cover, handling it like a born-again Christian opening his Bible.

Colonel Dorsey began reading aloud a chronicle of shared historical events that cemented our two Corps of Marines. I listened as he recharted the turbulent growth of the Vietnamese Marine Corps, his eyes never lifting from the Journal.

He read ". . . In June 1956 Lieutenant Colonel Croizat ended his Asian assignment when replaced by Lt. Col. William Wilkes as Senior Advisor. Colonel Wilkes' second entry reflects that Colonel Croizat had, in retrospect, assumed the stature of a founder, setting a standard of professionalism that future U.S. Marine advisors would aspire to achieve."

Colonel Dorsey had become so familiar with the writing style of each Senior Advisor that he would stop at a particular Journal entry, where he sometimes would silently read to himself, and then move on. Often he would say, "Here is an important entry," and then read aloud the exact entry.

July 1956—(Lieutenant Colonel Wilkes) One noncommissioned officer billet was upgraded to an officer position. This change coincides with the expansion of the VNMC to a second landing battalion and will enable a U.S. Marine Corps officer to be available to advise the individual battalions on a permanent basis.

Colonel Dorsey looked up at me and added, "U.S. Marines are still assigned and operating with every VNMC infantry and artillery battalion. President Nixon's Vietnamization program will eventually reduce this advisory relationship. We may have to eventually eliminate all battalion advisory billets."

He read from further entries:

September 1958—Vietnamese Marine officers began attending basic and junior courses at Marine Corps Schools, Quantico, Virginia. Vietnamese Marine noncommissioned officers began drill instruction training at the Recruit Depot, San Diego, California. U.S. advisors began teaching U.S. Marine Corps marksmanship training to Vietnamese troops.

* * *

May 1959—A third landing battalion is formed. The VNMC now number 2,276 officers and men. The Marine Advisory Unit expands its officer billets to support the new infantry battalion.

\* \* \*

June 1, 1959—The JGS directs the Vietnamese Marine Corps and ARVN airborne brigade to assume the mission of the general reserve force for the entire Republic of Vietnam Armed Forces (RVNAF). The VNMC becomes a separate service directly responsible to the JGS for any assigned ground warfare mission.

\* \* \*

August 1959—Lt. Col. Frank R. Wilkerson, Jr., while serving as the third senior Marine advisor, proposed to the VNMC that they adopt an official emblem and a distinctive uniform. A board

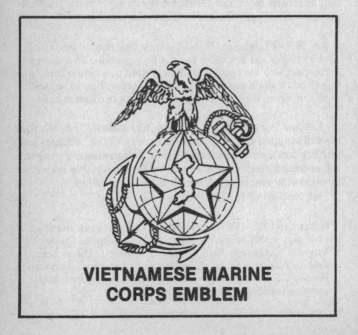

**VIETNAMESE MARINE
CORPS EMBLEM**

of VNMC officers selects an emblem similar to that of the U.S. Marine Corps. The VNMC also adopts a black and green tiger-striped camouflage utility uniform similar to that formerly worn in Indo-China by French commando units.

\* \* \*

October 1959—Lieutenant Colonel Wilkerson receives approval for U.S. Marine advisors to accompany their units into action.\*

\* \* \*

He interrupted his reading to state, "Gerry, Colonel Wilkerson and his advisor assistants became the first American servicemen to witness actual combat operations against the Viet Cong."

He continued.

May 1960—Maj. Le Nguyen Khang is appointed by President Diem as senior officer, Vietnamese Marine Corps. Wilkerson has also written, "This is an excellent choice as Khang is one of the first Vietnamese Marines to graduate from the U.S. Marine Corps Amphibious Warfare School at Quantico."

\* \* \*

May 1961—Vietnamese Marine Corps is increased to 3,321 officers and men. A fourth infantry battalion and other combat support units are also authorized.

\* \* \*

January 1963—Marine Advisory Unit increased to eight Marine officers and ten noncommissioned officers. Col. Clarence Moody is serving as the senior Marine advisor. "Moody was instrumental in having Lieutenant Colonel Khang deploy his brigade-sized VNMC in operations against the Viet Cong."

\* \* \*

Capt. Richard B. Taylor, U.S. Marine advisor, 2d VNMC Battalion awarded the first Silver Star medal to a Marine in the Vietnam conflict.

---

\*Similar entries to those cited in the Senior Advisor's Journal can be found in *U.S. Marine in Vietnam: The Advisory and Combat Assistance Era. 1954–1964.*

* * *

February 16, 1964—Maj. Donald E. Koelper, battalion advisor to VNMC, killed by Viet Cong terrorists. Posthumously awarded first Navy Cross for heroism in Vietnam conflict.

* * *

August 6, 1964—The U.S. Congress unanimously passes the Gulf of Tonkin Resolution. The advisory unit begins developing a contingency plan for expansion of U.S. advisory effort.

* * *

Colonel Dorsey was now completely engrossed in the journal and he searched for the next tab, folding back twenty-five to thirty pages.

"Nineteen sixty-eight was a big year for the Vietnamese Marines," he began. "In January the Vietnam Marine Corps had their infantry and artillery battalions deployed in three of the four military regions and also the capital military district."

Further entries included:

February 1968—The Viet Cong launch their Tet Offensive. Vietnamese Marines are flown to Phu Bai where they fight alongside U.S. Marines in the recapture of the provincial capital city of Hue. On 16 February Vietnamese Marines, accompanied by their U.S. advisors, battle their way to the southwest wall of the city, killing 618 Viet Cong, while suffering 113 Marines killed and 405 wounded.

* * *

October 1, 1968—The Vietnamese Marine Corps is expanded to division size. The VNMC activates a third brigade. The three infantry brigades are now task-organized, with supporting units similar to a U.S. Marine regimental landing team.

* * *

April 1, 1970—The VNMC activates its ninth infantry battalion. The Marine Advisory Unit increases its strength to sixty-eight officers and enlisted Marines.

* * *

June 13, 1971—Capt. Michael Dickey, advisor to the 7th Battalion, was killed in action, in Quang Tri Province.

Removing his last marker from the journal, Colonel Dorsey said, "I've only made a few entries.

"The day I relieved Col. Francis Tief as the senior advisor was 10 July 1971. The second entry reflects our initial planning to begin pulling the battalion advisors away from the individual units and consolidating them at brigade level.

"As you know, we've been directed to reduce the advisory unit by fifteen officers during April. The only way we will be able to continue to support the VNMC will be to establish a liaison team at each brigade headquarters. Advisors would then move out to the infantry battalions as the need arises.

"My latest entry records your relief of Lieutenant Colonel Swigert as the Assistant Senior Advisor." With that, he closed the Journal.

I was surprised when he said, "Gerry, you'll probably be one of the last U.S. Marines assigned to this advisory unit. It's just a matter of time now before all American servicemen will be limited to noncombat billets. I can foresee the day when our advisory unit will be deactivated and if U.S. Marines remain in-country at all, it will be within a centralized American Assistance Command."

He described what he foresaw as the wind-down in these terms:

"Our field tasks are almost complete. We need only monitor their logistical preparedness and this is where I want you to put your major efforts. The Vietnam War is ending for Americans; it will be just a matter of time before we all go home for good."

My first meeting with Colonel Dorsey drew to a close. He stood up, lifted the Journal from his desk, carefully placed it back on the raised credenza behind him and returned to the checklist on his desk. Before he could begin, however, Warrant Officer Francis, our adjutant, interrupted with the news that the Chief of Staff, Naval Forces in Vietnam was calling.

During their conversation, Dorsey mentioned my arrival, so the Chief of Staff scheduled the two of us for a meeting with Admiral Salzer at 1000 the next morning.

During the lunch that followed our meeting, he reviewed the advisory "chain of command." He astutely voiced his awareness that although the MAU was essentially an autono-

mous command, nonetheless his direct Senior Officer was Rear
Admiral Robert S. Salzer, Jr., Commander U.S. Naval Forces
Vietnam (NAVFORV). In turn, the admiral's immediate senior
was Gen. Creighton Abrams, Commander U.S. Military Assistance Command Vietnam (COMUSMACV).

I later learned that our Marine Advisory Unit had a direct
working relationship with the MACV staff on routine staffing
matters because the Vietnamization program had significantly
reduced the size of the U.S. Navy staff to the point where it
could no longer provide day-to-day interface between subordinate and higher headquarters. More NAVFORV personnel
reductions were scheduled during April, leaving the MACV
headquarters with the only fully manned intelligence and operations sections and tactical operations center (TOC) in
Vietnam. Because our MAU was still involved in field operations, it had full access to these important staff sections. Colonel
Dorsey encouraged me to become acquainted with the
NAVFORV and MACV staffs.

Just before 1000 the next morning, I met Dorsey at the
NAVFORV headquarters which was located in what had once
been a prominent French businessman's estate in an exclusive
area of old Saigon.

We were met by Capt. Robert Paddock, the Chief of Staff,
who ushered us into the admiral's office.

Admiral Salzer looked distinguished with his grey hair. He
was a trim fiftyish and appeared immaculate in his whites. Gold-
braided shoulder boards sat evenly on his broad shoulders and
the silver thread in his two-star insignia glistened. He stepped
from behind his dark oak desk to greet us on what was obviously just a routine courtesy call. Since the Admiral was quite
busy, we remained only long enough to complete the amenities.

During the ride back to the Bo Tu Linh Compound, Colonel
Dorsey reminded me that the next morning we would meet
with the Vietnamese commandant.

Starting my third morning in Vietnam, I noticed that the
newness of my tiger-striped advisor's uniform contrasted sharply
with the weathered green beret passed on from a former U.S.
Marine advisor. Checking the alignment of my web belt one

last time, I met Colonel Dorsey in preparation for my first meeting with the commandant of the Vietnamese Marines with whom I shortly would be serving.

The morning sun felt good on my back as Dorsey and I waited on the second-floor veranda of Marine headquarters for my introduction to Lieutenant General Khang. He thought that Khang would be particularly interested in my previous field experience and my knowledge of the material assistance programs we would administer on behalf of the U.S. government.

Promptly at 0830 a Vietnamese lieutenant stepped out through the double French doors and announced that the commandant would see us. With Colonel Dorsey in the lead we entered General Khang's large office. In keeping with Vietnamese custom, Khang waited until my introduction was completed and then reached out to shake hands.

I remember thinking, "He looks just like his picture." He was about five feet, six inches tall, stood almost ramrod straight, yet did not appear stiff. His dark-rimmed glasses were slightly tinted. He spoke very softly, but intensely, and I felt that beneath this gentle appearance was an undying bitterness for his North Vietnamese brethren.*

With the introduction over, we were offered tea as we sat around a plain coffee table. The open windows and French doors made the room very comfortable. The talk was light and friendly, with the general speaking first to Colonel Dorsey and then to me. Khang reminisced first on how the Vietnamese Marine Corps in the South had evolved from a few North Vietnamese river boat companies and commando units into a division-sized force of Marines. Its sustained excellence as a fighting force made it one of the two elite units of the armed forces of the Republic of Vietnam. He spoke with special pride when he told me that two of his three infantry brigades, namely

---

*General Khang's biographical summary mentioned his birth in Hanoi, and the fact that in 1954, at the time of the partition, he had made the decision to leave that part of his homeland rather than live under a communist government. Some eighteen years had elapsed since the French had surrendered at Dien Bien Phu and his hatred for the North Vietnamese had hardened through a hundred battles. He had been the first commander of the 3d Battalion and progressively risen to command all 16,000 of Vietnam's Marines.

the 147th and 258th, were deployed in Military Region One (MR-1) and were now occupying many of the fire bases built by U.S. Marines in the late 1960s. The 3d Brigade, the 369th, was now in the Saigon area.

It was indeed a most pleasant introduction to my new role in Vietnam. Dorsey ended our meeting by informing General Khang of my forthcoming trip to MR-1, describing it as a three- to four-day orientation visit to get acquainted with the U.S. advisors deployed with Vietnamese Marines along the 17th Parallel separating the two Vietnams. This visit would take place just before the Easter weekend to permit me to return to Saigon while Dorsey spent a well-deserved holiday with his family in the Philippine Islands. Upon hearing this, Khang asked me to relay his best wishes to all the advisors deployed with his brigades.

In the short walk from the commandant's office to the Marine Advisory Unit headquarters, several Vietnamese Marine NCOs saluted us as we passed. I noticed they had glanced at the Vietnamese Marine Corps rank insignia sewn on our left uniform pockets. Colonel Dorsey's black patch with four stripes, similar to a Navy captain, identified him as the senior U.S. Marine. My newly sewn on rank insignia of three broad stripes showed my equivalent Vietnamese rank was full commander or "trung ta."

After we returned to the advisory headquarters, Colonel Dorsey indicated that I should begin my orientation visit to the VNMC base camp and hospital the next day. Thanking him for the background and guidance, I left his office and returned to my quarters in the gathering twilight. I felt good about my new assignment and was personally looking forward to the logistical management challenges I would be experiencing in the months ahead.

# CHAPTER TWO

# VIETNAMIZATION: THE BEGINNING OF THE END

As the 1972 Easter period approached, the monsoon season was ending in the northernmost provinces of South Vietnam commonly referred to as Military Region One (MR-1). There was a growing feeling of tranquility among the people as nearly seven years of heavy fighting appeared to have diminished into occasional harassing incidents. Highways long closed were open and filled with traffic, which stimulated the rebirth of a growing economy. Marketplaces in Quang Tri City, Dong Ha, Hue and Cam Lo, humming with the incessant chatter of bargaining Vietnamese, were full of food and wares. Around them it appeared that an ugly war was slowly dying.[1]

Indeed, the U.S. Marines from the 3d Division who had made the initial landing in 1965 had long ago left their base camps and redeployed to Okinawa. The previously intense battle area known as "Leatherneck Square" remained only a dim memory.[2] Other old battle areas such as the "Rock Pile" and Khe Sanh were now silent, with jungle growth rapidly covering the scars of war. With the war changing and slowing, combat bases such as Con Thien and Gio Linh had been designated Alpha 2 and Alpha 4.

In these areas a thousand U.S. Marines had earlier bled and died protecting the city of Dong Ha from North Vietnamese regular forces. Now, two years after the 3d Marine Division had withdrawn, the 1st and 3d ARVN Divisions replaced the 120,000 departed Americans. The most northern of these Vietnamese Divisions, the 3d, was filled with two newly activated Vietnamese Army regiments whose level of training and readiness was not the highest. These two divisions and two additional Vietnamese Marine infantry brigades were now all that guarded the northern boundary, and the most direct route to Hue, the ancient capital of Vietnam, approximately forty miles to the south.

Much had happened since President Nixon had met with South Vietnamese Premier Nguyen Van Thieu on the island of Guam in 1969. It may be recalled that during a press conference on 25 July 1969, the president announced a new foreign and security policy aimed at bringing about peace on both the negotiating and battle fronts.[3] The "Nixon Doctrine" was the beginning of an accelerated effort to strengthen the South

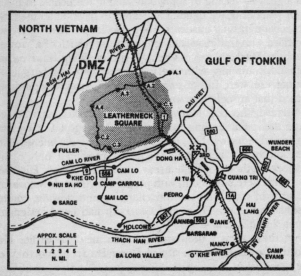

"LEATHERNECK SQUARE." IN NORTHERN QUANG TRI PROVINCE

Vietnamese Armed Forces (RVNAF) and disengage the U.S. from the war, an alternative course of action taken in the face of the deadlocked peace negotiations in Paris.[4]

For more than a decade preceding promulgation of the Nixon Doctrine, Southeast Asia had claimed the almost singular attention, efforts and commitment of the national resources and policy directions of the U.S. decisions by four American presidents had, over the years, transformed the nation's role in Southeast Asia from providing a few advisors to a massive conventional battlefield involvement. By April 1969 over 550,000 American troops had been committed to the defense of the Republic of South Vietnam. However, in time it also became a presidential option to decrease the use of American troops in leading the fight for the defense of South Vietnam and to shift the burden of that role to the Vietnamese themselves.

The primary objective of the Nixon Doctrine was the achievement of a long-lasting peace through negotiations. The president's policy was based upon three premises: willingness of the parties to negotiate, ARVN strength and a workable partnership.[5] With the South Vietnamese armed forces intended to assume the leading role in the fighting the U.S. could withdraw from the war without negotiating with the North Vietnamese. There was, however, one basic flaw in this strategy: should the North Vietnamese elect to do so, they were capable of launching an attack when the American strength had been drawn down to very limited combat power.[6] U.S. political and military leadership tacitly recognized the fact that a successful communist attack could topple Premier Thieu and the Republic of South Vietnam.

Notwithstanding this fact, the immediate goal of the U.S. was to initiate a phase-down of American troop involvement in the war. The Vietnamization program would be implemented in three phases. The first, and politically the most urgent, consisted of turning over to the Vietnamese the responsibility for ground combat against the communists. The second phase was for the U.S. to provide material assistance that would enable the RVNAF to achieve self-reliance. This also involved an increase in the U.S. providing sufficient artillery, air, naval gunfire and other support capabilities to permit the RVNAF to assume the complete ground combat role. The final phase saw the further reduction of the American presence to that of a military advisory role. It was envisioned that the advisory role and assistance presence would be gradually reduced as South Vietnam grew in strength until such military assistance was no longer required.[7]

The Vietnamization program was not to be confined solely to strengthening the military forces of the country. The program was also to include measures designed to help institute political stability, social reforms and resolve South Vietnam's major economic problems. In order to compete realistically with the influence of the communists, on their own ground, social reforms were required and long-standing social injustices had to be eradicated. Agrarian reform was a most important and necessary tool to bring about social and economic changes. Thus, the Vietnamization program was to provide a platform for the Vietnamese to create their own future by helping them build and safeguard their own nation.[8]

The reduction and redeployment of U.S. troops gradually changed the U.S. command and control structure. Thus, in MR-1 the departing 3rd Marine Division and III Marine Amphibious Force were replaced by the U.S. Army's XXIV Corps. On 13 June 1971, Secretary of Defense Melvin Laird announced that 90 percent of the combat responsibilities had been given to the RVNAF.[9]

Massive amounts of war materials were turned over to the Vietnamese forces. American bases passed to Vietnamese control as units of the U.S. Armed Forces departed for stateside or other bases. The American units that remained directed their activities toward logistics and pacification programs while awaiting their own orders to depart.

The year 1971 ushered in a period of improved security throughout the nation as South Vietnam's Armed Forces held the initiative on all battlefields and almost all the population of the South lived under the effective protection of the government. There was hope that, realizing defeat, the communists would eventually return to the North as the government of Vietnam (GVN) expanded its pacification programs to include community defense and development. ARVN forces themselves, long immobilized by pacification duties, began turning over territorial responsibilities to local units, known as Regional Forces (RFs) and Popular Forces (PFs). The goal of this transfer of responsibility was to release the regular forces for mobile operations while affording the RFs and PFs the opportunity to involve themselves in combating local Viet Cong guerrillas.[10]

With each drawdown of the 80,000 men in the 3d Marine Amphibious Force (III MAF), the South Vietnamese expanded their areas of responsibility and a new feeling of confidence was exhibited by the personnel in the armed forces. ARVN Popular Forces units moved back into village hamlets as the Regular Forces assumed an offensive role.

By all exterior appearances, the Vietnamization program was proceeding on schedule. I Corps remained quiet and by January 1971, almost all U.S. Marines had departed Vietnam with the last Marine infantry battalion, 2d Battalion, 1st Marines, returning to the U.S. on 26 March 1971.[11] The III MAF headquarters was transferred back to its permanent base camp on Okinawa on 14 April 1971.[12] Some units, most notably U.S. Marine aviation elements, withdrew at a slower pace. However, by 26 May 1971 Marine aviators had ceased flying air combat operations, although some low risk helicopter support and administrative flights continued through mid-June 1971. By July 1971 no U.S. Marine combat units were involved in the Vietnamese War and after six years of war the Southeast Asian Force In Readiness had completed its stand-down.[13]

On 1 July 1971 only two U.S. Marine units remained in South Vietnam, which together totalled less than 250 officers and enlisted men, doctors and corpsmen. The Marine Advisory Unit (MAU) which had been advising and training Vietnamese Marines since the mid-1950s had sixty-eight personnel. Sub Unit 1, 1st Air and Naval Gunfire Liaison Company (ANGLICO) had 180 personnel.* Both units were scheduled for

---

*By way of explanation, Marine Corps ANGLICO units are charged with the unique responsibility of coordinating naval gunfire and air support in any form for U.S. Army and allied forces. Liaison teams in Vietnam were still supporting the Vietnamese and Australian Armies and the Korean and Vietnamese Marines. These naval gunfire support (NGF) teams were responsible for controlling the fire of the U.S. 7th Fleet destroyers and cruisers along the country's entire coastline.

further troop reduction on 1 April 1972. If all proceeded as planned by 1 May 1972, the ANGLICO unit would be reduced to eighty-nine personnel while the Advisory Unit would be cut to thirty-two.

In the northern provinces an ANGLICO liaison team was stationed at Danang with naval gunfire (NGF) spotter teams assigned to the Vietnamese 1st and 3d ARVN Divisions. A small complement of ANGLICO naval gunfire spotters was also located with the Vietnamese Marines and their U.S. Marine advisors along the demilitarized zone (DMZ). Positioned on hilltop outposts, Alpha 2 and Alpha 1, they were alert to enemy activity, often calling suppressive fire missions against NVA mortar or rocket fire attacks.

By Christmas of 1971, enemy activity along the 17th Parallel diminished to its lowest level in six years, with U.S. naval ships receiving fewer and fewer requests for suppressive fire missions. By 24 March 1972, no U.S. naval gunfire spotters remained on an assigned basis anywhere in South Vietnam, except along the DMZ.[14] First Lt. David Bruggeman and four enlisted Marines remained positioned in an observation tower at fire base Alpha 2 along with their ARVN counterparts. This last remaining spot team was sheduled to be withdrawn during May as withdrawal plans called for all ANGLICO Marines to go home before the summer of 1972 had passed.

In January 1972, U.S. combat strength in South Vietnam had been reduced to 140,000 and by the end of April was to drop below 70,000.

Public confidence in the process of Vietnamization was high, although the U.S. government recognized that without American airpower the Armed Forces of the Republic of South Vietnam would not be able to defend itself adequately against an all-out NVA attack. Notwithstanding this awareness, the last U.S. tactical aviation squadrons were continuing their preparation to depart the country.

Despite the ominous indications that the communists were preparing for a general offensive, the U.S. and other free world allied countries maintained their disengagement policy and continued withdrawing their troops from South Vietnam at an accelerated rate.[15] In the process, combat support assets, such as command and control communications systems provided by the U.S. for the South Vietnamese forces, were also being substantially reduced. The draw-down on these command and control communication systems significantly reduced ability to react to any major thrust by the enemy and each reduction in U.S. personnel necessitated a commensurate reduction in an operational capability, such as the gathering of intelligence or the ability to project U.S. combat power.

In MR-1 the U.S. Air Force Direct Air Support Center (I DASC) at Danang had been reduced to a skeleton crew, sufficient to support a minimal operational commitment.[16] Where before a hundred officers and enlisted air controllers had controlled all air activity in the skies over Southeast Asia, there were now a mere seven officers and eighteen enlisted men to do the same job.

By March 1972, almost all remaining U.S. combat units had redeployed from MR-1. The 196th Infantry Brigade was ordered to stand down and to conduct only defensive operations around the Danang and Phu Bai air bases. Ground combat operations had become the sole responsibility of ARVN units supported by such U.S. tactical air and naval gunfire assets that remained and by the assistance of a few remaining advisors.

The backbone of South Vietnamese military forces that were responsible for the five northern provinces and MR-1 consisted of three ARVN infantry divisions—the 1st, 2d* and 3d—along with the 51st Regiment, the 1st Ranger Group and the 1st Armored Brigade. Other units organic to MR-1 included a combat engineer group and corps artillery units. Six Regional Force (RF-PF) battalions also contributed to area security in all five provinces.[17]

Lt. Gen. Hoang Xuan Lam, a native of Hue, commanded MR-1 and exercised control over all regular and territorial forces. General Lam, an armor-trained officer, was placed in command of the region shortly after U.S. Marines landed across Blue Beach in 1965. His headquarters was located in Danang.

---

*The combat experienced 2d ARVN REGT was reassigned from the 1st ARVN Division when the 3d Division was activated.

The general disposition of MR-1 forces saw the 3d Infantry Division, activated some eight months earlier, assigned to secure the northernmost frontiers of South Vietnam. This new unit of 11,203 soldiers had never fought a coordinated battle as a division, and its nine infantry battalions consisted of only marginally trained troops with little experience fighting in northern Quang Tri Province.[18] Most of the troops were natives of the region, but were not familiar with the terrain along the DMZ or hardened to the harsh, cold dampness of its weather. Further, the six battalions of the 56th and 57th Infantry Regiments occupied base camps and strong points in which ARVN soldiers had been located for years, and many of their families had recently moved into nearby villages.

In sharp contrast to the U.S. government's initiative to

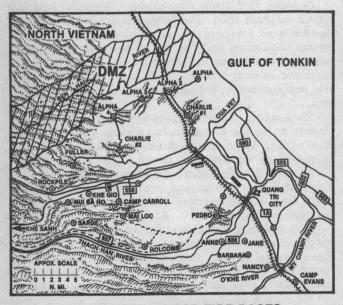

**SOUTH VIETNAMESE FIRE BASES,
QUANG TRI PROVINCE**

achieve a negotiated peace agreement, the North Vietnamese remained firm in their demands that the U.S. and other free world forces withdraw from South Vietnam. At the Paris peace talks there was almost no progress. By mid-1970 the communists were still insistent on their demands: a coalition government, neutrality and an immediate cease-fire. President Thieu rejected them all.

The persistence of the North Vietnamese in not compromising their ultimate objective of reuniting the two Viet nations was typically Asian and ultimately prevailed. Hanoi's leaders could not be swayed from their long-term pursuit to conquer South Vietnam. Almost simultaneous to the implementation of President Nixon's Vietnamization program, the North Vietnamese opted to escalate their efforts to unify the two Vietnams.

In 1970, ARVN forces felt confident enough to conduct cross-border operations into Cambodia and in 1971, a similar operation, Lam Son-719 was conducted into Laos.[19] The limited successes realized by the RVNAF in these two battles caused the communists to make a radical departure from the "war of attrition" which had been fought during the years prior to the 1968 Tet Offensive. Undaunted in his party's goal to create one Vietnam, General Giap began to plan large-scale attacks which would employ conventional methods of warfare. As always, Giap believed time was on his side, and, sensitive to the forthcoming U.S. presidential elections, he deliberately selected the year 1972 for the new offensive.[20]

To prepare for the invasion, North Vietnam requested huge quantities of modern weapons from Russia and communist China. During 1970 and 1971 unprecedented quantities of war supplies were shipped into North Vietnam. MiG aircraft, SAM (surface-to-air) missiles, T-54, T-55 and light, amphibious PT-76 tanks, 130MM and 152MM artillery pieces, 160MM mortars, 23MM and 57MM antiaircraft guns, and, for the first time, SA-7 heat-seeking antiaircraft missiles, were also added to the inventory being amassed for the next general offensive.[21]

This would be the largest offensive ever for the North Vietnamese Army. On only three previous occasions had that army ever approached operations on such a scale, namely, the

Dien Bien Phu campaign, the 1968 winter-spring (Tet) offensive, and the 1971 Operation Lam Son-719. The 1972 Easter drive would be called the "Nguyen-Hue Offensive."[22]

It was not by simple coincidence that Hanoi selected the code name Nguyen Hue. Nguyen Hue was the birth name of the Emperor Quang Trung, a Vietnamese national hero who, in 1789, maneuvered his troops hundreds of miles through

# THE NGUYEN HUE OFFENSIVE
## THE 1972 NORTH VIETNAMESE INVASION OF MR – 1

jungles and mountains, surprised and attacked invading Chinese and defeated them on the outskirts of Hanoi.

General Giap would, for pragmatic reasons, change his strategy from that of his 1968 offensive. The 1968 Tet Offensive was directed toward seizing terrain only briefly to achieve a psychological shock effect on a grand scale.[23] It was planned to permit key terrain to be seized and held to demonstrate actual control by communist forces. Further, in the 1968 offensive the objective was to contain the populace within targeted areas, whereas the 1972 campaign would be oriented toward driving them from the targeted areas. Heavy artillery would be positioned to fire into the South's major cities.

General Giap's plan contemplated the commitment of the entire combat force of North Vietnam consisting of some fourteen divisions, twenty-six separate regiments and supporting armor and artillery.

There were to be three major spearheads, the first of which would be directed across the DMZ into northern Quang Tri Province. The second thrust, initiated a few days later, would strike from the Cambodian border into Binh Long Province toward Saigon.[24] After initial successes in Quang Tri Province, the third spearhead was planned to be directed into Kontum Province in the Central Highlands. Thus, the stage was set for the communists to launch, in a conventional warfare mode, the largest offensive of the Vietnam War. It was an offensive designed to exploit the mobility, firepower and psychological shock action of armored elements consisting of Russian and Chinese T-54 and PT-76 tanks.

The northern cities of Quang Tri and Hue were to play special roles in the offensive. Hue, the capital of Thua Thien Province, and ancient capital of Vietnam, was the focal point of the history and culture of central Vietnam. Because Hue had played a major role in the 1968 Tet attack, its recapture by North Vietnamese forces was intended to inflict a catastrophic psychological blow upon the forces of the South.[25]

If the momentum could be maintained from these initial attacks, the major cities of Danang, Qui Nhon, Pleiku, My Tho and Can Tho further south were also ultimate targets of the offensive. It was perceived by the communists that loss of these cities could precipitate the fall of the remainder of the Republic of Vietnam.

As is common in military planning, in early December 1971, documentary evidence of North Vietnam's preparations for an invasion of the South began to be obtained from a variety of sources. It was learned that the general reserve divisions of the North Vietnamese Army were recalled from Laos back to North Vietnam where they were replenished and thereafter moved south. Other divisions followed, consisting, among others, of the elite 308th Division.[26] This unit had conducted the final assault on the entrapped French at Dien Bien Phu, and in early 1972 moved into an assembly area approximately twenty miles north of Leatherneck Square. In the long history of the Vietnam War, the 308th had left Hanoi to join in only one other major offensive.

General Giap was taking an exceptionally dangerous risk in committing his total military resources. A critical element in his planning for this offensive was the simultaneous attack in several major areas throughout the country, to disorganize and thus prevent the RVNAF from decisively committing its national reserves.[27]

Giap also directed his independent units to complement, protect and preserve the integrity of the regular army units. Independent regiments were to launch the leading diversionary attacks and interdict key lines of communications. His tactical reasoning was consistent with previous campaigns, in that independent units would encounter ARVN forces and tie down its reserve. At the same time elite NVA units would conduct the final assaults and capture the major objectives.

In MR-1, three independent infantry regiments avoided direct confrontations with ARVN forces and moved to their final staging areas. Protected from observation by a combination of monsoon weather conditions and darkness, these regiments would support the main attacks of the 304th and 308th Divisions. Two other independent regiments would operate in support of the attack by the 324B Division on the ARVN positions of the 1st Division west of Hue City.

To protect its logistical activities from interdiction by allied air, the NVA intensified and expanded a sophisticated air defense system consisting of antiaircraft artillery (AAA), and sur-face-to-air missiles (SAM). Indicative of this buildup were reports by allied pilots that, by early 1972, the intensity of fire near the DMZ was equal to that encountered in the Hanoi area. On 17 February 1972 the NVA in the DMZ fired over fifty Soviet-made SA-2 missiles, shooting down three U.S. F-4s.[28] Giap's massive hammer was set to drop.

The 3d ARVN Division was generally responsible for Quang Tri Province. Its headquarters, under Brig. Gen. Vu Van Giai, was located at the Ai Tu combat base. Two of the three regiments of the 3d Division had been activated less than six months. The 56th and 57th regiments were deployed over a series of hilltop strong points and fire support bases dotting the area immediately south of the DMZ from the coastline across the piedmont area on into the western hills. The command post of the 57th Regiment was located at fire support base (FSB) Charlie 1 while the 56th was headquartered at FSB Charlie 2. The 2d Regiment, formerly a component of the 1st Infantry Division, occupied Camp Carroll with two of its battalions at FSB Fuller and Alpha 4.[29] In addition to the 2d regimental headquarters, five batteries of artillery were positioned at Carroll for fire support across the division's crescent-shaped line of fire bases and strong points. Thus, Camp Carroll* was the largest ARVN combat base in Quang Tri Province.

In addition to organic units, the 3d Division had operational control over two Vietnamese Marine brigades, the 147th and 258th. The 147th Brigade was headquartered at Mai Loc combat base while Brigade 258 was located at FSB Nancy approximately ten miles south of Quang Tri city. The Marine infantry brigades were in every respect combat effective and generally positioned to form a strong line of defense facing west, the direction of most probable enemy attacks. They were both at full strength, well equipped and supplied through their own channels. In sharp contrast to the ARVN units, the Vietnamese Marines still had U.S. advisors assigned to the brigade staff and down to the infantry battalion level. Two ARVN reg-

---

*Camp Carroll was named after U.S. Marine Capt. J. J. Carroll, killed in action in 1966.

iments had small advisory teams but no Americans remained with their infantry battalions.

During January 1972, General Lam became concerned about the progressive buildup of North Vietnamese forces above the DMZ. He issued orders to all subordinate units, alerting them to be prepared for increased enemy activity during the Tet holidays. He was aware of the enemy's logistical buildup in the area north and west of MR-1 defenses, but still believed the communist Tet action would be limited to an increase in shellings and sapper attacks on ARVN lines of communication. Lam would reserve his concern for the time when the NVA divisions moved into staging areas on the west flank of Quang Tri Province and in western Thua Thien Province. Indications of these deployments were always seen prior to previous offensives.[30] In late March there was still no sizeable buildup in these traditional NVA staging areas.*

The South Vietnamese forces reacted effectively to enemy initiated activities throughout MR-1, and Tet passed in relative calm. Intelligence officers and tactical commanders, meanwhile, closely monitored and waited for signs of movement of NVA forces. Their correct prediction of the enemy's scope of activities for the Tet period reinforced their confidence that the enemy would probably not depart from his established pattern of making deliberate deployments, which would be detected, prior to launching any offensive.

By February, this assessment of the situation gained further credibility when it was revealed that the NVA 324B Division was moving into the A Shau Valley in western Thua Thien Province. This was a familiar and often-used staging area from which this enemy division launched attacks against Hue. What remained to be confirmed as definitive indications of a predicted offensive in MR-1 was the movement of elements of the NVA 304th and 308th Divisions into western Quang Tri Province.[31]

General Lam did not believe in the theory that the NVA might attack directly across the DMZ. The threat was there,

---

*The North Vietnamese 324 B Division had attacked the 1st ARVN Division units deployed west at Hue City, in the A Shau Valley.

but it had never happened before. As a result, he believed it was a no-man's land, consisting mostly of flat, exposed terrain, unfavorable for the maneuver of large infantry formations. He assumed that if the enemy should conduct such an attack, supported by armor, it could be quickly stopped, coming immediately under observation and fire from U.S. tactical air, ARVN artillery and armored forces in addition to the strategically located combat bases.[32]

General Giai, commander of the 3d Division, shared Lam's opinion, believing that any large-scale attack would come from the west, although he did not entirely rule out the possibility of an attack from the north. Intelligence reports had provided him with strong indications that the NVA had brought in surface-to-air missiles, additional 130MM guns, ammunition and armor in the area just north of the DMZ.

Around 19 March, it was confirmed that the NVA had expanded its air defense posture in the DMZ area. Twelve SA-2 SAM sites were identified in the areas just north of the DMZ, with four other sites ten miles further north. The AAA threat included 23MM and 37MM weapons grouped to comprise at least six high-threat areas.[33] With the installation of the SA-2 SAM missiles, providing an effective air defense envelope of up to 60,000 feet, the permissive environment required for the truck-killing, low-flying AC-130 gunship ended.

The NVA was becoming stronger and more threatening every day. On 28 March an SA-2 missile was launched from an area west of the DMZ that struck a four-engine AC-130 gunship. It went down in flames, killing all its U.S. Air Force crew. This loss caused the 7th Air Force to declare a "missile ring" along the DMZ.[34]

Thus, the NVA used its SAMs to restrict gunship combat operations and the U.S. Air Force's protective reaction removed the last opportunity for direct observation of the enemy buildup. With the U.S. air observation gone, the NVA increased its flow of supplies and equipment into the DMZ.

Beginning on 27 March, the NVA increased its artillery attacks by firing against the 3d Division's fire support bases in the DMZ area where, on the western flank, FBs Sarge and Nui Ba Ho received heavier than normal artillery fire. Concurrently, there was a marked increase in enemy ground activity along the ARVN forward defense line bordering the DMZ.

General Giai had other pressing problems in his 300-square-mile area of responsibility. His primary concern was to consolidate the recently occupied defensive positions to the west and to train and continue to prepare his new division for the much discussed NVA offensive. In spite of the ominous signs of an imminent attack, his staff continued to debate the problem of dominant terrain features, the most probable courses of action for the NVA, the disposition of divisional units, the configuration of their defense positions and, above all, how to employ his forces effectively in the event of an enemy offensive.

While his division staff was developing comprehensive plans for the defense of his area of responsibility, Giai initiated a program of rotating his units among the regimental areas of operation, to familiarize each of them with the terrain. It was also intended to eliminate the "fire base syndrome" among his troops.[35] Thus, on 30 March, the 56th and 2d Regiments began the scheduled rotation of their respective Tactical Areas of Responsibility (TAOR). The 56th Regiment was directed to take over the 2d Regiment's AO to include Camp Carroll, FSB Khe Gio and FSB Fuller; it would be primarily responsible for the northwest defense line. The 2d Regiment was directed to move into the 56th's AO which extended from the DMZ south to the Cam Lo-Cua Viet River and west toward the Laotian border.

Late in March, information was obtained by the South Vietnamese JGS that 29 March was to be the D-Day of an NVA general offensive. This information was sent to all ARVN units. The four national military regional commanders were directed to place their subordinate commands on full alert. The JGS, however, was still not certain where the main communist attack would be launched.[36]

General Giai's plan to rotate two of his regiments was also scheduled to begin on 30 March. For reasons we shall never know, he did not comply with the JGS alert or alter his planned rotation of units. Thus, around 0900, his two ARVN regiments began their exchange of tactical areas, with infantry units marching to their new areas. Tactical command posts (CPs) were vacated, unit radios shut down, antennas dismantled and placed aboard jeeps and six-by-six trucks. Thus, the 3d ARVN Division literally went nontactical for the duration of the rotation and was temporarily unable to perform as a viable fighting force. The Republic of South Vietnam's most northern boundary was ripe for invasion should the NVA choose this as its moment of decision; the right time to launch its offensive.*

I was to learn later that at approximately 1200, instead of supervising the 3d Division's relief of lines, General Giai and his U.S. senior advisor were planning to fly to Saigon for the holiday weekend. Giai, a proven combat commander, had somehow misread the North Vietnamese Army buildup. After ordering his division to execute one of the most difficult of tactical operations, he and his staff then violated every prudent tactical planning consideration in not supervising the timely accomplishing of that task in the face of the identified threat.

Such a decision by Giai was and is absolutely baffling. It is incomprehensible that a military leader, in daily contact with an enemy growing stronger daily and who has been alerted of an impending attack, would attempt to execute an intra-division relief of lines, and then plan a holiday of his own in the middle of it.

---

*Military manuals and doctrinal publications on the arts of war are replete with instructions on the techniques to execute a passage of lines or a relief in place. While the passage of lines is an operation in which a unit attacks through a unit in contact, a relief of lines is executed when the outgoing unit is on the defense. The combat mission and area of operation responsibilities for the outgoing unit are assumed by the incoming unit. For units of division size, the plan must specify as a minimum, the time of commencing and completing the relief and the priorities for use of the roadways involved. Under normal circumstances, the relief should be carried out in darkness or other conditions of reduced visibility.

To prevent severe degradation of the defensive posture, the relief should also be executed in stages. Every effort must be made to prevent the enemy from learning that a relief is taking place. Any major reduction in combat effectiveness should be avoided.

The methods for relieving fire support units must be clearly established. Normally the outgoing artillery unit remains in place until the units along the forward defense have been relieved. By using the in-place artillery units that are familiar with the fire support plans and the areas of operation, they are in position to fire during the critical periods of the relief of forward units.

Once the relief in place has begun, the division staff supervises the timing and movement of subordinate units. They should stay abreast of the overall situation so that they can react swiftly to any emergency.

Brothers can be deceitful. Deception between North and South Vietnamese had long been rampant. Both Vietnamese military and civilian hierarchies were infested with opportunistic agents and double agents. The timing of Giai's relief-in-place operation, the unprofessional manner in which it was executed, and his disregard of the warnings of a major attack, inevitably lead to the hypothesis of treason. The precise timing of the multitude of events about to unfold could not have happened just by chance. This would not be the first situation where South Vietnamese combat units were subjected to a military disadvantage because of the possibility of covert sympathies for the North Vietnamese enemy at the highest levels of government or their own military leadership.

One can only surmise the thoughts of the 30,000 North Vietnamese soldiers poised in pre-invasion positions. Their

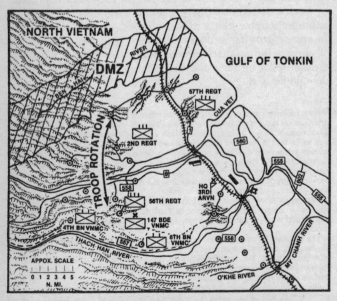

**MARCH 30, 1972 ROTATION OF ARVN REGIMENTS**

southern brothers were completely exposed as the long columns of infantry companies route-stepped between fire bases. Heavy cloud cover had dropped the ceiling down to 1,500 feet and covered most of Quang Tri Province. Hidden from the ever-watchful eyes of high-flying reconnaissance aircraft, the North Vietnamese division commanders must have been electrified by the military advantages presented to their assault forces.

# CHAPTER THREE

# NORTH TO MILITARY REGION ONE

It took another two weeks to complete my orientation and familiarization with the various U.S.-funded military assistance programs at the headquarters of Military Assistance Command, Vietnam (MACV). A special security clearance also allowed me access to the latest intelligence information and I particularly enjoyed the numerous briefings on the Viet Cong and North Vietnamese Army activities. As I sat through these briefings I was again aware that in every intelligence community there exist two diverse opinions on the enemy's intentions and capabilities. Alive and thriving in MACV's intelligence were the traditional opposites, the "doomsville" group and the "realists." Both groups agreed there had been a significant buildup in NVA forces in Military Region One (MR-1). The "sky is falling" pessimists were convinced the anticipated general offensive had been unexpectedly delayed. "It should have already happened," they said.

In contrast, more conservative pragmatists foresaw an offensive in the summer of 1972 which could be a major offensive. Neither group would predict where the main thrust would be focused; perhaps an attack in the central highlands designed to divide South Vietnam in half.

On 28 March, the night before my flight north to Quang Tri Province, the Marine advisors gathered at the Hoa Bien Bar. Maj. Bob Sheridan, a brigade advisor I'd known for a decade, was the most vocal of the group. He reminded me several times to take a couple of bottles of cognac along for the battalion advisors out on the distant fire bases. "Maj. Walt Boomer and Capt. Ray Smith have been out with the 4th Marine Battalion for over sixty days. Take them some cognac. Spend a night out there with them on Sarge," he repeated several times. "The war is about over; it's been quiet up there for months. You won't need a helmet or flak jacket. They know you're coming up, Colonel, and they're looking forward to seeing you." Before I could say anything, his deep voice demanded, "And take the mail. Jesus Christ, take the mail. They haven't had any in a week. If you forget it they'll shoot you as you step off the aircraft."

"Bob, you'll never change, you're beautiful," I retorted.

I was up early next morning and encountered perfect spring weather in Saigon.

The U.S. Air Force flight from Saigon to Phu Bai would take just over three hours. Except for me, all other passengers were Vietnamese. The crew chief had removed all the canvas seats to permit maximum use of the floor space. As a hundred-plus Vietnamese Marines walked aboard the aircraft, they dropped their packs and propped them up along the aircraft's bulkheads for pillows. When every possible square foot of space was taken, the rear ramp was closed.

The ramp's closing signaled a rush for territory as each passenger attempted to squeeze out a little more space. Hundreds of arms and legs became intertwined as bodies bent around packs, rifles and fellow Marines. Three dark-eyed, teen-aged Marines cautiously sized up the lone COVAN, then laid their heads on my legs. Others followed; I was trapped and destined to serve as a pillow on the flight north.

It was a smooth flight but, for a reason I could not identify, I was uneasy. Although I tried several times to think of other things, it didn't work because the apprehension was too strong. The gut feeling that something was about to happen lingered. It remained with me until we landed at Phu Bai. I finally pushed the feeling away as the aircraft swung off the runway, and the ramp doors opened. Fresh air rushed in. The aircraft came to a complete stop but the engines were kept running while we disembarked. When the last Marine was on the ground, the ramp doors were closed and the engines whined to a high pitch as the aircraft moved toward the runway for the flight south to Danang and then home to Saigon. "Ah," I thought, "those Air Force folks sure lead a hard life."

I watched the aircraft's camouflaged wings bend as it lifted off and listened as the roar of the engines faded away. The Phu Bai airfield was silent again. I was struck by the silence. During my 1967 tour, Phu Bai had been one of the busiest airfields in South Vietnam. Once the hub of U.S. military activity in the northern provinces, now the latticework of steel aircraft bays stood empty. The grass in the parking areas, into which a hundred helicopters used to swoop between operations, now moved only by the wind. It gave me an eerie feeling.

Time and President Nixon's Vietnamization program had changed the war. The Americans, who had spent millions building an airfield, had returned home. Phu Bai airfield, left as little more than a ghost town, was kept alive by an occasional Air America, VNAF-123 or U.S. C-130 replacement flight.

I was met by Maj. Jim Joy who had a Huey helicopter waiting to lift us the sixty miles northwest to Marine Brigade 147's field headquarters at fire support base Mai Loc. The U.S. Army pilot flew north following National Highway 1. In sharp contrast to the mid 1960s, the two-lane asphalt roadway was filled with civilian vehicles. Narrow gravel feeder roads leading to the main north-south highway were also heavy with foot and small truck traffic.

"This is the first time the sun has been seen since January," Joy's voice came over the helicopter's intercom system. "On the flight down here, we flew over fire base (FB) Nancy where Brigade 258 is located. We could see the Marines there swimming in the river just outside the base perimeter."

He continued, "The monsoon season up here is just ending. Last November we had over fifty inches of rain. December and January were just as bad. Everything we have is wet and rusty or covered with mildew.

"I've asked the pilot to fly us north at about 1,000 feet and to follow along Highway 1 until we get to Quang Tri City. From there our flight will take us north to the city of Dong

Ha, west along old Route 9 and then back south to our brigade (CP) at FSB Mai Loc. Later today I've arranged for you to receive a briefing on where the 3d ARVN Division units and our Vietnamese Marines are positioned along the DMZ."

"Quang Tri City is just ahead," Jim said. "It's a boomtown compared to the mid-1960s. There are over 20,000 people living there now. You'll be able to see that the ARVNs have a large military compound inside the old Citadel walls. On the west side of the city you can see the main highway and bridge that leads on north to the city of Dong Ha."

Flying over Quang Tri, we could see the blacktopped Highway 1 stretching northward after crossing the Thach Han River.* Two miles further north the two-lane roadway passed between an airfield and huge camp complex on the east side. On the west side was a series of giant fuel tanks surrounded by earthen berms.

Jim continued to direct my attention to the major installation below. Adjacent to the fuel farm was a well laid-out base camp. In quick succession he pinpointed the revetments of a sprawling ammunition dump, the headquarters of the 3d ARVN Division and the U.S. army advisor compound. "That is the Ai Tu combat base," he said. "That big bunker in the center of the compound is the South Vietnamese principal command and control center for Quang Tri Province. We'll visit there tomorrow." He turned his head away toward Dong Ha City.

As we approached Dong Ha, Jim began to point out the old U.S. 3d Marine Division campsites south of the city. Two large steel and concrete girdered bridges, spanning the Cam Lo-Cua Viet River, dominated the green pastoral countryside below. Passing over the abandoned Dong Ha airstrip, the Huey banked to the west and flew along Highway 9 towards Cam Lo. Off to our right was Leatherneck Square, the DMZ and North Vietnam. Joy pointed out the Con Thien hilltops and the small village of Cam Lo just before the helicopter turned south toward Mai Loc. From the air, Leatherneck Square and the surrounding areas looked very peaceful.

Shortly after landing, he introduced me to his brigade ad-

---

*Vietnam's Highway 1 parallels the East Coast from Saigon to Hanoi.

visors. Capt. J. D. Murray was the assistant senior brigade advisor. He had been awarded a Navy Cross during a previous tour in Vietnam.

Capt. Earl C. "Skip" Kruger was the logistics advisor. I quickly learned he had a rare sense of humor and also that he was seldom caught without his portable cassette player and Kris Kristofferson tapes.

I was surprised to discover another U.S. Marine officer living in this tent area who was not part of the advisor team. First Lt. James Edwards was the executive officer from the Marine detachment of an aircraft carrier. He had never served on the ground in Vietnam. While ashore in Danang, Edwards had run into several Marine advisors, and, as only Marines can do, managed somehow to get permission from the ship's captain to remain ashore in order to spend four or five days of orientation in a "secure area."

His Missouri humor coming to the surface, Joy said, "Colonel, the Mai Loc combat base hasn't received an incoming artillery round in over two years. The lieutenant is safer here than on the streets of Danang." I agreed, it seemed perfectly all right for Edwards to get some field experience.

It had been a beautiful afternoon, so we sat outside the tents and bunkers and watched the evening sunset. Captain Murray had set up a map board, orienting it to the terrain around us. FSB Mai Loc sat in the center of a twenty-mile, U-shaped valley that opened toward the sea. J.D. would point to a terrain symbol on the map and then carefully locate that same position on the ground. He first identified the hilltop FBs Sarge and Nui Ba Ho which were situated along a mountain ridgeline overlooking Route 9 and the old Vandegrift fire base.

The 4th Vietnamese Marine Battalion was responsible for these two bases. Their mission was to guard the far western approaches into the northern provinces. Their senior advisor was Maj. Walt Boomer and the assistant advisor was Capt. Ray Smith. The battalion was divided into two tactical groups as was the custom of the Vietnamese Marines. The Alpha command group was on FB Sarge. Two rifle companies and the 81MM mortar platoon were located there along with the battalion commander's headquarters units.

The Bravo command group led by the battalion executive

officer and accompanied by Captain Smith was located on Nui Ba Ho Mountain approximately 1,000 meters to the north with the remaining two rifle companies.

I interrupted J.D. to ask whether the Captain Smith on Nui Ba Ho was the same officer who fought so valiantly during the Tet Offensive and at Khe Sanh in 1968. J.D. confirmed that he was the same man, then a lieutenant in A-Company, 1st Battalion, 1st Marines, where he was repeatedly cited for his uncommon bravery. Twice recommended for the Navy Cross, both commendations were subsequently downgraded to Silver Star medals.[1]

J.D. said, "Later tonight Major Boomer will radio in from his bunker on FB Sarge. We will confirm to him that you'll remain at his position overnight. Tomorrow, at 1130, a U.S. Army Huey will pick you up at the 3d ARVN Division headquarters and fly you out to Sarge. The same Huey will return to pick you up about noon the next day.

"Earlier this month, General Giai, commanding general, 3d ARVN Division, helicoptered out to FB Sarge. While he was out there, Walt got his field diary out and went over his daily sightings of enemy troops with him. Major Boomer isn't an alarmist, but he did express deep concern about the steady increase in enemy activity. He felt that something significant was going on to the west, out toward the old U.S. Marine Corps base at Khe Sanh. The general listened and agreed that something could be building in the western mountains but he felt he did not have sufficient troop strength to conduct an offensive operation out toward the Laotian border."[2]

Major Joy interjected, "The last couple of nights both Sarge and Nui Ba Ho have been probed by enemy troops. During the daylight hours Walt has been coordinating with a U.S. forward air controller (FAC) and he and Smith have successfully run several air strikes on NVA sightings. At night they have used aircraft flares to locate and then call in artillery on enemy movements.

"On the evening of the twenty-second a B-52 ARCLIGHT* strike was run on an NVA logistic target Walt had

*ARCLIGHT—Code name for a B-52 bombing strike.

identified. The rolling thunder of 750-pound bombs saturated the area. Walt had observed the ARCLIGHT's rippling explosions as over 300 bombs hopscotched across the jungle terrain. He later reported a Vietnamese Marine reconnaissance team found evidence the strike had been partly successful. We passed this information back to higher headquarters.

"Earlier today Walt had artillery fire called on NVA troops spotted on Route 9. He thought they were moving toward Sarge from the old U.S. Marine FSB Vandegrift.

"Heavy rains on Sarge and Nui Ba Ho for the past ten days have prevented ARVN helicopters from resupplying the 4th Battalion. Yesterday Walt reported that the Bravo command group on Nui Ba Ho was almost out of food."[3]

At the moment, heavy artillery fire erupted to our north, interrupting J.D.'s briefing.

"Those are the ARVN artillery pieces at FSB Camp Carroll," he said. "There are about five batteries up there with twenty-two guns. Four are the long-range 175MM guns, the rest are 155 or 105 howitzers. The Vietnamese Marines have one battery of 105s dug in up there."

J.D. pointed behind me. "On the mountain ridgeline directly behind us is FB Holcomb," he said. "The brigade has two rifle companies from its 8th Battalion there. Maj. Emmett Huff, its senior advisor, is currently in Texas on R&R leave. Capt. Clark Embrey now is the senior U.S. Marine with the 8th." Embrey, sitting beside me, added that "FB Holcomb Marines had also had several recent encounters with Viet Cong or NVA. They're not certain which right now. The two companies have also had numerous daytime sightings, which means that during the hours of darkness there is a hell of a lot of enemy moving around up there."

A skillful briefer, Murray waited until Embrey was finished speaking. He pointed next to FB Pedro on the map and then pointed due east back toward the ocean and Quang Tri City.

"The 1st VNMC Battalion is located at Pedro. On the evening of the 25th one of the battalion's patrols ran into an NVA force. They killed several, but had several Marines wounded. The Marines got their wounded back to Pedro but the heavy

rains prevented the ARVN med-evac helicopters from flying
a rescue mission. Two of the wounded died before they could
get them out.

"Maj. Bob Cockell and Capt. Larry Livingston are with the
1st Battalion. We'll be visiting them on Easter Sunday."

Always very proper, Major Joy concluded the briefing with
the advice that: "Tomorrow morning we'll drive into the 3d
ARVN Division headquarters at the Ai Tu and Quang Tri
combat bases. I've made arrangements for you to meet Colonel
Murdock and the staff of his Advisory Team 155. We'll also
visit their division tactical operations center (TOC) and their
sensor read-out bunker. After lunch the Army helicopter will
fly you to FB Sarge."

Talking late into the night with Major Joy, I made a list of
the health and comfort items he felt the advisors could use.

"Keep the mail coming as often as possible. The monsoon
rains have really been depressing, and mail is all they live for
up here!" Major Joy was sensitive to his officer's needs. He was
a highly experienced infantry officer and obviously a very respected leader of Marines, and it was (no pun intended) a joy
to observe his leadership.

As the evening waned, little did either of us realize that
this peaceful time together would be our last good night's rest
for weeks to come. The heavy rains during the night further
heightened the stench of mildew in the blankets and in our
damp clothes. Just before dawn the rains stopped. The skies
remained overcast with a solid cloud cover to 1,000–1,500 feet.

Shortly after 0830, Joy, Captain Murray and I climbed into
a jeep and began the drive toward Cam Lo. The whole valley
was quiet; no artillery firing, no signs of any enemy activity.
It had the appearance of another peaceful morning in Quang
Tri Province.

Captain Murray was driving. Jim sat in the back seat pointing
out the various artillery batteries at Camp Carroll, the much
fought over jungle outcropping known as "The Rock Pile" and
the other major ARVN fire bases of Fuller, Charlie 2 and 3.
Several Vietnamese Marine vehicles were following about a mile
behind us. The red clay roadway was still wet, so there were

no dust clouds. When we passed through Dong Ha, he identified the Catholic church and reminded me it was Holy
Thursday.

We arrived at the 3d ARVN Division headquarters around
0930 and went straight to the senior U.S. advisor's headquarters. The division's encampment area was well kept, with neatly
trimmed grassy areas and concrete walkways between the long
rows of corrugated tin-roofed tropical Ely huts that were probably erected by U.S. Navy CBs years earlier.

The Ely hut occupied by the division commander was located beside a massive sandbagged bunker. A white star on a
small red sign identified him as Brig. Gen. Vu Van Giai. We
walked quietly by the general's combination office and living
quarters into the nearby U.S. Advisory Team 155 headquarters. Col. Fred Murdock, U.S. Army, was the senior advisor.
He gave us a general area briefing and invited us to visit his
G-3 advisor in the 3d Division's TOC. During our visit, Murdock confirmed my flight to FB Sarge at 1130. Afterwards, we
left his headquarters and walked the short distance to the 3d
ARVN Division TOC.

An informal briefing had been arranged in the advisors'
G-3 area. The TOC bunker dominated the division headquarters area. Surrounded by a six-foot wire fence, it loomed
like a huge river barge turned upside down, the biggest bunker
I had ever seen in Vietnam. At least ten feet of sandbags had
been placed along the northern wall and on its flat roof. The
faded insignia of the 101st Airborne Division still adorned the
eastern entrance, reminding all who entered of a bygone era.

The bunker's interior was compartmented, separating the
key advisors' G-3 operations section from the ARVN artillery's
fire support center (FSC) and U.S. naval gunfire and Air Force
air liaison teams. The separation of the supporting arms coordinators under the present low level of enemy activity apparently presented no real difficulty.

Team 155's G-3 advisor, Major Wilson, met us as we entered. He guided us to his tactical operations area. The 3d
Division's counterpart G-3 section was located in two rooms
directly across a jointly used briefing area from the G-3 watch

officer's working space. The advisors' G-3 watch area was a ten- by twelve-foot room, with tactical radios arranged along the back wall just above a work bench. As I anticipated, a battered chart with unit callsigns and radio frequencies, written in blue grease pencil, was displayed directly above the work bench. One of the G-3 officers reminded me that two channels of radio communications were established to where all units of U.S. advisory personnel were in the field with South Vietnamese units. "The ARVN infantry battalions do not have U.S. advisors assigned to them anymore," he said. "Our U.S. Army advisor radio communications extend down to where the last American is deployed. The ARVN's communication system serves as the primary radio link. The U.S. advisor's radios provided a backup link in confirming the tactical or logistical situation." Wilson moved over to a large tactical map and began to point out the major units of the 3d Division.

"The 2d ARVN Regiment is most experienced but does not have any U.S. advisory personnel attached. The 56th and 57th Regiments both have U.S. Army advisors at the regimental level. Lt. Col. Bill Camper is serving as senior advisor with the 56th and a Maj. Joe Brown is his deputy advisor. Lt. Col. Twichell and Major Figardo were assigned to the 57th Regiment."

Camper was identified as the most experienced advisor. He had first served with the 2d Regiment in 1964-65, and up until 14 March, was with the 2d. Colonel Murdock felt the 56th Regiment, which had no advisors, could better use his field and training expertise. The 56th had only been activated three months earlier, and still was having many start-up problems. Camper had indicated recently that the quality of the 56th's leadership was poor, but was hopeful it would improve with time.[4]

Major Wilson's generalized briefing complemented what I had received from Captain Murray. He explained that two regiments of the division were deployed on a series of outposts along the DMZ from National Highway 1 westward to the mountains. The remaining regiment occupied the major fire base, Camp Carroll, bordering the highway, Route 9, leading into Laos. He also pointed out the three key artillery bases supporting the division: Charlie 1 and 2 as well as Camp Carroll.

The two brigades of Vietnamese Marines, under the operational control of the 3d ARVN Division commander, completed a defensive area along the western mountain ridges that protected the populated areas of central and eastern Quang Tri Province.

Major Joy nodded agreement when Wilson said, "Marine Brigade 147 at FSB Mai Loc complements the ARVN regiment at Carroll to form the major defensive line against any attack from the west."

"Colonel Turley spent last night at the advisors' camp in Mai Loc," Jim added. "Later this afternoon he will helicopter out to FB Sarge and spend the night there."

Wilson continued to identify other South Vietnamese Army units in the area.

"On the east side of Highway 1, extending out to the ocean, regional forces of Quang Tri Province occupy small outposts. These forces are not under General Giai's operational control, but instead are commanded by the province and Gio Linh district chiefs. The division commander monitors their actions and dispositions, but, he has no direct responsibility for either. It is interesting to note there is no unity of command for ARVN military forces immediately below the DMZ."

Other units included the 1st Armor Brigade which was also operating in the division's area. "The newly activated 20th Tank Battalion has the only U.S. M-48 tanks in-country. They were provided to the South Vietnamese as part of President Nixon's Vietnamization program. The battalion is just completing its final training tests and should be certified as a combat-ready unit within a few days."

Wilson just began to sum up the divisions' training activities when his G-3 advisor's radio net became active. A report was being received from Maj. Tom Gnibus, reporting for the Marine advisors at FSB Mai Loc.

"FBs Sarge and Nui Ba Ho have reported numerous enemy troop sightings and heavy artillery fire on both of their positions."

Major Joy moved over to the G-3 watch officer's radio and requested permission to call Maj. Walt Boomer to get an immediate assessment of the 4th Battalion's situation.

To insure the enemy could not listen to his transmission, he switched the radio to the "secure voice cypher mode." The watch officer's small radio loudspeaker volume control was increased so we in the watch area could also listen.

Boomer responded to his call sign, "Mike," and Capt. Ray Smith's also came on the radio net as "Mike-1." He reported, "Shortly after daylight the NVA began to shell us here at Sarge and at Nui Ba Ho." His assessment was that it was not a routine artillery attack because it was too heavy and too concentrated. "Our Alpha command bunker has received two direct hits," he said, "but miraculously no one was hurt. We have a number of Vietnamese Marine casualties. Both my position and Smith's have been raked by artillery and rocket fire. So far this morning we've been hit with about every caliber weapon the NVA has."

I had yet to meet Boomer, but I was impressed with the calmness with which he described the situation. His initial report would later prove to be an accurate assessment of the enemy situation in the western mountains. He was no stranger to combat. I remembered that his Officer's Qualification Record (OQR) recorded the award of the Silver Star medal in 1966-67 for his heroic action as the infantry company commander of Hotel Company, 2d Battalion, 4th Marines.

He continued, "At 1100 this morning, a patrol from the 4th Battalion's 1st Company on Nui Ba Ho made contact with a company-sized unit; they are still in contact at this time." Smith joined in to report he had also observed three other NVA units of approximate company size moving toward his position. He and the battalion executive officer had been requesting artillery fire support from both FSB Mai Loc and Camp Carroll. Boomer added, "The sky is so overcast, TAC Air cannot be used up here right now. We would like some air when these clouds lift."

In the G-3 watch area, we were listening intently as Boomer continued:

"It looks like this could be their big push. Captain Smith

[who spoke fluent Vietnamese] indicated he and his counterpart had been listening to the North Vietnamese artillery observers' radio transmissions and they had been making adjustments of down to ten meters on their target areas. The NVA's fire is as accurate and as heavy as we have ever experienced up here. We're all OK now, but there is probably a big battle coming our way!"

Boomer closed off his transmission by saying that he would begin sending hourly situation reports.

Major Joy briefly went over the situation on the western flank. He felt that, under the circumstances, he should return to Brigade 147's headquarters at the Mai Loc combat base as soon as possible. Jim requested permission to use Team 155's command and control helicopter (CC Bird) to return to FSB Mai Loc, but it was not immediately available. At this time, Wilson also said that my planned flight to FB Sarge would be delayed for awhile.

It was almost noon. There was no further immediate action to be taken, so Joy, Murray and I walked to the Team 155 dining hall to eat lunch.

On our way over to Advisory Team 155's compound, Murray suggested we stop by the Army's sensor read-out bunker to see what enemy movement reports had been received. It was a classified area with an armed soldier at the bunker entrance. After confirming our identification, he allowed us to enter. An impressive-looking Army warrant officer was on watch. He gave us a hasty, but well-organized, briefing on the U.S. electronic surveillance systems operating in the northern provinces.

"This is the only ground-surveillance station north of Danang," he said. "We have been alerted that our station will be deactivated during May. Most of the technology is still classified, so it will not be turned over to the ARVN when we close down."

Using the map, he pointed out where the unattended seismic detectors were operating. A variety of surveillance systems had been planted to cover the DMZ and likely avenues of approach out of the western mountains. Any movement near the emplaced devices would register an electronic signal in the read-out bunker.

The primary purpose of the sensor systems was to detect enemy infiltrations. The warrant officer said, "They enable us not only to find the enemy but also to keep track of his movements.

"As an example, during the past three weeks our sensors have reported heavy vehicle movement on Route 9, west of FB Sarge toward the Laotian border. Truck movement reports have tripled in the DMZ area. Many of our sensor string activations have signaled both wheeled and tracked vehicle traffic. This past week we have been getting solid readings during daylight, and this has never happened before. There sure is a lot of NVA activity out there."

It was an enlightening briefing on a new and important technological capability that enabled a field commander to place sensors at great distances from his forces that could alert him of any foot or vehicle movements. They were "silent sentries," ever-watchful day and night, reporting any type of movement to a centralized monitoring headquarters in all kinds of weather. Once implanted, seismic detectors require no further support and work without assistance. In sharp contrast, inserted reconnaissance teams are always subject to discovery, need food and water, and often require emergency extractions after detection. In our walk to the Army's dining hall, the three of us agreed that sensors of all types could replace deep reconnaissance teams in some future war.

On entering the dining hall we were invited to share a table with Maj. James E. Smock, an Army armor officer who was the senior advisor to the 20th Tank Battalion. He was fresh out of the field where the battalion had just completed its final training test. Smock was proud to note the 20th had the only M-48 medium tanks in Vietnam and felt they were finally combat ready. (This chance meeting and some interesting insight on the readiness of the 20th Tank Battalion would prove to be beneficial the next time I spoke with Jim Smock.) He impressed us with his extensive training program that the ARVN tankers had successfully completed. We wished him well with his unit, then left as it was time to get back to the division's TOC.

It was just 1200 noon. As we were leaving, the thunder of artillery could be heard to the north and seconds later artillery rounds began to impact around us. Quang Tri airstrip just across Highway 1 to our east also began receiving incoming fire. The runway was hit several times. More rounds were falling on the 3d Division cantonment areas.

We ran for safety to the TOC bunker. When we arrived, both the ARVN and U.S. watch officers' tactical radios were receiving attack-by-fire reports from all ARVN fire bases.

The NVA's Easter offensive had begun. Little did we realize at that time that during the next ten days some of the most unique events of the Vietnam War were going to occur.

# CHAPTER FOUR

# DAY ONE: EASTER OFFENSIVE

At noon, 30 March 1972, the North Vietnamese Army launched its largest offensive of the Vietnam War. A well-coordinated attacking force of three divisions with supporting units crossed the DMZ along the Ben Hai River and invaded south into Quang Tri Province. Heavy artillery barrages preceded NVA infantry advances which were supported by over four hundred armored fighting vehicles, artillery and mobile AAA and SAM batteries. The enemy's long-range 130MM field guns poured fire on the outposts and fire bases of the 3d ARVN Division. Hundreds of 122MM rockets, 130MM artillery rounds, and other ordnance slammed into Camp Carroll, Mai Loc, Sarge, and Nui Ba Ho, Alpha 2 and 4, Charlie 1 and 2, the Dong Ha and Quang Tri combat bases. Every major ARVN installation was pounded by deadly-accurate concentrations of fire. Each fire base location was known to the enemy and it was easy to target for massed fires because the same locations had been used for years by both U.S. and ARVN forces.

Two of the 3d Division's infantry regiments were in the process of exchanging positions and moving toward FSB Carroll and Charlie 2, when thousands of artillery rounds struck the exposed troops causing instant death and chaos.

The 2d Regiment was being replaced at Camp Carroll and the outposts at Khe Gio and FB Fuller by the 56th Regiment. After only three weeks of deployment along the DMZ, the 56th

.now had to assume full responsibility for the northwestern anchor of the crescent defense line for Quang Tri Province. In turn, the 57th Regiment had just recently completed its move into fire bases Alpha 1, 2 and 3 and Charlie 1, a coastal and piedmont area extending from the Gulf of Tonkin inland for fifteen miles.

With the 56th ARVN Regiment were two U.S. Army advisors, Lt. Col. William Camper and Maj. Joe Brown. Camper was an experienced field advisor who had already served with two other ARVN regiments. His first tour in 1964–65 was with the 3d ARVN Regiment, 1st Division in the Hue City area. When he returned to South Vietnam in late 1971, he was initially assigned to the 2d ARVN Regiment, 3d Division now located at Camp Carroll. In March 1972 he was reassigned to

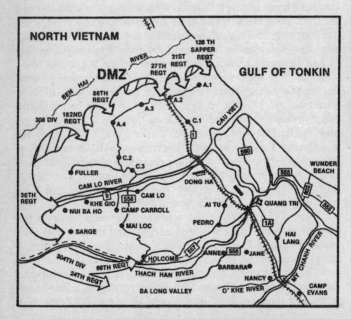

**INITIAL THRUST OF NVN OFFENSIVE**

the recently activated 56th Regiment.[1] During the shift of positions the regiment had been ordered to move in a movement-to-contact formation from Charlie 2 southwest to Camp Carroll. The leading battalion was to move through Cam Lo, turn west on Route 9 and march onto the FB Khe Gio. Camper positioned himself with Lt. Col. Pham Van Dinh, the regimental commander, while Major Brown made plans to displace with the regimental logistic support trains.

The regiment's headquarters was to follow the lead battalion with the logistical support trains in trace. Another battalion moving alongside the command element was to move as flank security, north of the Cam Lo-Cua Viet River, to FB Fuller. Just before noon, the 1st Battalion reached Khe Gio. The regimental command element moved forward into Camp Carroll and replaced the 2d Regiment which in turn began its own displacement, north to Charlie 2.

Colonel Camper later recalled:

> The attack on us began as heavy artillery fire. It was well-aimed fire estimated to be Soviet 130MM guns. In the first hour we received in excess of 200 rounds. The incoming rounds almost immediately destroyed all the radio antennas that were standing above our deep bunkers. The incoming fire caused tremendous morale problems since the South Vietnamese were not used to being on the receiving end of artillery, not accurate artillery fire.[2]

His jeep and radios were destroyed in the first hour. The NVA artillery knocked out the fire base's generators and power lines leading to the underground command and communication bunkers and most telephone lines.

Camper said:

> It was difficult for the regiment's staff to operate in the darkness underground. The ARVN had become accustomed to American-style briefings with the big maps, plastic plexiglass boards, iridescent pencils, lights, all the comforts of home. I don't think too many of them gave much forethought to having no lights. I had a box of candles which I passed out to the TOC; we operated on that for awhile.[3]

The 56th's First Battalion, moving toward FB Fuller to relieve a battalion of the 2d Regiment, was also hit by intense artillery fire. The effect was instantaneous and devastating. The battalion never reached its destination, having lost all communication with its regimental headquarters. Without being exposed to any NVA attacking ground forces, the battalion simply dissolved and elements could not be relocated for several days.

The effect of this intense attack on the regiment was almost prophetic, since shortly after his assignment Camper's initial assessment of the quality of its officers and enlisted personnel was:

> The regiment was in bad shape. It did not have the quality of officers that the 2d Regiment had. It did need advice. I was told the 56th and 57th were formed from enlisted men who were deserters, offenders from the 1st Infantry Division. They were sent north as a punishment and also as a deterrent because they could not escape the DMZ area very easily. This may have been true. I have no verification of this.[4]

The 57th Regiment had been adjusting to its new tactical area of responsibility (TAOR) bordering the coastline. (Lt. Col. Heath Twichell, Jr., was serving as senior advisor to Lt. Col. Do Zeon Gioi. Maj. Wallace Fajardo was deputy senior advisor.)

The regimental headquarters was located at Charlie 1 along Highway 1. Its 1st Battalion had two companies positioned around the regimental command post and two companies in training south of Quang Tri City. The 2d Battalion, with four rifle companies, was deployed along the south edge of the DMZ. Their CP at Alpha 2 had two rifle companies patrolling along the DMZ. The regiment's reconnaissance company was located near the coastline at Alpha 1.[5]

The NVA began to increase its activities in the 57th area of responsibility on 28 March when FB Charlie 1 was struck with approximately 300 rounds of 122MM rockets. On the 29th and 30th of March, sporadic artillery fire again struck Charlie 1, Alpha 2 and 3. Because of the 200–300 rounds striking each fire base the 1st Battalion's two rifle companies south of Quang Tri were brought north to Charlie 1 on 30 March.

Deadly concentrations were simultaneously striking FSB Mai Loc, FB Holcomb and Dong Ha combat base. Every ARVN strong point was paralyzed under a withering rain of steel.

The massive artillery offensive was followed by ground assaults. T-54, T-55 and PT-76 tanks would eventually spearhead four attacks out of the DMZ. Two were to be directed against positions of the 2d Regiment in the vicinity of FSB Fuller and FSB A-4 (Con Thien). The other armor drives would move south paralleling National Highway 1, attacking the 57th Regiment at Alpha 1 and Alpha 2. Further inland, the NVA's westernmost assaults were intensified against FBs Sarge, Nui Ba Ho and Holcomb.

South Vietnam's entire northern boundary lay open to the largest enemy attack of the Vietnam War. Over 30,000 men from elements of the 304th and 308th Divisions, along with three separate infantry regiments of the B5 Front, two tank regiments, and five artillery regiments, entered the ground campaign of the Nguyen Hue Offensive in a decisive struggle for control of the South.

The unexpected direction of the assault across the DMZ caught the South Vietnamese forward elements when they were disorganized and only partially settled into defensive positions. The troops of the 56th and 57th were marginally trained and unfamiliar with the terrain in their new AOs. Also, the ARVN defenses in the DMZ area were designed primarily to counter infiltration and local attacks.[6] These positions were not prepared to give depth to the battlefield or interlocking support. Tragically, there was no active 3d ARVN Division defense plan against an invasion from a conventional warfare attack.

With the news of the massive attack, activity at the headquarters, 3d Division at Ai Tu reached fever pitch. The troop billeting and support area for both the ARVN and U.S. advisory team began receiving long-range 130MM fire and casualties began to mount. Radio communication nets were disrupted as antenna systems were destroyed from the blast and fragmenting shells.

In the division's TOC, reports of the attacks were radioed

to General Lam's MR-1 headquarters. His American counterpart, Maj. Gen. Frederick J. Kroesen, Commanding General, First Regional Assistance Command (FRAC) received his first alert of the attacks through the U.S. advisory communication channels.

Lam notified his JGS headquarters in Saigon. No immediate action was taken to reinforce MR-1 because the JGS was convinced, and had long anticipated, that any major North Vietnamese attack would come from the west instead of the north. The enemy's crossing the DMZ, they believed, would demonstrate a blatant violation of the 1954 Geneva Accords. "It just won't happen," said Lam. It was obvious that he and his staff had focused on what they believed were the intentions of the NVA, not their capabilities.[7]

Lam did review the forces available to him in MR-1 to meet the new threat. He then directed Marine Brigade 258, in a reserve position at FB Nancy, to move north. The 1st Armored Brigade's 20th Tank Battalion was also alerted to redeploy north. As Major Smock had told us, the battalion had only been activated a short time earlier and was in the final phase of its first major field training exercises. Thus, the battalion had never fired a shot in anger and was scheduled to be announced as operational on 30 March 1972.

Shortly after noon the 1st Armor Brigade's field headquarters received a frantic message from General Lam's MR-1 headquarters to halt the field test and return the 20th Tank Battalion to Quang Tri where it was to be placed under the operational control (OPCON) of the 3d ARVN Division. One tank company was to move directly to the city of Dong Ha.[8]

Col. Raymond R. Battreall, who was chief of staff of the Army advisory group to the 1st ARVN Armored Brigade, could not understand the order to halt the final phase of the 20th Tank field test. He and Brig. Gen. Toan, ARVN chief of armor, flew to Ai Tu combat base and met with General Giai. Both officers were briefed on the North Vietnamese action along the DMZ. There appeared to be no immediate threat to the city of Dong Ha, and the 3d Division still didn't comprehend what was really happening to its ten most northern fire bases. General Toan, with advice from Colonel Battreall, suggested to General Giai that it would be unwise and premature to commit the 20th Tank Battalion. Instead, it would be better to hold the fifty M-48 medium tanks together, to be committed as a counterattack force as soon as Giai could clarify the situation and determine where a counterattack should be launched.

Giai was further persuaded that since the tanks had been actively involved in a week of field training, he would get better service out of the battalion if whatever time was available was fully devoted to maintenance. The battalion's tanks returned to Quang Tri combat base on the afternoon of 30 March where they immediately went into a crash maintenance program.

Around 1800 Col. Ngo Van Dinh received an order from Giai to displace his Marine Brigade 258 to Dong Ha combat base.[9] Maj. Jon Easley, USMC, the senior brigade advisor, alerted his COVANs of the impending move. Two of colonel Dinh's three infantry and his one artillery battalions were ordered to move out just after darkness. The 6th Infantry Battalion, located on nearby FB Barbara, would remain in place, but was alerted to be prepared to also move north on order.

The 7th VNMC Infantry Battalion, under the command of Major Hue, had been stationed in Danang since 4 February 1972 where it served as strategic reserve for MR-1. Maj. Andy DeBona, USMC, was the senior advisor to this unit with Capt. Ronald Rice, USMC, as his assistant.

During one of the 7th's patrolling actions, Marines of the battalion had uncovered a cache of fifty North Vietnamese flags. DeBona and Rice quickly decided that they would be invaluable for barter. Such things as eggs, steaks, spare parts and weapons mysteriously became available when an enemy flag was offered in trade.

As DeBona was later to recall, 30 March started out like any other day.

Ron Rice went out on a "steak and eggs" mission at 1000 with two flags. Major Hue, his S-3 officer, two Vietnamese company commanders, and Rice were passing the afternoon playing a Vietnamese-style poker game. At 1400, with no prior warning, the battalion received the order to move out. The mission was to reinforce the Marines at FSB Mai Loc.[10]

At 1600, the battalion was loaded and aboard trucks ready to move, directed to drive straight through. No security or fire support would be planned to cover their eighty-kilometer motor march because speed of movement and time was considered crucial.

They moved out precisely at 1600. Rice had still not returned from his "morale run" and DeBona waited for him. DeBona said, "He came back around 1630 and we caught up with the battalion just south of the Hai Van Pass." They drove throughout the night with all vehicle lights blazing, giving mute testimony to the urgency of their mission.

South Vietnamese villagers, who had become complacent because of the enemy's infrequent attacks, were suddenly caught up in the sounds and effects of an expanding battle. Villages and hamlets located in northern Quang Tri Province near the ARVN fire bases were struck by artillery and rocket fire. ARVN soldiers from the 3d Division and regional forces, seeing their hamlets under siege, left their units to protect their wives and families. Some returned to their units; many did not.

Thatched-roof huts caught fire from the fragmenting white-hot shells. Frightened civilians, defenseless before the impacting shells, began to sense the impending calamity. Fear gripped every village, adding to the chaos.

Three regiments of NVA artillery continued to pound all twelve major ARVN fire bases through the afternoon hours. There was no letup on these attacks. NVA infantry units advanced out of the cover of the DMZ toward the most northern defensive line of Alpha 1, 2, 3, and 4 and FB Fuller. In the west, elements of the 308th Division were moving into assault positions against FBs Sarge and Nui Ba Ho.

South of Mai Loc, on FB Holcomb, two rifle companies of the 8th VNMC Battalion were in heavy contact with elements of the 304th Division. Headquarters of the 8th Battalion located at Mai Loc had lost radio contact with one of its companies as the numerically superior enemy force appeared to be positioning itself for an assault to overrun FB Holcomb. This base was an important strong point that guarded a natural avenue of approach into Quang Tri City; hence its loss would be a drastic setback.

All South Vietnamese infantry units were demanding artillery support but there were not enough tubes to respond or crews willing to service them under fire. The on-rushing enemy exploited the failure of the ARVN forces to fire counterbattery or deliver accurate fire on otherwise lucrative troop concentrations. There were just too many targets. From the forward fire bases came continuous requests for artillery support, while back within the ARVN artillery battery positions, crews were abandoning their guns and seeking protection from the incoming steel. South Vietnamese gun crews, unaccustomed to being on the receiving end of an artillery attack, were hesitant to remain on their guns. Thus, when it was needed the most, ARVN counterbattery fire was drastically reduced because of fear in the gun pits.

Because of the inferior or inadequate ARVN counterbattery fire, the enemy was able to increase the intensity of its artillery attacks on the western flanks. Located on FB Sarge, with Major Boomer, were two U.S. Army enlisted men who maintained an electronic listening post. Trained to operate special communication equipment, their mission was to gather information from North Vietnamese radio circuits. Shortly after noon, their bunker was hit. During a lull in the shelling, Boomer crawled over to find their bunker enveloped in flames. There was no sign of life. He later recalled that the bunker had taken a direct hit early in the fire attack. The round had in all likelihood passed through the aperture and exploded inside, killing both young men instantly. These soldiers were the first Americans to die in the Nguyen Hue Offensive.*

Around 1500, the NVA began to mass their infantry for an assault on Nui Ba Ho. Capt. Ray Smith, USMC, with the Bravo command group, radioed Boomer that the enemy was staging for a major ground assault as NVA began to supplement their artillery fire with very accurate 82MM and 60MM mortar preparatory fires onto the northern segment of Nui Ba Ho. Shortly afterward, Smith reported that the mortar position had just been hit and that every member of their mortar

---

*The Pentagon MIA-POW Center has identified these two soldiers as SP-5 Gary Westcott and SP-4 Bruce Crosley, Jr.

crews had been killed. By dusk, the NVA had worked their units almost to the perimeter wire of Nui Ba Ho. NVA artillery and mortar crews began to orchestrate the final destruction of the hilltop outpost. There was doubt in the minds of the besieged defenders whether they could hang on to Nui Ba Ho through the night.

In the 3d ARVN Division TOC bunker there was a great deal of confusion as to the overall situation. The U.S. Army advisory team, like the 3d ARVN Division staff, had not prepared for a major attack across the DMZ. Caught off guard, the division and the advisory team found themselves paralyzed by the intensity and accuracy of the North Vietnamese artillery attacks. Radio reports received in the TOC were more often emotional than factual.

The advisory team's compound was receiving sporadic incoming fire. Most of the young soldiers and NCOs of the team had never experienced an enemy attack by fire. Frightened, they scrambled into long neglected sandbagged trenches and remained there through the night.

Major Wilson, the G-3 advisor, set up a 24-hour watch. A report was received in the division TOC that two U.S. Marine advisors had been killed on FB Holcomb. Major Joy and I both knew there were no U.S. Marine advisors with the two VNMC infantry companies on FB Holcomb and we were quickly able to verify that this report of U.S. casualties was erroneous.

At this point I decided to remain in the division TOC bunker and monitor the activities of the VNMC's units and pass this information on to Major Wilson. As a visitor to the northern area, I had no command responsibilities, but offered to work under his guidance. He accepted this arrangement and invited me to set up an additional VNMC advisor's radio net in his G-3 watch area.

At 1600, Major Joy received a call that Col. Nguyen Nang Bao, commander, Marine Brigade 147, was sending a Vietnamese Air Force helicopter to pick him up and deliver him back to Mai Loc. Just before he left, Joy said, "Colonel Turley, I'm going to leave Captain Murray with you here in the division TOC."

Together, Murray and I established radio contact with the

advisors at Mai Loc, Sarge and Nui Ba Ho. We found a yellow tablet and opened a G-3 journal of events. This would become the primary record of events maintained by the U.S. advisors during the next five days.

Also located in the G-3 watch area of the 3d Division's TOC were two U.S. Marines from Sub Unit One, 1st ANGLICO. First Lt. Joel Eisenstein was the officer in charge of Team 1–2. Through him I learned that an ANGLICO naval gunfire spot team was located on Alpha 2, which was in as desperate a situation as were the Marines at Sarge and Nui Ba Ho.[11]

Eisenstein and his senior NCO, Sergeant Swift, had been closely monitoring his spot team's status. First Lt. David C. Bruggeman, Sergeant Newton, Corp. James Worth and two other enlisted Marines were deployed on Alpha 2 having arrived several days prior to 30 March 1972. Their mission was to support the infantry and artillery units by directing naval gunfire and any other supporting arms necessary to engage the enemy in the areas north, east and west of Alpha 2. They were outfitted with the standard USMC radios and other communications equipment to permit them to communicate with aircraft as well as U.S. naval ships. The team was stationed in an old French tower and when not on duty slept in the underground portion of the structure. They were also to assist spotting for the Vietnamese gunners at the fire base. In exchange for their services, the Vietnamese infantry battalion provided them security.

FB Alpha 2 was located north of the village of Gio Linh, along the main north-south highway, situated upon a little finger of ground that had steep slopes along the northern edge. The ground surrounding the fire base, and particularly to the west and northwest, consisted of gently rolling small hills. There were no trees in the area as they had all been destroyed by shell fire. There was a considerable amount of underbrush and short vegetation covering the ground in all directions. The base was shaped in an elongated oval with its axis running north and south. The oval could be divided into four separate sectors. The first sector, the northernmost, was where the artillery, consisting of a battery of six 105MM howitzers, was positioned, generally in an arc along the northern edge of the oval. In the second sector, below the artillery, stood an old French fortress. The word "fortress" is probably a misnomer, as the fort was nothing more than an observation post, twenty-five to thirty feet tall, constructed of concrete with an underground basement area. The entrance faced south and had several steps rising to the ground level. The tower provided unobstructed observation in all directions while an area behind, some thirty-five to forty yards long, was used as a helicopter landing zone.

In the third, southernmost quadrant of the fire base were two rows of sandbagged Quonset huts in which were stored the supplies, motor vehicles and other odds and ends of the Vietnamese personnel who manned the base.

The base's primary defense was centered around the howitzers, augmented by a row of foxholes stretched around

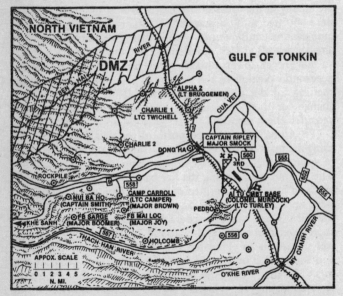

**US ADVISORS AND THEIR FIRE BASE LOCATIONS**

the perimeter of the fire base and along the edges of the hill. There were several rows of concertina wire and other obstacles stretched out for ten to twenty yards outside the foxholes around all the sides of the fire base and also at the entrance and exit to the base located at the southernmost portion of the hill.

The NVA began their siege on Alpha 2 at approximately 1215 on 30 March. Lieutenant Bruggeman immediately reported the unusually heavy volume of artillery fire on their position as he and his spot team reported the conduct of the battle from their observation post. Shortly after the invasion began, Bruggeman radioed Lieutenant Eisenstein in the 3d Division TOC that the ARVN artillery batteries were not responding to calls for fire. He reported that instead of remaining on their guns, the South Vietnamese gunners had abandoned their gun pits and were hiding in their bunkers. There was no counterbattery fire.

Initially, only one U.S. Navy destroyer was positioned off the coast.[12] That vessel, the U.S.S. *Buchanan* (DDG-14) quickly moved in to a position close to the shore and began to deliver accurate naval gunfire support on enemy targets around Alpha 1 and 2.

On the far western flank, FSB Mai Loc was under heavy artillery attack as Major Joy's helicopter approached the airstrip. He directed the pilot to set down near the front gate of the Huong Hoa district headquarters, disembarked and began to move on foot toward the Mai Loc combat base. About halfway there he flagged down a Vietnamese Marine truck and rode into Mai Loc in the midst of incoming artillery fire.

Upon arriving, he found Brigade 147's command element had moved into an underground bunker where Colonel Bao's staff was operating effectively. The advisors' sandbagged bunkers were heavily damaged. Maj. Tom Gnibus, USMC advisor to the 2d Artillery Battalion, had moved into the brigade operations bunker and was working closely with its fire support coordinators.

Colonel Bao was frustrated in his efforts to get reinforcing fire for the 4th Marine Battalion positions on Sarge and Nui Ba Ho. His repeated requests for reinforcing fires from Camp Carroll had produced little results. When the twenty-two guns located at Camp Carroll were in fact shooting, the direction of fire was primarily to the north. Also, as the gun crews sought shelter, Camp Carroll's counterbattery fires were becoming less intense and less effective, allowing the NVA's offensive momentum to accelerate and intensify.

As darkness neared on the first day of the NVA's Nguyen Hue Offensive, all ARVN combat bases were reeling under the continuing heavy artillery barrages. During the first day over 11,000 rounds had struck South Vietnamese fire bases and surrounding villages. The greatest pressure from ground attacks was experienced on the western flank, especially around FBs Sarge and Nui Ba Ho.

FB Nui Ba Ho had several platoon and squad-sized positions outside the perimeter's wire. At approximately 1800, one platoon-sized outpost 600 meters to the north known as E-4 came under intense small arms and B-40 rocket fire. This was followed by three "human-wave" ground attacks. The Vietnamese Marines manning outpost E-4 repelled these assaults, inflicting heavy casualties on their attackers, and held the position. At 1830 a squad outpost located on the east side of Nui Ba Ho came under heavy ground attack from their north. That position was overrun and of the defenders only seven wounded Marines made it back to Nui Ba Ho that night.[13]

Simultaneously, another squad position on the south side of the fire base perimeter was assaulted. The Marines at this position repelled the first attack but were overrun by a second and larger assault. Only a third of the squad survived and made it back to Nui Ba Ho. Losses were mounting, as the NVA had troops on three sides of Nui Ba Ho. The pressure was building.

Capt. Ray Smith remembered:

After full darkness fell, ground activity slackened off considerably. However, throughout the night Nui Ba Ho received incoming mortars and thrown TNT charges. Twice during the night, the defenders of E-4 killed three-man recon or sapper teams inside their position.[14]

At approximately 2000, a U.S. Air Force AC-119 Stinger gunship began to orbit above Sarge and Nui Ba Ho. Low cloud cover blocked out the aircraft's view of Nui Ba Ho and prevented Smith from using the aircraft's machine gun platforms on the encircling enemy. Major Boomer then attempted to use a radar-emitting transponder to direct the aircraft against NVA positions. They could not complete a lock-on of the electronic position locating device, so the aircraft's guns could not be assured its fires would avoid friendly troops.[15]

Exposing himself to intense artillery fire, Boomer then attempted to use an infrared strobe light to enable the aircraft to locate the target area. As a last resort, the air crewmen dropped parachute flares in an attempt to have the two advisors direct the aircraft to their location. This proved frustrating and fruitless, as cloud cover had dropped to a few hundred feet above their hilltop positions. With the weather deteriorating, the aircraft departed the area, leaving behind an increasingly desperate situation.

Immediately after the AC-119 had departed, the NVA renewed and increased their probes on Sarge and Nui Ba Ho. Back at Mai Loc the VNMC's 2d Artillery Battalion was attempting to improve its responsiveness to the 4th Battalion's call for fire. The Vietnamese Marines, like the ARVN artillerymen, continued to leave their guns whenever the enemy's rounds impacted in their area. The 2d Battalion's officers exposed themselves to the incoming fires to convince their gun crews that the only way they were going to stop the artillery from coming in on them was to start hurting the NVA by shooting back. Capt. David Randall, USMC, an artillery advisor, repeatedly exposed himself by working directly with the 2d Battalion's battery commanders to get the artillerymen to fire their howitzers while undergoing attacks by fire. This was to no avail.

Back along Highway 1, the Quang Tri airstrip had suffered numerous hits during the day, but the runway remained operative. Around 1800, Colonel Murdock's U-21 aircraft returned from Saigon. He briefly visited the division TOC bunker and then retired to his quarters for the evening. I doubt that he slept.

Around 2000, the TOC began to settle in for the night. The staff and advisors plotted units on their tactical maps and made a preliminary assessment of the unprecedented intensity of the enemy's attack. The tactical situation that came out of this was confusing to both the ARVN and the American advisors.

Major Wilson and I had spent most of the afternoon in his G-3 watch area attempting to coordinate the array of supporting arms available to the division. In addition to the ARVN artillery and naval gunfire, both U.S. and VNAF air support was available. Although low cloud cover prevented tactical aircraft from operating, other air assets could be utilized. Recognizing that the only currently usable air power would be ARCLIGHT (B-52 strikes), Combat Skyspot and LORAN (radar controlled) bombing, we began to prepare air requests for their support.

Maj. David A. Brookbank, USAF, was serving as the air liaison officer (ALO) to the 3d ARVN Division and his liaison team consisted of a captain and two airmen. Brookbank had just joined Advisory Team 155 on 6 March 1972 and was still in the process of establishing a counterpart relationship with his opposite number in the VNAF ALO. Brookbank had just made his March report in which he summarized:

> The period 6 March–30 March can be characterized by a low level of activity and relatively ineffective performance on the part of the VNAF, ALO, VNAF FACs and helicopter operations. The most serious and obvious flaw in the VNAF structure at Quang Tri was the lack of command leadership, whether it is attributed to the ALO or FAC and/or helicopter detachment commanders. There is a definite lack of senior ranking command supervision of any major VNAF operations conducted for the 3d ARVN Division in this time period.[16]

Major Brookbank proved to be one of the most resourceful U.S. officers in the TOC. He and his air liaison team worked in coordination with the division G-3 to process air requests from all units. His personal stamina and ability to operate under the most difficult of conditions immeasurably aided the South Vietnamese forces.

Brookbank's team began submitting requests for close air support missions. Hard targets were identified for bombing the next morning. The advancing NVA divisions were presenting some of the most profitable targets of the war, but only if the weather would break.

As dawn approached, we received the worst possible forecast; an extremely heavy storm front extending directly across the DMZ. It was doubtful if any close air support missions could be run during the next twenty-four hours.

It was to be a long and fateful night for the division's twelve fire bases and also for the few of us in the TOC bunker. In coordination with the 3d Division staff, the advisors attempted to develop an assessment on the combat effectiveness of units, their locations and their casualties. Equally important was the logistical status of all friendly units. The ARVN artillery batteries had been firing sporadically for eight to ten hours and would be needing ammunition replenishments. Both the South Vietnamese and U.S. advisor radio nets were used to obtain operational and logistical reports from three besieged regiments.

Prior to the NVA offensive, the Marine advisors at FSB Mai Loc were twice daily making radio contact with their advisory headquarters at the Bo Tu Linh. When the NVA began their attack on FBs Sarge and Nui Ba Ho, Major Boomer made numerous radio reports to Major Joy at FSB Mai Loc. Since it was an unusually heavy attack, the situation of the 4th Battalion was also radioed the 350 miles south to Saigon. When the first reports of heavy contact were received, Captain Izenour, at the Bo Tu Linh, immediately set up a round-the-clock radio watch to assist the besieged Marines where possible.

When Boomer reported 75 percent of FB Sarge's northern defenses had been destroyed by indirect fire, Izenour carried this information to the MACV intelligence center. Initially, the watch officers doubted the speed with which he had obtained the information on the accuracy of the damage. However, several hours later, a similar report arrived through normal radio channels from FRAC headquarters in Danang. This first report on the intense shelling of FB Sarge did alert the MACV staff that there were strong indications the NVA was undertaking its first major combat action along the DMZ in months.

Unfortunately, the lack of a steady flow of information on

the fluid situation in northern Quang Tri Province resulted in failure to identify early on that the anticipated NVA offensive had been launched. Isolated from the distant battlefield, the MACV staff did not fully appreciate the significance of the sketchy details and generally remained inactive, simply waiting for more details.

In the MACV operations and intelligence centers, the U.S. watch officers checked with their South Vietnamese JGS counterparts only to learn that General Lam's MR-1 operational center had not yet reported any heavy fighting in the 3d ARVN Division's area of responsibility. However, both the U.S. and the JGS operation centers did begin to make radio and telephone inquiries to their subordinate headquarters in the northern provinces.

Information was also being sought from the 3d ARVN Division and regional forces by General Lam's staff in Danang and from the South Vietnamese JGS headquarters in Saigon. The inevitable radio and telephone calls began around 1800, all of which sought immediate answers to both relevant and ridiculous questions. The staff of both the division and Team 155 responded as best they could under the circumstances. Difficulties arose when well-meaning U.S. MACV staff officers in Saigon would bypass the U.S. FRAC staff in Danang to get the latest update. Telephone calls in the TOC bunker were answered by whoever was closest to the phone. In this fashion both accurate and misleading information was passed on, leading to more frequent inquiries seeking further clarification on Team 155's earlier reports. Chaos prevailed.

Around 2200, the advisor's G-3 telephone rang again. It was connected to the Danang headquarters through a radio relay system. FRAC operations center was confirming to us that the weather forecast for 31 March looked very unfavorable. We were directed to "continue to request B-52 strikes and high altitude radar bombing missions, but don't expect any TAC Air."

This, of course, meant all of our supporting fire would have to come from the ARVN artillery units or the U.S. Navy gunfire ships off the mouth of the Cam Lo-Cua Viet River. Although the U.S.S. *Buchanan* was eager to respond to our gunfire requests, its twin 5/54″ guns could only fire inland approximately ten miles. Its main turret gun could strike targets around Alpha 1 and 2, Charlie 1 and the city of Dong Ha. The South Vietnamese fire bases located further inland, to the west of Highway 1, would have to be completely supported by ARVN artillery batteries; batteries that were becoming less and less responsive to the increased requests for fire support of the infantry regiments.

Hourly situational reports were coming in from the COVANs at Sarge and Nui Ba Ho where situations were continuing to deteriorate. One favorable aspect of the overcast skies and climatic condition was an improvement in radio communications between FB Sarge and our position in the division TOC bunker. From this we learned that NVA infantry had now been sighted on all four sides of Sarge and Nui Ba Ho.

The only positive sign of encouragement in the TOC came when Marine Brigade 258 reported its arrival at the Dong Ha combat base. Colonel Dinh's brigade had moved its motor column from FB Nancy under total blackout conditions. This move, in spite of the darkness and the refugees struggling along Highway 1, went well. The lead elements moved into their new assembly areas at 2300 as Brigade 258 assumed the mission of division reserve.

The bridgade's 3d Infantry Battalion brought up the rear of the column and entered the old USMC Dong Ha combat base just in time to receive rocket and artillery attacks, which continued throughout the night. Most of the rounds impacted around an ARVN battery of 175MM guns, just north of the brigade's hastily selected CP.

The 3d Marine Battalion was given the mission of base defense and as the only uncommitted infantry battalion was designated as 3d ARVN Division Reserve. Major Binh, an aggressive commander, had two COVANs, Captains John Ripley and James Johnson, assigned to his battalion.

Ripley had previous combat experience in Vietnam. He had served three years in a force reconnaissance company, during which time he attended the Army's airborne and ranger courses and Navy's underwater swimmers course. He had also been assigned duty with the British Royal Marines where he commanded a company. He was nearing the end of his one-year tour as an advisor. During the previous eleven months he, his assistant, Captain Johnson* and Major Binh had become exceptionally close in their advisor-counterpart relationship. Long hours had been devoted to discussing Viet Cong and North Vietnamese military tactics. Over the months, the rapport between Binh and Ripley epitomized the fusion of leadership and advisory roles first envisioned by Colonel Croizat eighteen years earlier.

Maj. Jon Easley, Brigade 258's senior advisor, radioed Maj. Jim Joy at Mai Loc of his arrival. They updated each other on VNMC units and the location of all U.S. advisors.

The 3d Division's G-3 officers were extremely pleased when Colonel Dinh radioed the news of his brigade's arrival at the Dong Ha combat base. Almost immediately after the division TOC had received the report, Marine advisors confirmed the brigade's arrival through their radio nets. A ray of hope arose as both the Vietnamese and Americans experienced the first dual-channel radio report reconfirming the validity of a parallel reporting system.

On into the night the enemy's artillery and rocket fire harassed ARVN strong points. At approximately 0200, the VNMC's 7th Infantry Battalion from Danang arrived at the main gate of the Dong Ha combat base. Major DeBona remembered:

> It was extremely quiet when we arrived. We moved into an assembly area with our vehicle lights blazing. The battalion was slow getting its lights off. Fifteen minutes later the NVA threw a thirty to forty-five artillery barrage around us. Major Hue quickly ordered his four infantry companies to move southwest to the village of Throm Truong Chi. The battalion arrived and set in about 0430.[17]

The 7th Battalion was alerted to prepare to move west along Highway 9 in the morning. Its mission would be to keep the road clear between Dong Ha and Cam Lo because this roadway served as the primary supply route for FB Camp Carroll and

---

*Johnson was on R&R leave on 30 March 1972.

FSB Mai Loc. If Route 9 was closed off by the NVA, a helicopter resupply effort would be the only means of keeping the fire bases replenished.

Earlier in the day, at General Abrams' Headquarters in Saigon, the MACV staff released two messages to the Chairman, Joint Chiefs of Staff in the Pentagon, Washington, D.C. Although Abrams was in Bangkok on leave, his staff properly alerted American authorities of the NVA's activities along the DMZ.[18]

The first message reported:

> Enemy-initiated indirect fire attacks have significantly increased in the DMZ area during the past three days. Their purpose appears to be to screen the movement of men and materials through the DMZ, while it could be a coordinated effort against ARVN units in Quang Tri Province. While the situation is not critical at this time, it appears to be developing. There are indications of increased pressures, especially against FBs Sarge and Holcomb. General Lam appears to be reacting well within his resources.[19]

As events were later to show, this initial report on the North Vietnamese spring offensive couldn't have been more misleading.

# CHAPTER FIVE

# DAY TWO: GOOD FRIDAY

The crescendo and reverberations of the unrelenting North Vietnamese artillery bombardments were further heightened by the low-clinging clouds. The solidly overcast sky placed a protective blanket over the NVA's assault forces pressing south. VNAF and American aircraft could fly helplessly around on top of the overcast, but could not seriously interfere with or assist in the ground battles below.

At first light, the enemy opened fire on Nui Ba Ho with recoilless rifles from four or five different positions. This was followed immediately by another mass ground assault on the north section. Captain Smith observed the 4th Battalion's own recoilless rifle crew fire four rounds of beehive ammunition into the assaulting formation. The thousands of flechettes, looking like tiny darts, tore through the NVA assault elements and repelled them at the wire. Leaving at least 100 dead in the perimeter wire, the enemy withdrew, but only long enough to reorganize and return fire, killing two gun crews and wounding a third replacement crew, silencing the Marine's recoilless fire.

Later that morning, a U.S. FAC, requested the night before, arrived on station. Despite marginal weather conditions, he surveyed the situation around FBs Nui Ba Ho and Sarge and attempted to locate enemy artillery firing positions to the west. With the assistance of the FAC three suspected gun positions were located and counterbattery fires placed on them to good effect by the 105 batteries at FSB Mai Loc. Supporting fire from the 175s at Camp Carroll was also requested. Their response was slow and ineffective.

On FB Sarge the NVA continued to move deliberately up the steep slopes. It was only a matter of time before their assault would be launched. The condition of the defenders worsened as poor visibility limited the placing of accurate artillery fire against the enemy units advancing on the 4th Battalion's fire bases.

Down in the valley at FSB Mai Loc, Brigade 147 headquarters was continuing to receive incoming fire from the enemy's long-range 130MM artillery. This fire, while demoralizing, was not effective because the NVA was using only point-detonating fuses. Had they been delayed action fuses, the shells would have penetrated the underground bunkers before exploding. This would probably have brought about a collapse of the Marine brigade's willingness to remain under the intense fire of the Soviet-made guns.

Individual efforts were now being made to locate the enemy artillery positions as advisors moved through the impact areas to examine the shell holes for the telltale signs that accurately revealed the direction of the enemy gun positions. Their crater analyses quickly revealed that the NVA was following the Soviet practice of emplacing artillery pieces just outside the range of U.S. 105MM and 155MM howitzers. With careful planning, the attackers had located their guns just outside the 10,500-meter maximum range of the 105MM howitzers and the 14,800-meter range of the 155MM howitzers. Then, by exploiting the 27,500-meter range of the Soviet 130MM guns, the North Vietnamese were able to attack the fire bases with very little threat from ARVN counterbattery fire. Only the U.S.-made 175MM gun had sufficient range to counter the NVA's massive artillery attacks. However, the four 175MM guns at Camp Carroll, and the four located at Dong Ha, failed to respond effectively. Each time the ARVN 175MM batteries would fire, the NVA would counter with a heavier barrage. ARVN cannoneers, frightened by the incoming rounds, abandoned their guns to seek safety, permitting the NVA to win the artillery duel.

Just south of the DMZ, the enemy's early morning artillery attacks on Alpha 1, 2, 3 and 4 and Charlie 1 and 2, were also intensified. The NVA's reconnaissance and sapper units were probing ARVN strong points in preparation for infantry assaults. Leatherneck Square was saturated with the enemy's artillery and 122MM rocket fire as these bombardments struck military targets and once-peaceful villages indiscriminately.

General Giap's deliberate decision to strike the populated areas created havoc in every village and caused desertion in the ranks. The villages of Dong Ha and Cam Lo were transformed into infernos, and thousands of persons who had felt secure in the villages and hamlets hugging the DMZ were now terrorized by the wanton destruction.

After eighteen hours of continuous artillery bombardment, homeless, frightened refugees from the countryside began to stream onto the roadways. What started as a trickle near the DMZ turned into a torrent of human misery. Peasants, clutching their meager belongings and often driving their cattle before them, moved onto Highways 1 and 9 in their southward flight to the safety of Quang Tri City.

Anticipating this, North Vietnamese artillery fire was preplanned to strike key road junctions. Intermittently, 130MM rounds and 122MM rockets would cut down the helpless peasants in their exodus, briefly opening gaps in the long line of refugees. Only blind fate seemed to decide which families would become the latest victims in the carnage and which, dazed but unscathed, would survive and push on. Once opened by the shell bursts, the gaps would close again as the injured and dead were carried away or simply pushed off the roadways. As the fleeing waves of refugees left Gio Linh, Cam Lo and Dong Ha many believed they would die before the sun set on this, the so-called "Good Friday" of the Christians' Easter season.

In the headquarters of 3d ARVN Division, General Giai and his staff were still trying to assess the enemy's order of battle. The three infantry regiments of the division had all reported heavy casualties and the situation on the fire bases just below the DMZ was confusing and beginning to show the dreadful signs of disintegration. Communications with the forward elements were repeatedly interrupted as radio antennas were shot away.

Around 0700 I radioed Major Easley, the senior Marine advisor to Brigade 258, and learned that the brigade had experienced a difficult night at Dong Ha trying to find cover from the 130MM artillery fire. I decided to attempt to reach their position by jeep while Captain Murray remained in the TOC monitoring Vietnamese Marine activities.

Leaving the headquarters was slow since refugees and military vehicles hindered our movement, but the driver and I encountered no artillery fire during the seven-mile drive north to Dong Ha combat base. Upon arriving, VN Marines directed us to Brigade 258's CP where I found the brigade advisors in an Ely hut with large holes dug in the floor. This arrangement provided both shelter from the rain and ready access to trench lines whenever the enemy's artillery struck their area.

Majors Jon Easley and Regan Wright and I met for the first time. Wright, the senior artillery advisor, 1st Artillery Battalion, was the first to declare that he did not particularly enjoy being on the receiving end of an artillery attack.

Our brief meeting was beneficial as we shared our views on ominous battle signs and also cleared up the many rumors that had arisen. We were also able to account for all U.S. Marine advisors, a fact of no little concern to us.

Around 0930, I returned to the division TOC at the Ai Tu combat base. The flow of refugees had dramatically increased, with most of the civilians moving in a stupor. Incoming artillery rounds continued to impact on the TOC and the ARVN and advisory team's troop compounds. It was apparent that this was going to be another day of continued attacks. Several of Team 155's troop billeting huts had been destroyed. Though no lives were lost, the Americans had become frightened. By this time they could see the endless line of refugees moving along Highway 1 just outside their compound.

In the TOC, the ARVN personnel were still rebounding from the onslaught of the enemy and were vainly attempting to orchestrate their defensive firepower. Indecision and confusion reigned. The 3d ARVN Division, which had never before functioned as a combat team, was stalled and did little or nothing to aid its beleaguered fire bases. More and more of the division staff's time was devoted to personal concerns and to their families located near the division headquarters. Discipline was seemingly nonexistent.

Throughout Day Two of the offensive incoming artillery at Alpha 2 increased substantially. Lieutenant Bruggeman reported that he was fearful of a major ground attack, as they were beginning to receive small arms fire. He and his troops were doing the best they could to direct naval gunfire to suppress what was obviously a buildup of enemy forces. By evening it became apparent that if the ARVN artillery and infantry troops on Alpha 2 did not have the resolve to develop a creditable defense, the fire base would be overrun.

The position was fast becoming untenable and Lieutenant Eisenstein was monitoring the situation on his NGF radio net and expressed deep concern for his Marines. He and Bruggeman began to develop an emergency evacuation plan of their Naval Gunfire Spot Team.

Late in the afternoon, the U.S. Marine advisory unit's G-2 intelligence officers came into the 3d Division TOC. Captains Thomas O'Toole and John Theisen had flown up from Saigon on 30 March and had spent the night under artillery attack at the Dong Ha combat base with the COVANs of Brigade 258.

O'Toole was scheduled to rotate home in two weeks. He had brought Theisen to Quang Tri Province to visit the U.S. and ARVN intelligence sections located along the DMZ.

O'Toole was one of the most respected combat intelligence officers in the Marine Corps. With a knack for cutting through the mass of data from the numerous competing intelligence agencies, he had the ability to extract the precise piece of correct information. As a former enlisted NCO, he had previously been assigned to the American Embassy in Moscow. From this assignment he was commissioned as a second lieutenant. Not content with sifting through raw data, he had become a FAC and, during his earlier Vietnam tours, he had been awarded numerous air medals and a Bronze Star for heroic actions. O'Toole was known as a "doer," and fate had brought him to the 3d Division's TOC.

The arrival of O'Toole and Theisen appeared to me as a godsend since the intelligence section of the 3d Division staff had been almost totally unproductive during the first thirty hours of the NVA offensive.

Following a quick handshake, I directed O'Toole to locate the intelligence advisor of Team 155 and assist him where possible. Captain Murray had been standing on our G-3 radio watch for over twenty-four hours, so I told Theisen to relieve the weary officer. After a hurried briefing on both VNMC brigade locations, radio callsigns, and the status of the ARVN fire bases, Theisen assumed the G-3 watch. Murray, who vehemently protested his relief, moved into an adjacent room, lay down on the wooden deck and quickly fell asleep.

O'Toole located the Army G-2 advisor. He found that Capt. J. M. Oseth, U.S. Army, was new to his assignment and to the intelligence field. As O'Toole was shortly to report to me, "The G-2 advisor was completely overwhelmed by the events of the past couple of days."

I responded that it was indeed a bad situation but time was working against us and criticism couldn't help anyone now. In order to bring some order out of this mess, we needed help. I told Tom, "Get with the ARVN staff and the Air Force liaison section and find out the latest information on the NVA's push on Alpha 1, 2, 3 and 4."

I wanted him to find out if the ARVN units were going to hold and what the status was of the ARVN fire bases along the DMZ. Major Joy, at Mai Loc, was keeping us current on the western flank fire bases. O'Toole nodded and moved off to locate his new counterparts.

The steady NVA pressure on the westernmost ARVN positions, curtained from attack by the dust rising from the incessant artillery pounding and low cloud cover, became overwhelming. The enemy's artillery fire into Nui Ba Ho became even more accurate than the day before. Captain Smith reported that movement on top of their hill was extremely dangerous, especially on the critical north face. Recoilless rifle fire from the NVA had collapsed a large part of the perimeter trench line and several of the larger bunkers. Throughout the early afternoon, the enemy continued to reduce the hilltop position with artillery, mortars and recoilless rifle fire.

During the previous night, the 4th Battalion's position at E-4 had been bypassed by enemy infantry, although the encircled platoon of Marines continued to bring fire into the flanks and rear of enemy units attacking the Nui Ba Ho perimeter. Smith later recalled that the heroic actions of this platoon inspired the Bravo group to put up an even greater resistance to the numerically superior enemy force.[1]

At approximately 1500, another ground attack was launched against the north face of Nui Ba Ho with the enemy units coming up over a saddle and hitting the north wire.

After endless hours of seemingly fruitless effort to obtain artillery support, a Marine battery of 105s at Mai Loc finally came to the aid of the beleaguered garrison at Nui Ba Ho. The battery-fired, air-bursting, time-fused ammunition helped to repel several more assaults. One of the enemy's 75MM recoilless rifles was destroyed by a direct hit from one of the Marine 105MM rounds.

By 1700, the two rifle companies of the Bravo group, 4th Battalion had suffered so many casualties on the north face that the executive officer, Major Hoa, was forced to relocate Marines from his south and eastern perimeters to replace the losses. At 1730, a company-sized enemy force was sighted moving toward the south side of Nui Ba Ho. The Marines could see they were pulling a large, wheeled gun up the slope. Orbiting overhead, an airborne controller identified the wheeled gun through the broken overcast and for the first time since the Nguyen Hue Offensive began, called in a close air support mission for the 4th Battalion. Two U.S. F-4s made runs on the enemy force before the weather closed them off. Their air strikes were effective and dispersed the enemy. Smith estimated the NVA suffered ten to twelve casualties and the gun never reappeared.[2]

As darkness closed in, the NVA again assaulted the north sector of Nui Ba Ho. This attack was repulsed but the Marines suffered more casualties. With the darkness the cloud ceiling dropped below the top of the hill, adding fog to the night.

A Stinger C-119 gunship arrived on station, but the pilot could not locate Nui Ba Ho through the fog and was unable to fire. Parachute flares were dropped in a fruitless attempt to locate the Marine positions. At approximately 2130, one flare drifted low enough to cast some light through the heavy fog. Under the eerie light of the descending flare, the surviving Marines discovered the north slope was covered with infiltrators.[3]

Major Hoa called for artillery illumination but the heavy fog hindered its effectiveness. Capt. Dave Randall, back at FSB Mai Loc, was monitoring all requests for fire support from Boomer and Smith.

At almost the same time, one of the company commanders radioed back to the Bravo group bunker and requested that the Marines on top of the hill stop throwing hand grenades down into their positions. Since by this time there was no one left to man the interior defensive lines, Captain Smith and his counterpart assumed that the NVA had infiltrated Nui Ba Ho and were the source of the grenades. At 2205 one of Major Hoa's Marines called from a perimeter radio and informed him that he had been in NVA hands on top of the hill minutes before and that the NVA were surrounding the command bunkers on the hilltop.

At this point the two Marines decided to go outside their bunker in order to better tell what was happening. As they left, the radio man in front of Smith had trouble with his radio set and was held up for a couple of minutes. Smith finally passed him and went to the bunker entrance. As he looked out he could make out about five enemy troops some three meters in front of the bunker. The Bravo commander had already vanished and Smith could see no friendly troops. He heard familiar voices calling to each other on the south slope of the hill. The NVA and Smith were confused, but Smith was able to run past them without being detected. As he approached the group of survivors huddled against the southeast corner of the wire, he realized they were afraid to go through the wire because of the booby traps. By this time it was obvious the position was lost, so he grabbed the two nearest Marines and threw them into the wire. Major Hoa suddenly appeared and the two officers directed the assembled troops in a single file for passage through the gap in the wire. As they were doing this, from no more than five feet away an NVA soldier began firing over their heads. Smith turned and fired, knocking him down. Realizing that fire would bring more NVA from the hill to their position, he moved up to the head of the column, which was held up at the outer strands of concertina.

Once again the young Marines were afraid to go through the wire because of the booby traps and mines emplaced earlier. Ray Smith recalled:

> I felt that haste was essential so I threw myself, on my back, over the wire. (I recall thinking—foolishly—that the radio on my back would protect me if I tripped a mine.) Once I hit the wire, all hesitation ended and the twenty or thirty Marines started across fast, mostly over me. I got pretty tangled in the wire, and in my haste I tore most of my clothes off and cut my hands and legs quite a bit. As soon as all the Marines had cleared the wire, I called for artillery fire on the hill.[4]

The remaining heroic defenders of Nui Ba Ho were swallowed up in the night and the dark jungle. At 2140 on 31 March, the base was lost to the enemy and all contact with the 4th Battalion Bravo group was lost.

Major Boomer radioed the news that the NVA had overrun Nui Ba Ho. In the short time he and Smith had been together they had become good friends and he was convinced that Smith, along with all the Vietnamese Marines, had "bought the farm."

With little time to reflect upon the loss of friends and fellow officers, the 4th Battalion Marines on Sarge began to fight for their lives. During the day, they had acquitted themselves valiantly. Despite being subjected to extremely heavy shelling, the battalion's 81MM mortar platoon had faithfully supported its troops throughout the battle. By evening every member of the platoon had been wounded or killed.

When Nui Ba Ho fell, Major De, the battalion commander, and Major Boomer agreed it would only be a matter of time before Sarge itself would be overrun. Major De was torn between staying and fighting to the last man or pulling off his position in an attempt to save what was left of his battalion and fight again another day.

Just after midnight, De made the decision to pull off FB Sarge since there was no letup in the enemy pressure to overrun the fire base. Artillery, recoilless rifle and mortar fire pounded every square foot of the hilltop. At 0340 on 1 April, Boomer made his last radio transmission from FB Sarge. His voice was surprisingly calm and did not reflect the past thirty-six hours of heavy combat.

"Uniform, Uniform,* this is Mike . . . moving . . ."

All communication with the 4th Battalion of the Vietnamese Marine Corps was then lost.

Back in the relative safety of the 3d ARVN Division TOC bunker, we felt the loss of a fire base and other positions in such a short period of time was almost unbearable. The tension drained us of whatever strength remained. We had all tried to help by requesting artillery support from the ARVN. Through U.S. channels we sought immediate B-52 strikes and SKYSPOTS; anything to halt the enemy assaults. Our best efforts were inadequate. The loss of an entire battalion of Marines absolutely overwhelmed the Vietnamese and Americans. In the TOC bunker we were entering our second night without sleep and the weariness was beginning to affect all of our temperaments. We were relearning that the mental strain on staff officers, though not as hazardous, was equal in its intensity to the strain on field advisors.

Earlier in the evening, Colonel Murdock appeared in the TOC. He apparently had had a previous conversation with his G-3 advisor, and indicated that Major Wilson was on the verge of physical exhaustion and required immediate relief; he would have to be evacuated for battle fatigue. Murdock said to me, "I would like you to assume the duties as the U.S. G-3 advisor in the TOC until I can get another Army officer up from Danang or Saigon."

Although Wilson was forty or fifty pounds overweight, I was astonished that any officer could actually become battle fatigued in thirty-six hours. I reminded Murdock that I was a Marine and as a visiting staff officer had no command responsibilities in Quang Tri Province. However, because of the unique situation we were experiencing, I would do as he requested.[5]

---

*3d ARVN Division callsign.

We both agreed that I was the most logical and perhaps only immediate replacement for Major Wilson. Initially Wilson and I had worked closely together, but by the morning of the second day he was spending less and less time in the G-3 watch area. His progressively longer absences eventually caused him to lose contact with the fast-moving combat situation. His two U.S. Army captains remained in the G-3 watch area and provided valuable continuity to me and Captain Murray. The four of us were fast becoming a cohesive operations section.

Murdock recognized our team effort, saying he appreciated my help. He added he could not remain in the TOC to direct Advisory Team 155's actions in support of the 3d Division staff. I would also have to handle this. He would be moving with General Giai, the division commander, who would be helicoptering to all his units to show his presence and try to restore confidence within his division.

NVA artillery rounds were impacting around our bunker as we were talking, so our conversation was brief. Yet it was an unexpected combat assignment that would eventually affect my own Marine Corps career and that of several U.S. Army officers.

Major Wilson was not in the G-3 area when Nui Ba Ho and FB Sarge fell. I had Captain Theisen call him on the telephone to advise him of the losses. Shortly thereafter, I telephoned General Kroesen's First Regional Assistance Command (FRAC) in Danang to report the loss of the two fire bases. I also reported, "the location and state of Maj. Walter E. Boomer, USMC, and Capt. Ray L. Smith, USMC, is unknown at this time."

Day Two of the Nguyen Hue Offensive drew to a bloody close. In Saigon at MACV Headquarters, General Abrams' staff would neatly report the day's activities to the Chairman of the JCS. COMUSMACV's message (now declassified) amplified the few details then known on the development in northern Quang Tri Province. Thirty-six hours after the offensive had begun, neither the Vietnamese nor the U.S. military commands had correctly identified the invasion as the main attack of North Vietnam's 1972 general offensive. General Abrams' personal message read:

1. The enemy launched attacks by fire and ground probes against targets in northern MR-1. While the situation is not critical at this time, it appears to be developing. There are indications of increased pressure, especially against FB Nui Ba Ho (YD00510), Sarge (YD028478), and FSB Holcomb (YD118431). Attacks by fire reported to average on the order of 200–300 rounds at each location and appear to be consistent in intensity. Precise types of rounds are unknown at this time.

2. A late report indicates that a forward installation of the RRU* on FSB Sarge received a direct hit and the bunker collapsed. Condition of U.S. personnel and equipment unknown at this time.

3. General Lam appears to be reacting well within his resources. However, there are requirements for U.S. support. Bad weather limits TAC Air although combat SKYSPOTS are being flown in for support. Fixed wing gunships are limited due to the SAM rings which now extend as far south as FSB Sarge.

4. It is anticipated that requests for ARCLIGHT diverts will be forthcoming.[6]

The U.S. commander's assessment of the second day of the spring offensive was later to be recognized as having no perception of the hell, death and destruction taking place along the DMZ. For some reason the MACV staff did not take the initiative to dispatch officers north and make an on-site assessment of the NVA's activities. Perhaps the Easter weekend created sufficient complacency to hold off any immediate action by these staff officers, who were comfortable, secure and in Saigon.

*Radio Reconnaissance Unit.

CHAPTER SIX

# DAY THREE: HOLY SATURDAY

For the third straight night, North Vietnamese artillery continued to strike the cities of Dong Ha, Cam Lo and the remaining beleaguered ARVN fire bases. To the U.S. and Vietnamese military leaders located in northern Quang Tri Province, there was no doubt that the scope of the offensive, the massive numbers of men, buildup of artillery involved, and the intensity of their attacking forces meant that this NVA assault across the DMZ constituted the main attack of their 1972 offensive.

It was also the first time in six years that the South Vietnamese were having to go it alone on the battlefield. It was an Asian war and to an Asian "saving face" and avoiding personal embarrassment is more important than losing one's life. This belief probably contributed to the early successes of the North Vietnamese Nguyen Hue Offensive since the ARVN leadership was reluctant to report the reality of the situation: they had been deceived by the enemy, besieged under the heaviest artillery attack of the Vietnam War, and were further surprised by the employment of massive quantities of Soviet armor. Their inability to regroup and contain the attackers was the ultimate embarrassment for South Vietnam's political and military leaders. They had lost face. Perhaps, if they waited, the situation would improve. This had often been the case before and perhaps it would happen again. At each level of command, the truth of the combat situation was avoided.

Lt. Col. Camper at Camp Carroll reported his difficulty in getting accurate information concerning the 56th's fire bases.

> It hurt when we reduced our U.S. advisors. I found out at the regimental level I could not tell what was happening down at the battalions and companies. Without that information, it was difficult for me to properly advise and assist the regimental commander. There were a lot of false reports to save face which resulted in extremely drastic losses of territory and personnel.[1]

Not identifying the intensity of the NVA's Nguyen Hue Offensive early on played directly into the hands of the enemy. Col. Hoang Ngoc Tung, assistant J-2, JGS in Saigon, was later to write:

> As it turned out, it was up to three days after the enemy attack was launched in MR-1 before it aroused any major concern in Saigon.[2]

This hesitancy by the ARVN leadership to report fully the perilous situation in the northern province caused some strained relationships with advisory personnel. In order to justify the sudden requirement for quantum increases in naval gunfire missions, TAC Air sorties, B-52 ARCLIGHT and SKYSPOT (radar) bombing strikes, the tactical situation was being reported by the advisors as it was happening through U.S. communications channels.

In the 3d Division TOC, requests for naval gunfire were passed directly to the ships steaming into the Gulf of Tonkin. The captains of the U.S. destroyers were subsequently reporting their supporting actions through Navy command channels. Although the Navy's ships had become the main U.S. supporting arm, they were still under the operational control of the Commander, 7th Fleet, not COMUSMACV. COMM-SEVENFLT headquarters was immediately retransmitting these operational reports to the Commander-in-Chief, Pacific (CINCPAC), in Hawaii. This resulted in Admiral McCain there having more detailed, accurate, and timely information and being better informed on the NVA offensive than General Abrams. Abrams was furious at the inefficient flow of tactical information to his Saigon headquarters from MR-1.

Comdr. William J. Thearle, USN, commanded the U.S.S. *Buchanan* (DDG-14). Thearle and his crew responded magnificently to the call for assistance from Lieutenant Eisenstein's naval gunfire spotters. When the *Buchanan* went to full battle stations and began to deliver suppressive fires on the enemy, the ship properly reported its actions in "high precedence" naval messages. Fire missions for naval gunfire increased in intensity almost by the hour, and Thearle requested augmentation from other U.S. destroyers. By 1 April, four destroyers were off the Cam Lo-Cau Viet River delivering fire on the enemy. The deployment of these and other ships all resulted from voice radio communication from the 3d Division TOC. The Navy was committed to the defense of Quang Tri Province before General Abrams recognized the crisis or asked for additional assistance.

Because of inclement weather conditions, no tactical air support was brought to bear on the North Vietnamese ground forces. Naval gunfire became the only reliable source of supporting arms during the first forty-eight hours of the offensive. History will record that the U.S. destroyers were of immeasurable value in holding back the North Vietnamese attack down Highway 1 to Dong Ha and Quang Tri City.

The U.S.S. *Buchanan* later received credit for destroying four PT-76 tanks,* definitely a first for a U.S. destroyer operating in South Vietnamese waters. Hundreds of rounds of ammunition were being fired on NVA troops and vehicles and at the end of each day, Navy gunfire expenditure reports were submitted identifying the types of targets fired upon. Often the ships included personal assessments on the situation ashore and identified U.S. Marine advisory personnel. Eisenstein, Turley, and later Captain Ripley, began to appear in their "flash" precedence messages to CINCPAC in Honolulu.

Other U.S. operational support centers began to receive

---

*A lightweight amphibious tank of Russian design. Mounting a 76MM main gun, it was widely used by the NVA because of its cross country mobility.

hurried calls for assistance. The U.S. Air Force Direct Air Support Center (I DASC) in Danang was saturated with air support requests.[3] The reduced crew of air controllers responded as best they could. Initially, only high level, B-52 strikes and radar bombing missions could be employed against the enemy. However, by the third day of the Easter offensive, U.S. tactical fighter aircraft were alerted and ready to strike, whenever the weather cleared sufficiently to permit them to do so.

All of these U.S. elements were providing support or preparing for surge efforts while the South Vietnamese military leadership had still failed to recognize that the time for the test of President Nixon's Vietnamization program had arrived.

Time and weather conditions continued to work for the enemy and the momentum of the NVA's conventional warfare attacks was accelerating. Armor and infantry units of the 308th and 324B Divisions were moving into assault positions on the most northern fire bases. It may be that the North Vietnamese, in "knowing their enemy" anticipated the slow response of their southern brothers to the tactical surprise of an all-out invasion.

Around 0400, on the third day of the offensive, there was a sudden lull in the enemy's artillery attacks. In the 3d Division TOC, the Americans gathered in the G-3 watch area to review the situation. With the loss of FBs Sarge and Nui Ba Ho, ARVN's western defenses were free to fall back toward FSBs Carroll and Mai Loc, where a new defensive line could be established. Also, the continued overcast still precluded close air support. The NVA maintained the momentum of its offensive. Somehow the ARVN had to contest the enemy.

It was at this time that I was told by Lieutenant Eisenstein that he had requested Colonel Murdock's authority to evacuate the naval gunfire spot team from Alpha 2. Eisenstein had approached the colonel on the evening of 31 March and requested helicopters or any other assistance to extract his five U.S. Marines. Murdock's view of the Alpha 2 situation was different from the lieutenant's and he denied the request.

During the night, enemy infantry units were reported to be encircling Alpha 1, 2, 3 and 4. On Alpha 2, the naval gunfire spot team was the northernmost contingent of U.S. troops in South Vietnam and it was, therefore, understood by everyone in the G-3 watch area that should the predicament on Alpha 2 deteriorate we Americans would attempt some type of rescue mission.

Dawn was breaking on a heavily overcast morning. It was dark and dreary, seemingly appropriate for Holy Saturday. First light revealed thousands of refugees along both lanes of the Highway 1. They were bewildered peasants who didn't know where they were going, but were just heading south.

Around 0600, on the third day of the offensive, Major Joy called to report he had just established radio contact with the survivors of the Nui Ba Ho attack. Captain Smith, along with his counterpart Major Hoa, were with a group of forty to sixty Vietnamese Marines and moving toward Mai Loc.

Radio communications during the day to the exhausted remnants of the Bravo group of the 4th Battalion were intermittent as they continued to move eastward toward Mai Loc. At noon they arrived at a location called E-45, an artillery fire base approximately 3,000 meters due west of FSB Mai Loc. From there, the group moved to a village north of Mai Loc to obtain food. However, little food was found and the column moved on. By mid-afternoon, the 4th Battalion's Bravo command group, and what was left of two rifle companies, took up positions northeast of Mai Loc. Only about 69 Marines had finally made it back from Nui Ba Ho out of an initial strength of over 300.

Later, Captain Smith recalled their escape through the jungles infested with North Vietnamese around Nui Ba Ho. As the last Marine cleared the barbed wire of the abandoned fire base, they formed into a column and moved down the east slope. Smith called for artillery fire on the hilltop behind them. A driving rain storm engulfed the battle-weary Marines, covering their escape but reducing their visibility to a few yards. As the drenched Marines moved due east, they could hear enemy soldiers behind them and off to their left flank, but no contact was made. As their column reached the valley floor, NVA units were again heard along the stream. After a short halt to let the enemy pass, they moved directly across the stream, and about halfway up the slope and turned to follow the contour to the south and east. Several times during the night, Smith could hear enemy units moving in the low ground on their right and on the ridgeline to the left. He and his counterpart tried to stay on a mid-slope position to avoid the enemy who seemed to be everywhere. Smith later stated:

> As I had the only radio and had very little communication with any friendly forces, we couldn't be certain of where friendly air strikes and artillery would be landing. Throughout the night, I personally was more worried about friendly fires than the enemy.[4]

Smith had sufficient reason to worry. Once they reached position E-45, they moved to the ridgetop where better time could be made. On more level ground the column's pace increased as they all shared the unspoken sense that the enemy was not far behind and was, in fact, closing in on Brigade 147's headquarters at FSB Mai Loc. There the survivors hoped they would be safe.

Major Hoa, the Bravo commander, was completely exhausted and suffering from exposure, lack of food and sleep. He experienced severe cramps and was unable to walk. The other Marines were in almost the same condition and didn't respond when asked to carry their commander.

Reaching deep within themselves for strength, Ray Smith and one Vietnamese enlisted man took turns carrying Major Hoa on their backs for the last two or three miles.[5] Once again the intangible bond of loyalty between a COVAN and a Vietnamese Marine commander was stretched, but never broken, under the most trying of combat conditions.* Together they had gallantly fought against an overwhelming, numerically superior force, then survived a desperation march, and reached safety together. Upon reaching the village of Mai Loc, the Marines had their first food in over two days as the Bravo command element of the 4th Battalion returned.

The North Vietnamese divisions continued to press south in assaults on the ARVN fire bases. Artillery fire increased,

---

*Capt. Ray L. Smith was awarded the Navy Cross for his actions around Nui Ba Ho (See Appendix D).

with hundreds of rounds striking Alpha 1, 2, 3 and 4, Gio
Linh, Charlie 1 and 2 and Camp Carroll. By 0800, the most
northern bases along the DMZ were under direct infantry attacks. ARVN artillerymen continued to crawl into their make-
shift shelters instead of remaining in their gun pits to conduct
counterbattery fire. They, and thus we, were rapidly losing the
battle and the war.

The situation at Alpha 2 was not uncommon to the South
Vietnamese on the other fire bases. Lieutenant Bruggeman's
spot team had remained in the old French observation tower
despite the heavy artillery fire. From their vantage point they
radioed back to the advisor's G-3 watch officer that the ARVN
troops of the 57th Regiment had abandoned their 105MM
howitzers as well as the foxhole positions on the northern slope
of the fire base. NVA infantry was now visible on three sides
of their position.

It was around 0840 when Bruggeman's radio report was
received by Lieutenant Eisenstein. He immediately located
Colonel Murdock and requested permission to launch an
emergency helicopter evacuation. Murdock gave tentative approval to begin the necessary planning and pre-flight coordination briefing, but the mission was not to be launched without
his final approval. Eisenstein left the TOC and went over to
the Quang Tri airstrip only to discover that there were no U.S.
helicopters in the landing zones.

It was an agonizing wait until a U.S. Army Huey, piloted
by WOs Ben Neilsen and Robert Sheridan, arrived. The pilots
agreed to conduct the rescue mission, but said they would have
to wait for helicopter Cobra gunships to provide covering support for the lightly armed troop helicopter.

The shelling of the division and Advisory Team 155's troop
billet and work areas continued. Eisenstein was fearful the helicopter would not be able to remain at the airstrip. While they
awaited the gunships, he developed a fire support and ex-
traction plan. Once again the five-inch guns of the U.S.S.
*Buchanan* would be called upon to provide the main covering
fire as the helicopters attempted the rescue.

The *Buchanan,* and the U.S.S. *Joseph P. Strauss* (DDG-16), which had just arrived on-station, were requested to lay a heavy line of fire on the northern portion of the fire base. On Eisenstein's signal, the spot team would leave the tower and move to the southeastern corner of Alpha 2's helicopter landing zone. Because a number of U.S.-made ANPRC-25 radios had already been lost by the South Vietnamese units, and out of fear that the NVA probably was listening to all transmissions on its nets, Lieutenant Bruggeman specifically was not told the planned direction or exact time of approach for the helicopters. Bruggeman's "secure voice" (cypher) unit had been damaged, causing all voice transmissions to be in the clear, accessible to anyone on the same radio frequency.

Upon arrival, the two U.S. Army Cobra gunship pilots conferred with Eisenstein and the Huey pilot. On his tactical map, he showed them their destination, the approach route and where naval gunfire was planning to strike the enemy. None of the pilots was familiar with the Alpha 2 area, but all were willing to attempt the rescue.

Eisenstein finished his orientation briefing, saying that he understood that Alpha 2 was almost completely surrounded and that there would probably be much ground fire. The Army pilots expressed no hesitation at such news, but soon it was to be their time to be severely tested.

With the rescue mission assembled and ready, Eisenstein found a telephone and called the advisor's G-3 section requesting Colonel Murdock's final approval to launch. However, Giai and Murdock had already departed the headquarters to meet with ARVN commanders on the fire bases. Lt. Col. Heon, Executive Officer, Team 155, could not be located. Time was becoming critical, so Eisenstein told Sergeant Swift to "get Colonel Turley's permission. We can't wait for Murdock to return."

Swift was near me in the TOC. He quickly briefed me on the situation and asked my authority to launch the rescue mission.

I hesitated. Time was passing, and Swift pleaded, "Please, Colonel, let them go. Lieutenant Bruggeman says he can see NVA troops all around Alpha 2."

A decision had to be made at once and it was not a pleasant

one. If the helicopters and their crews were lost, I would be responsible. I was assuming more responsibility than I had authority to handle. On the other hand, inaction on my part would have further eroded the confidence of the Americans around me.

My mind raced, not helped by the silent eyes watching as I searched for a solution. My heart was pounding so loudly it must have been heard by people standing close by. Lives were at stake either way.

A hundred thoughts flashed in my mind. (First, I'm only helping out here on a temporary basis until an Army officer arrives from Danang. Second, where is the Team 155's executive officer? He should be the one to countermand the colonel's order. This is an Army unit; I'm a Marine; I don't have authority to act; my trip up here was only to visit; I'm already involved more than I should be.) My thoughts were soon interrupted by Swift, who again implored.

"Please, Colonel, let them go." He was now directly in front of me awaiting my action.

My indecision had already taken several minutes in the watch area, now silent except for the radios beside us which were actively echoing a naval gunfire mission. My career as a Marine had taught me one thing—to make decisions and be responsible for the outcome.

"Tell him to launch," I said. I felt relieved, because clearly it was right to attempt the rescue of our men.

This was a far more momentous decision than I had ever realized. It was the correct action to take under such conditions and I had to do what was right. But, until this moment I had been a passive participant in the NVA's Nguyen Hue Offensive and all of my earlier actions were taken in a liaison role as I moved about the battle area and was basically little more than the bearer of information between Vietnamese Marine units and their COVANs. Unexpected conditions had suddenly arisen and all too quickly I was thrust into the center arena of the battle. I was now in a position of authority. The equation had changed.

Swift grabbed the telephone and shouted, "Colonel Turley says, 'Go!' "

The crews climbed into the three helicopters and lifted off the landing zone. Lieutenant Eisenstein, who knew how the ground sloped away from the fire base, initially proposed a low approach from the southeast. If the pilots could stay low enough, they could fly virtually undetected by anyone positioned on the north or northwest side of the fire base.

The plan almost worked. However, the Cobra gunships, following in trace, did not stay as low as the Huey aircraft. Eisenstein's helicopter skimmed the treetops until it reached an easily recognizable area from where he was able to point out the final heading into Alpha 2. The Huey pilot identified the fire base to the gunships. As they proceeded overhead and began firing machine guns and rockets north and northwest of the fire base, the Huey "flared" in preparation for landing on the northwest corner. Just seconds before the attempted landing, the entire fire base was suddenly engulfed in a tremendous cloud of smoke. The NVA gunners, detecting the approach, had patiently waited, and just as the helicopter attempted to rise up out of the valley, they pounded the fire base with 100 artillery rounds.

At great risk to himself and his crew, the Huey pilot pressed on with his rescue mission. Naval gunfire was now impacting to the north and northeast of the fire base as they landed the Huey thirty to thirty-five yards from Lieutenant Bruggeman and his team. Sergeant Newton recognized Eisenstein as he and one crewman jumped from the helicopter and ran across the landing zone to the huddled Marines. Newton was attempting to carry a wounded Marine toward the helicopter. It was Bruggeman, who had suffered a serious head wound during the last artillery attack. There was no movement from the officer and his body was limp. As Newton and two other Marines carried the radio equipment and rifles to the churning helicopter, Eisenstein and the Army crewman grabbed Bruggeman and placed him on the helicopter. Several wounded South Vietnamese staggered out from behind a bunker and, almost without thinking, Eisenstein grabbed them and threw them aboard.

Lieutenant Eisenstein counted his troops. One was missing. "Where is Corporal Worth?" he called out.

Sergeant Newton didn't know, but pointed toward a bunker. Eisenstein ran back across the landing zone, yelling "Worth, Worth!" He began searching the bunkers around the landing zone. The bunkers turned out to be empty. Worth was nowhere in sight and the enemy's incoming fire was increasing. Corp. James Worth* would have to be left behind.

Moving back toward the helicopter Eisenstein noticed for the first time a number of body bags, each containing a dead South Vietnamese soldier, neatly stacked along one side of the landing zone. He could see wounded soldiers everywhere. As he climbed back aboard, several ARVN soldiers on the far side of the landing zone were struck by NVA small arms fire.

Other Vietnamese moved toward the helicopter and were attempting to get aboard. Eisenstein later recalled:

> The look of desperation was all about them. I will never forget the look in one Vietnamese's eyes as he stared at me across the skid pad of the helicopter. We were slowly rising and he was trying to make motions to get aboard. I had to take my foot and push him back into the crowd that was gathering underneath the helicopter. He was holding an M79 and we were staring right at each other. The thought raced through my mind, and I can remember it to this day, 'That son of a bitch is gonna blow us out of the sky with that M79. If he can't go, he's not gonna let anyone else go either.'
>
> As we slowly rose, more artillery rounds began to fall and the pilot abruptly rolled the plane towards the southern portion of the fire base and then tucked down below the hill and along the roadway. I remember, as we banked, seeing a large group of NVA soldiers circling around into the open on the southwest portion of the fire base and just outside the wire.[6]

The pilot stayed low to the ground along Highway 1 until he was safely away from the fire base and then rose several more feet above the tree line as they zipped past the city of Dong Ha. Eisenstein held on to a canvas seat harness and sat on the floor of the helicopter cradling Bruggeman in his arms.

---

*Today Corp. James Worth, USMC, remains missing in action (MIA), another casualty of those desperate days.

With one hand around his chest to keep him from sliding out of the helicopter, Eisenstein's other hand supported his wounded comrade's head.

Eisenstein remembers screaming into the intercom system for the pilot to call ahead for a medic. "Report we have seriously wounded U.S. personnel aboard."

The helicopter flew south over the highway clogged with refugees and landed at the Ai Tu combat base near the division TOC. It was just 1340 hours, with a little more than two hours having elapsed since I had approved the mission.

A Navy corpsman was waiting for the aircraft, along with several Army medics. Although the Ai Tu combat base was still under artillery fire, the medics assisted Sergeant Newton in placing Bruggeman onto a stretcher. First aid treatment began immediately. The two gunships took off; their helicopter rescue mission was complete. My decision had been the correct one.

Eisenstein, Newton, and the other two Marines walked over to their billeting area in the Team 155 compound. An emergency med-evac helicopter arrived and Bruggeman was placed aboard. In less than a minute the helicopter lifted off and turned south toward Danang.

Shortly thereafter, the U.S. Navy corpsman reappeared and handed Eisenstein Bruggeman's identification tags. He said that Bruggeman had died while being transported to Danang.

In the meantime, Eisenstein began to debrief the spot team on their actions while at Alpha 2. It was then that he heard about the event which had probably cost Bruggeman his life. Sometime during the previous evening, one of Bruggeman's enlisted Marines had had his helmet stolen by an ARVN soldier. The next morning, as the NVA increased artillery fire, Bruggeman gave his helmet to the Marine whose helmet had been taken. Tragically, as fate so often works, Bruggeman was the only person to be wounded from these fires. As he assembled his team for their rescue flight, an enemy shell exploded nearby, fragments striking him in the back of the head. Thus, on Holy Saturday, 1 April 1972, he died a hero as a result of trying to protect one of his Marines.

# CHAPTER SEVEN

# COLLAPSE OF THE NORTHERN FIRE BASES

Alpha 1, 2, 3 and 4, the four major fire bases located directly south of the DMZ, had been holding out against numerically superior North Vietnamese forces but were now being reported encircled; the enemy was closing in.

At 1045, fire base Alpha 4 (Con Thien) was evacuated. As an infantry battalion of the 2d Regiment was escaping through the wire on the southern perimeter, the North Vietnamese were overrunning the hilltop's main command and control bunkers. Artillery fire was directed at ARVN soldiers retreating down the narrow dirt road already crowded with refugees. Soldiers, RFs and PFs melted in with the civilians as the mass of humanity moved south toward Cam Lo and Route 9. All were pounded indiscriminately by the 130MM guns of the NVA.

Each day since the Nguyen Hue Offensive began, General Giai and Colonel Murdock flew around in Giai's Huey to visit his units. Giai was certainly no coward and he was reported everywhere trying to restore confidence. His style of leadership was to be forward and seen frequently by his men. As a new brigadier, he was more comfortable commanding in the field than managing his division from a sandbagged bunker. Often he was gone for four or five hours at a time. His absence was felt in the TOC because few decisions were ever made without his approval.

At some time during Holy Saturday, while away from the

division headquarters, Giai made a decision to evacuate Alpha 1, 2, 3 and 4 and fall back to a new defensive line.

Previously, he and Murdock had discussed a voluntary withdrawal of all ARVN forces to the south side of the Cam Lo-Cua Viet River because the line of old U.S.-constructed fire bases had never been intended as an actual main line of resistance. It was thought wise to move the units out of static positions and gain freedom of maneuver for the regiments. Likewise, it could gain time and create a free fire zone by withdrawing all friendly elements between the DMZ and the Cam Lo-Cua Viet.

In a withdrawal operation, the objectives are normally to reduce the enemy's combat power by avoiding a decisive engagement, thus gaining time. Buying time by giving up terrain is the goal, and to utilize the slackening of combat to reposition and regain a military advantage in the maneuver. This was not achieved by the withdrawing ARVN forces.*

Under the dire circumstances facing him, General Giai's decision to withdraw south of the Cam Lo-Cau Viet River was probably the best he could have made. He took a bold military risk to save his beleaguered subordinate units and to gain time.

Within the 3d Division's TOC, the U.S. advisors were completely unaware of Giai's decision to withdraw. His decision was made while he was in the field encouraging his commanders and trying to restore their confidence. More significantly, officers of his staff did not inform their American counterparts that they had been directed to execute one of the most difficult of combat operations, a withdrawal operation

---

*Detailed coordination and effective command and control are essential to any successful retrograde maneuver. Centralized planning must be conducted at the division level, and terrain, firepower, demolitions and limited offensive actions are exploited to slow, confuse and deceive the enemy, as well as to make him pay a high price in casualties and time in exchange for ground gained.

Night withdrawals are favored over those by day in order to preserve freedom of action, obtain secrecy and surprise, and reduce casualties. A withdrawal by day under direct enemy pressure is normally avoided since such a maneuver is usually under enemy observers' fires with resulting heavy casualties.

In the execution phase of a deliberate division-sized withdrawal, the three infantry regiments normally withdraw by echelons, with rearward positions, assembly areas and routes of movement assigned prior to initiation of the withdrawal.

In addition, the division's artillery and tank assets are coordinated to obtain the maximum supporting arms capability as the repositioning is underway.

under intense enemy pressure. However, there was no staff action initiated that resembled a collective effort to plan and execute the withdrawal of 3d Division units from north of the Cam Lo-Cua Viet River.

It was a time of great confusion. In thirty-six hours, one infantry battalion had simply disappeared from its assigned fire base, ARVN counterbattery fires were negligible and artillery support to the fire bases themselves could best be termed sporadic and unresponsive. All radio communication systems had been degraded with administrative nets repeatedly interrupting the traffic on the remaining tactical nets; two fire bases had been completely overrun—in short, the enemy had the momentum and the edge in all parts of the battlefield. Monsoon weather prevented air support from being unleashed against the NVA.

Except for the few U.S. advisors still out with the 56th and 57th regiments and the two Marine infantry brigades, the flow of timely battle information to Advisory Team 155 was very limited. The G-3 watch officers were not informed of Giai's withdrawal plan until Murdock returned to the TOC late in the afternoon. We clearly were reacting rather than planning to act.

The initial withdrawals from Alpha 1, 4 (Con Thien) and several regional force positions by ARVN accounts were considered orderly. On Alpha 2 the withdrawal was executed with haste and a loss of control by the ARVN commanders. A battery of 105MM howitzers was abandoned because the trucks that had been ordered to move the six howitzers never arrived. These guns were left behind in their firing positions and not rendered unuseable.

Traditionally, the capture of artillery pieces represents a significant battlefield victory since the loss and defeat of such weapons is often attributed to loss of control by unit leaders. Leadership within the 57th ARVN Regiment was clearly waning. The key blocking positions held by the 57th, across Highway 1, were unraveling, and opening to the enemy the most direct route toward Dong Ha and Quang Tri City.

The loss of FB Alpha 4 had the effect of activating a line of falling dominos. With the flow of reliable information from the ARVN regiments remaining poor at best, the advisor's G-3 journal recorded the loss of the northern defensive line as follows:

*1 April: 1450*   FB Fuller     Evacuated (2d Regt.)
                  FB Alpha 2    Evacuated (57th Regt.)
                  FB Khe Gio    Evacuated (56th Regt.)

FB Holcomb, occupied by Vietnamese Marines, fell to the NVA at 1430.[1]

About an hour earlier, Marine Brigade 258 headquarters received an order to move back to the Ai Tu combat base and assume responsibility for the overall security over the division headquarters and Quang Tri combat base. Colonel Dinh immediately located his senior brigade advisor, Maj. Jon Easley, and together they planned the relocation to Ai Tu.

Upon arrival at Ai Tu combat base, Dinh was to assume operational control of the 6th Marine Battalion with its one battery of artillery moving north from FB Barbara. The 6th Battalion would be responsible for the perimeter defense of Ai Tu.

Shortly before 1500, Brigade 258 arrived at Ai Tu and began to set up its command post in several old, dilapidated bunkers. Within minutes after their arrival, Ai Tu and adjoining Quang Tri combat bases came under heavy attack by enemy 130MM artillery. Upwards of 800–1000 rounds struck the area.[2] The American advisors' compound also received heavy incoming fire. The enemy's barrage was to be their heaviest and lasted for over ninety minutes. For the first time we at the division headquarters were being subjected to the same intense artillery attack as all ARVN fire bases had been receiving during the past three days. Such sustained shellings had a devastating physical and psychological impact upon the personnel manning the division headquarters.

The TOC was hit several times, although the ten feet of sandbags covering the bunker's heavy timbers absorbed the projectiles and the force of the blasts. Except for the noise and momentary shaking of the timbers and dust, we remained secure.

It was during this artillery attack that Lt. Col. Norm Heon

came into the G-3 watch area and informed me that he "recommended the total withdrawal of all U.S. personnel." It was obvious, however, that no one was going to move until the NVA artillery attack ended. Nothing more was said.

As the artillery fire subsided, Major Joy radioed in the good news that they had made contact with a small element of their 4th Battalion located in a deep ravine near E-45. "We're not sure who's in the group or how many there are. We'll let you know as soon as we hear something on Major Boomer." Several more hours would pass before they sent further details.

When Brigade 258's command element moved into the TOC, it seemed that its narrow hallways were lined with people. At that time, the following units were located in the bunker: 3d ARVN Division TOC staff sections and selected personnel; Brigade 258 staff; U.S. Army Team 155 personnel; Marine advisors, Brigade 258 and me, with two other advisors from the Marine advisory unit's Saigon headquarters. Additionally, there always seemed to be ARVN personnel wandering in, through, and out of the TOC for no apparent reason.[3]

The Americans began to take the lead in the TOC. As we all began to become more involved in its operation, coordination problems became more evident.

Shortly after 1800, Lieutenant Colonel Heon came back into the G-3 watch area. He called me aside from the other U.S. officers to tell me word had been received from Danang that all U.S. personnel were to be evacuated. Helicopters had been requested and were expected momentarily. The troops in the advisory compound would go first, then everyone here in the TOC.

"How about the U.S. advisors in the field? How are they going to get out? We can't leave without them," I said.

Heon didn't answer, and an awkward silence ensued. We were both exhausted from lack of sleep and the strain of the last three chaotic days. There was no more to be said. I walked away.

He had his orders. As the executive officer, he was responsible for over eighty Americans in the advisor compound. Their safety rested heavily on his shoulders.

His troops were mostly logistical support and administrative service soldiers, whose presence was not vital to the continued operation of the TOC. The nonessential troops could be moved without the loss of any of the advisor's tactical or supporting arms radio communications.

In the TOC were twenty to thirty U.S. soldiers manning the communication equipment. If this section were to be evacuated, all U.S. communication facilities north of Danang, eighty kilometers away, would be lost, for it was the only command and control center that knew the difficult and dynamic tactical situation and was accurately reporting it through U.S. channels. To evacuate the bunker and abandon the South Vietnamese military at such a difficult, confusing and deteriorating time would be tantamount to destroying the 3d ARVN Division.

"God, where do we go from here?" I thought.

The incoming artillery had slowed to one or two shells a minute. I had been wanting to make a head call for hours. Maybe fresh air would help me think about all the options. The narrow main passage was crowded with Vietnamese. Most had settled in on the plank flooring, their packs and rifles stacked everywhere. As I stepped over them, they would look up and their eyes would ask if everything was still all right. A smile or a thumbs-up gesture always got them to smile. A full understanding of our different languages was not necessary to communicate the desperate combat situation.

An iron gate, six feet outside the entrance, was the only opening in the high chain link fence around the bunker. It was still light enough to see where I was walking. A light breeze brought the smells of burning buildings and gun powder to my nostrils. Except for a few earlier head calls, I hadn't left the TOC, so I was unprepared for the devastation that had been inflicted upon the division headquarters. About half of the Ely huts had been hit and some were still burning. Their corrugated tin roofs had either been blown off the two-by-four wooden frames, or grotesquely twisted by fire. Four or five jeeps stood empty where they had been hit. White-hot artillery fragments had struck everything. Tires were flattened, vehicle canvas burned, and windshields shattered. The scene reminded me of a war movie—"It looked so real." I had never seen more devastation in one place, even in Korea.

The fog of war seemed to be thickest within the bunker itself. I walked to the side of a destroyed jeep and relieved myself. Alone, I began to wonder just how and where my casually planned "orientation visit" was eventually going to end, since it had turned into a personal dilemma I had neither anticipated nor sought out. As a visiting staff officer, I was far more involved in assisting a unit of another service than tradition or the structure of military command allowed. Fate had put me and a number of other Americans together under dire circumstances.

As I mused, my thoughts included questions as to what could possibly be done to help the situation. The Vietnamese Marines could not be abandoned, for it was clear to me that as long as the two Marine brigades stayed, their COVANs would also remain. We advisors at the TOC could not leave Captain Smith and Major Hoa, nor the other Marines of the 4th Battalion, after their epic march to Mai Loc. One could only wonder at the fate of Majors Boomer and De. Corporal Worth was still missing in action (MIA). If we could locate him, it might be possible to make another try at a helicopter rescue. There were no easy options; eighteen years of trust simply could not be betrayed in an instant. We, U.S. Marines and COVANs, would remain with our counterparts, no matter what the U.S. Army and ARVN decided to do.

The Vietnamese Marine infantry units had performed as well as could be expected up to this point. They had lost ground—several fire bases—while fighting tenaciously against overwhelming odds. In doing so, they gained time for the South Vietnamese military to respond. They had lost ground but certainly not their will or ability to fight.

In sharp contrast, ARVN units without American advisors showed little desire to hold their positions. Their infantry regiments were slow in reporting and South Vietnamese artillery batteries demonstrated little willingness to man their guns. ARVN leadership was indecisive, lacking the conviction that they could win on the battlefield.

Just three days earlier, the 3d ARVN Division and Team 155 were proudly expounding on their "ring of steel" across the most northern province of South Vietnam. Now its "steel" remained unmanned and often in abandoned artillery gun pits. Cannoneers and their officers were too frightened to respond to the fire missions requested of them. Their inability to shoot effective counterbattery fire was hastening the disintegration of the 3d ARVN Division.

The NVA's battle plan apparently was working on all fronts. Colonel Camper reported intensified artillery attacks on Camp Carroll. Late Sunday afternoon he said that their perimeter was receiving its first ground attacks.[4] In neutralizing the largest artillery base in Quang Tri Province, the NVA was eliminating the biggest danger to the attacking infantry forces.

North Vietnamese infantry units were also closing in on FSB Mai Loc. For a short period during that afternoon, an Air Force FAC was able to get under the low overcast and orbit over Mai Loc. The pilot and his airborne observer sighted several groups of enemy 3,000 meters west of the Mai Loc combat base complex. One group was spotted carrying a 57MM recoilless rifle.

By mid-afternoon the road leading from Dong Ha to Cam Lo (Route 9) and then south to Mai Loc was blocked by the North Vietnamese. The NVA had progressively built up their forces along the only road into Camp Carroll and further south to Mai Loc. Unless immediate offensive action was taken to reopen Routes 9 and 558, ARVN fire support bases would become critically low on ammunition.

Earlier in the day the 7th VNMC Battalion had been ordered to move by truck convoy from their bivouac position along Route 1 out to FSB Mai Loc to provide support to Brigade 147. The plan was to turn west on Route 9 and proceed to Cam Lo, then south to Mai Loc.

The ARVN truck drivers were apprehensive because of the enemy's artillery attacks on the roadways, holding up the convoy twice. The first occasion was when the truck driver, directly in front of Major DeBona's jeep, lost control and overturned. Ten Marines were killed, six seriously wounded. Major DeBona, a big-shouldered, rugged Marine known for his courage and physical strength, repeatedly tried to pull the trapped Marines from beneath the truck and did extract some before moving on. Time was crucial because the convoy could so easily be targeted by the NVA forward observer team. Before the convoy reached Route 558 on its way to Cam Lo, radio reports were received that NVA armor was in Cam Lo and reports of tank noises were being received over ARVN radio nets. In the TOC, however, there had been no actual sightings reported.

Major Hue, the 7th Battalion commander, halted the convoy for the second time, disembarked his four rifle companies and began to walk south to Mai Loc. A seasoned commander, he cautiously moved his companies by leaps and bounds. One company would move forward to take the high ground, then the rest of the battalion would close and then another company would move toward the next high ground.

As the battalion passed Camp Carroll on the west side of Route 558, Major DeBona noticed the ARVN artillery was shooting variable time (VT) fuses. The guns were firing to the west, and only seconds later, the projectiles were exploding as air bursts along a low ridge line. He remembered thinking the NVA infantry must be closing on Camp Carroll's western perimeter.

Major Hue continued his march to FSB Mai Loc. The lead elements of the battalion arrived around 1530, while the fire base was under intermittent artillery fire. The NVA would attack with ten to twelve rounds. During one of the relief periods, DeBona ran over to Brigade 147's underground bunker to pick up classified radio forms so the 7th Battalion and advisors could tune their radio on the same frequencies. He rejoined Hue after the battalion had deployed into an area a half-mile west of Mai Loc's short dirt runway. As the 7th Battalion was settling in, it made contact with an estimated platoon of enemy. Other enemy groups were reported moving toward the Mai Loc combat base area.

Since Holcomb, Nui Ba Ho, Sarge, Fuller and Khe Gio were gone, the ARVN western defenses had fallen back to Camp Carroll and Mai Loc combat base. Both these strong points were primarily artillery firing positions and were not prepared for infantry assaults. Now, with the only passable road into their positions blocked by the enemy, their survivability became questionable.

The 3d Division had recognized early on that the NVA were

sending small infiltration teams ahead of their assault forces. By the morning of the 31st, the NVA artillery forward observer (FO) teams had infiltrated between the ARVN fire bases into positions on the north side of the Cam Lo-Cua Viet River. From these hidden locations, they began to direct accurate artillery fire on to vehicle traffic moving east and west along Route 9. One such FO team was discovered in the vicinity of Cam Lo. Both NVA soldiers were killed, and their radio and targeting materials were captured.

It was apparent that the NVA was targeting all South Vietnamese military vehicles moving through two critical road junctions. The first of these was the main intersection just south of the Dong Ha Bridge where Route 9 originates and begins its westward direction toward Cam Lo, eventually reaching the Laotian border. This junction was receiving almost continuous 130MM fire. The road junction at Route 558 and Route 9 was also receiving heavy fire.

The NVA's 122MM and 130MM artillery could and did strike the ARVN military vehicles moving along the south side of the Cam Lo-Cua Viet River with deadly accuracy. National Highway 1 and Route 9 were the South Vietnamese primary resupply routes to their fire bases. When the North Vietnamese artillery observer teams began also to interdict Route 558, the ARVN lifeline to the VNMC on the western bases was severed.

To sustain the artillery batteries, emergency helicopter resupply missions were undertaken. Although Camp Carroll and FSB Mai Loc had been fully resupplied on 29 March, by the morning of 1 April, FSB Mai Loc was so low on 105MM ammunition that Brigade 147 was firing 155MM projectiles on what normally would have been 105MM targets. Early that afternoon FSB Mai Loc was resupplied by helicopter with 400 rounds of 105MM. At the rate the batteries were shooting, this meager supply would only last them through the night.[5] Major Joy radioed the TOC that more emergency resupplies would be necessary in the morning.

He also said the U.S. Army CH-47 pilots had earlier been receiving fire as they were making their approach to land. As the Chinooks came in to drop their external loads, Captain

Randall heard NVA artillery fire going off to the west, then, just as the helicopters were releasing their load, the enemy's artillery rounds would impact in the landing zone. It was clear that the NVA's artillery observers were watching every helicopter approach into FSB Mai Loc and Camp Carroll. Helicopter resupply missions would become even more difficult as the enemy closed in on both fire bases during the night.

As darkness settled on Quang Tri Province, FSB Mai Loc and Camp Carroll were still being struck by an assortment of NVA artillery weapons. In the vicinity of Cam Lo, another NVA artillery forward observer team was discovered and the warrant officer and two assistants comprising it were killed. Their radio equipment was recovered along with a tactical map showing ARVN positions along Route 9. It was apparent there was little they did not know about the dispositions of the ARVN units. NVA infiltration teams had now been sighted on both sides of the Cam Lo-Cua Viet River.

At 1800 one of the 3d ARVN Division's G-3 officers came over to the advisors G-3 watch area to inform us that the two regimental headquarters located on fire bases Charlie 1 and 2 had been ordered to withdraw. All ARVN units were to be repositioned south of the Cam Lo-Cua Viet River. There were a number of questions that immediately arose in the minds of the American advisors, but the flow of information back to division headquarters continued to be sketchy and answers were not easy to come by. We weren't certain as to when the evacuations had in fact begun, the order of withdrawal, or the time schedule to actually abandon the fire bases. If we knew the ARVN planned sequence of withdrawal, B-52 ARCLIGHT strikes could be requested to destroy the fire bases and also provide a curtain of protection to the rearguard units.

With these evacuations, the 3d ARVN Division had lost all seven of its major fire bases north of the Cam Lo-Cua Viet River. It was apparent from the report of the Vietnamese officer that some control had been lost within the units of the division as the order to evacuate was disseminated down to the ARVN infantry companies in contact with the enemy.

There were also other areas of immediate concern. First, were both command and control bunkers destroyed? Had all radios, telephone systems, and classified materials been removed or destroyed? If not, had the radios and classified materials, at least, been removed to preclude the threat to ARVN communications security? Third, what was the status of the artillery batteries? Were the batteries evacuated, or were more guns left behind?

Of critical concern was the sensitive U.S. sensor read-out bunker at Charlie 2. Was it destroyed? If so, where was its classified equipment? The ARVN officer professed to know nothing more.

I directed the G-3 advisors to pass this latest information on to the FRAC watch officers in Danang. Within a few minutes, a G-3 operations officer called back and asked for almost the identical information we had just sought from our ARVN counterparts. Our response was equally unsatisfactory to him as we could say little more than, "Yes, we'll pass the information along as soon as we find out what is happening."

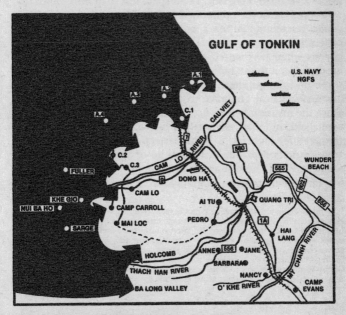

**SITUATION 2 APRIL**

CHAPTER EIGHT

# BEDLAM AT 3D DIVISION HEADQUARTERS

Shortly before 1900, Colonel Murdock entered the division G-3 watch area. In the previous days and nights I had been working as his G-3 advisor, I had spent less than thirty minutes with him. He never mentioned my decision to order the helicopter rescue into Alpha 2, nor did he ever countermand any orders I had given to his Team 155 advisors. On earlier occasions when he entered the G-3 watch area, he would look around, listen to the radio traffic, but never remain more than three or four minutes. Also, throughout this period he had given no tactical guidance to assist our U.S. advisory effort. Since the invasion began, no meetings of the U.S. advisors had been held, nor had any written operational summaries been prepared for higher U.S. headquarters. Most reports were voice transmissions over our tactical radio or radio telephone links with the FRAC headquarters in Danang.*

This time, however, Colonel Murdock motioned to me and

*Captain O'Toole was also making periodic radio reports directly back to the MAU Headquarters in Saigon. Captain Izenour would then immediately drive to the MACV Intelligence Center and pass along his latest information. Initially the MACV personnel would not accept his reports as reliable because they had not come through official channels. As the flow of information slowly reached Saigon, the Captain's earlier report proved to be completely accurate. By the third and fourth days of the Offensive, these same officers were telephoning Izenour at the Bo Tu Linh for his latest information on the combat activities in MR-1.

asked that I join him. We walked into the common map area between the ARVN G-3 and the advisor's watch areas. He began by telling me General Giai was relocating the division headquarters into the old Citadel in Quang Tri City. The move would take his headquarters outside the range of the NVA's 130MM guns. His advisory team would therefore also relocate to Quang Tri City. Lieutenant Colonel Heon would have to move the five miles south and set up the new advisory compound. As the senior American, I was to remain in the division's TOC bunker and take charge of all supporting arms. I was dumbfounded at the prospect of such an overwhelming task under the circumstances and I said so.

"Colonel, you can't split the division's G-3 operations and intelligence sections away from the U.S. supporting arms, air and naval gunfire, and still integrate these assets into the battle effectively." He agreed that it was an extremely difficult tactical situation and said I would have to do the best job possible. He remained adamant as to both my assignment and the relocation plans.

We stood alone beside the 1:50,000 tactical map of Quang Tri Province. We were talking to each other, but neither of us heard the other. Colonel Murdock didn't have much time. He had to join General Giai.

I tried to protest. "Sir, I can't do what you're asking. This is an ARVN and U.S. Army operation. I'm a Marine. Christ, I'm just visiting up here. Until yesterday I thought FRAC was a misspelled word. I don't even know your regimental advisors out on Camp Carroll and Charlie 1. I'm still not certain just what the division's new defensive plans are. You said I'd be relieved from filling in as your temporary G-3 advisor hours ago. Where is my relief?"

He was talking at the same time and we were resolving nothing.

I said, "I'll stay with the Vietnamese Marines. I'll help out in any other possible way. You've had several army colonels in and out of this TOC in the past two days." I was too tired to keep arguing and when I stopped Murdock told me to stay. "You've got it. It is an operational emergency. Someone will be brought up to relieve you as soon as possible."

We were both frustrated, each uncomfortable with the other, both groping for words. There were no easy solutions in this damn war. Almost mechanically he brought out an open pack of cigarettes and put them in my hand. "Good luck," he said.

I thought, "Christ, this can't be real, it's like a movie. I'm getting his last pack of cigarettes." After three days in combat, we were strangers. He still didn't know I had never smoked.

At 1900 the G-3 watch officer's entry recorded:

> Colonel Murdock and staff have departed this position. We are setting up a major CP under command of Lieutenant Colonel Turley.[1]

General Giai's speedy withdrawal from Ai Tu had an immediate demoralizing effect upon the remainder of the 3d Division headquarters. A series of rumors of the impending move had circulated during the afternoon. It was no surprise when the decision was made to shift the division's CP south to Quang Tri City.

In retrospect, Giai's decision was the best alternative to his staff's remaining under the enemy's shelling. However, the manner in which the relocation was executed had a devastating impact upon the remainder of the division. There was no written order or planned sequence for displacing his headquarters staff without interrupting the division's communication support to the three infantry regiments and two Marine brigades still locked in combat with the enemy.

Rather, at the command to displace, ARVN staff officers and their enlisted men simply stood up, grabbed their personal gear, and left the bunker. Radios were left on and simply abandoned; maps and classified materials lay where last used and were unguarded. For at least thirty minutes complete bedlam existed.

Outside the TOC the scene was duplicated to an even worse degree. Order melted into chaos as frightened men, who had ceased to be soldiers, ran for the nearest vehicle. Emotions were high; officers and troops clambered aboard jeeps and trucks and often before a truck was completely loaded an officer would scream at the driver to "get moving." The most senior officers

left first with Vietnamese helicopters swooping in to pick up
the ARVN colonels and the Vietnamese Air Force liaison personnel. The melee continued into the night. Even darkness
couldn't hide the unprofessionalism of the personnel of the 3d
Division CP as they literally scrambled for safety. It was a dark
and tragic day indeed.

Observing the debacle were other ARVN soldiers and Vietnamese Marines. The 6th VNMC Battalion, providing security
for the division headquarters, watched as files and office
equipment were first moved outside the TOC bunker and then
abandoned by soldiers running after already overloaded trucks.

At a time when a carefully planned and executed face-saving
move would have had a tempering effect upon the division,
firm leadership from the top was nonexistent. Confused by the
disorder around them, South Vietnamese radio operators began
radioing their observations to fellow communicators located
away from the division headquarters. Thus, it was only a matter
of hours before all elements of the division were aware of the
hasty withdrawal to Quang Tri City. On the besieged fire bases
at Charlie 1 and 2, rumors abounded that the division headquarters at Ai Tu had been abandoned. The rippling effect of
such rumors further eroded the South Vietnamese resolve to
fight.

As large troop helicopters began lifting U.S. advisory team
155 personnel out, the compound was still receiving occasional
artillery fire. Here also the scramble into CH-47 Chinook helicopters was uncoordinated. Frightened American soldiers carrying radios and stereo equipment scurried from the Ely huts
to the landing zone with desperation on their faces. Understandably, these support troops just wanted to get away from
the enemy's artillery and as helicopters settled into the compound, groups of the frightened soldiers rushed to get aboard.

In Team 155's disorganized haste to evacuate its advisory
compound, many weapons and other equipment were abandoned. Murdock would later certify the "combat loss" of twenty-
two machine guns, three 81MM mortars, eleven ANPRC-77
radios, a telephone switchboard, plus numerous other items,
with the statement, "These items could not be evacuated without
seriously jeopardizing the lives of the personnel of Team 155."[2]

Interestingly enough, only one American in the advisory team compound was slightly wounded during the first three days of the NVA offensive.

During this turmoil there was one unfortunate incident involving an American officer. Shortly after Team 155 had evacuated to Quang Tri, this officer, who had been designated to remain, was discovered leaving the TOC bunker. Because of his special skills it was critically important that he remain. Captain O'Toole noticed the officer had all his personal gear and was moving toward the bunker's entrance. He reported this to me and I was able to stop him. The officer was deeply frightened by the incoming artillery and said he wanted to leave. I ordered him back to his station.

About forty-five minutes later the same officer again was observed trying to leave the bunker. This time I caught him by the arm and ordered him back to his section. He hesitated. I said,

> Captain O'Toole, this officer has twice attempted to leave his assigned duty post. I'm going to give him a direct order which I want you to hear. ____, you are ordered back to your section because your help is crucial to our employment of U.S. supporting arms. If you attempt to leave again, I'll place a formal charge of "desertion under fire" against you.

I looked straight into the officer's eyes and said, "You, sir, and I will be the last Americans to leave this damned bunker. If I catch you trying to desert, I'll personally blow your head off. Now, get back to your duties."

It was an ugly moment I will never forget. The officer did return to his section. Although I observed him several times later on, we never spoke. There was nothing that could be said. He was still afraid, but he was performing his coordination duties. He had been caught up in the panic that was so prevalent in the bunker when the personnel of the 3d Division began leaving.

The major battles on Day Three of the NVA offensive had been fought. Of these, a hundred skirmishes had occurred, but only a few would be recorded. It was a battle between Asian brothers, in which no quarter was given. The northern invaders had carried the day and, under the cover of the gathering darkness, would reposition and replenish their assault forces. The NVA's first major objective, the capture of Quang Tri City, had still not been achieved. At first light, the Nguyen Hue Offensive would continue.

Amazingly enough, the tenacity of the NVA's massive conventional attack across the DMZ still had not been accurately understood or reported in Saigon. Neither the South Vietnamese military leaders nor General Abrams' MACV headquarters had received a comprehensive report on the war in Quang Tri Province. In Saigon there was still a firm belief that the battle across the DMZ was only a deceptive secondary attack and the NVA's main attack, yet to come, would be in Military Region Two (MR-2) through the central highlands. In spite of the loss of ten major fire bases south of the DMZ, the South Vietnamese JGS ordered a brigade of airborne troops to be flown into the Pleiku-Kontum area, an area with little enemy activity.[3] General Abrams' daily personal operational summary report (OPSUM) to the chairman, JCS, Pentagon indicated that "The time of attack in Kontum Province is approaching. Most of the provinces in MR-2 are on alert status."

His assessment of the situation in northern MR-1 was as follows:

The pattern of events is beginning to stabilize. The situation in Quang Tri is bad and it is going to get worse. The ARVN units have been fighting against human wave attacks with minimal air support and generally ineffective artillery support. The enemy SAM and long-range artillery coupled with poor weather conditions have almost completely blocked out all air support. As a result, the enemy's offensive is gaining momentum. Unless the conditions restricting air support change in the next twenty-four to forty-eight hours, it is a certainty that the enemy will control virtually all of Quang Tri Province outside a line encompassing Dong Ha and Quang Tri City . . . All allied bases remain in friendly hands with the exception of Holcomb. The ARVN company withdrew from that area yesterday to alternate defensive positions.

I have just been informed that a tactical emergency has been declared in that area.

In summary, the situation throughout RVN appears to be developing. Weather as well as the SAM threat north of the DMZ continues to hamper operations.[4]

In what remained of the 3d ARVN Division TOC we, of course, were unaware of Abrams' OPSUM. With both ARVN and Americans leaving, the bunker was still in a turmoil. Everyone was concerned for his personal safety. Emotions ran high, tempers were short, words between U.S. military personnel were both excusing and accusing. Only thirty Americans, soldiers, airmen and Marines would remain in the TOC.

In the midst of all this, the incoming artillery fire continued unabated. Radio reports on the collapse of the ARVN fire bases were continuing to be received. The Americans at FRAC headquarters in Danang and the MACV staff in Saigon were calling directly to the advisory team's G-3 watch officers, seeking the latest tactical information so they could update their own commanders.

Before Colonel Murdock departed the TOC, he allowed me to keep certain elements of his advisory team at Ai Tu. To assist in fire support coordination, the U.S. Air Force liaison section, the U.S. naval gunfire liaison team, and the B-52 ARCLIGHT strike officer, U.S. Army Maj. James Parrish, along with the team's communication officer, Maj. J. F. Neary, were selected to remain.

In addition to Neary's lieutenant assistant, nine of his soldiers volunteered to remain behind. This latter contingent was a godsend because without this superbly led and professionally knowledgeable group of communicators, all our efforts would have been for naught. To a man, they shared our fears. Hell, we were all afraid but we remained at our stations.

In any fast-moving, dynamic combat situation, a field commander must have some means of controlling his forces and its supporting arms. Without a reliable command and control communications system, commanders command in name only and are ineffective leaders. The striking difference between the command and control communications channels of the 3d ARVN Division was that the Americans made their system work in spite of the disarray around them. When communications broke down between the ARVN units, they accepted the loss because "it was the enemy's offensive," whereas the Americans kept trying to establish an alternative link.

Major Neary repeatedly demonstrated his exceptional abilities as a communicator. He was everywhere, overseeing the repair of malfunctioning radios and checking the operations of radio relay vans and telecommunications systems. Throughout the ordeal he strived to maintain a high degree of communications security. His personal attention to monitoring voice radio transmissions prevented tactical information from falling into the hands of the enemy.

The Team 155 communication section was located directly behind the line of radios in the G-3 advisor's watch area. A small opening two feet square had been cut between the two areas. During periods of heavy radio traffic Neary would pull back the small door and then appear at eye level with the G-3 watch officer. For those of us on watch, our adrenalin was obviously high. We were excited and feeling the strain of the battles. Often in our haste to respond to an advisor's radio call we would begin speaking into the radio handset before the scramble (cypher) device had become fully activated. As a result, our voice transmissions would be garbled or incomplete.

Through all of this Major Neary was untiring and exceptionally patient with us. His head always seemed to be in the opening and he would say, "All squelch. Say it again. Wait a full two seconds before you begin to talk. Say it again, Colonel. Again, sir, repeat your last transmission."

God, I thought, he's always there looking at me. Doesn't he ever sleep? Does he have a whole body, legs? All I've ever seen is his face telling me "All squelch," or "Say it again." He was an irritant, yet we all felt secure because he was there. Once, when he wasn't looking at us, we agreed that his nickname would be "Major All Squelch"—a small bit of levity which helped relieve the tension in the bunker. So far as I am aware, Major Neary never knew of his nickname, which remained our section's secret.

Neary was demanding of all the watch officers. Because of his pursuit of excellence, even in the face of death, the communication system manned by the Americans remained a viable commander's tool throughout the heaviest artillery bombardments that the North Vietnamese directed at us. His young soldiers were inspired by his "can-do" spirit and quickly sought to emulate their major. No problem was insurmountable, and they repeatedly demonstrated their versatility in maintaining the critical communications systems in the TOC.*

Upon the relocation of the 3d ARVN Division to Quang Tri, their complete command and control system was left in place at Ai Tu. The communications facilities of Team 155 along with part of its support personnel also remained at the Ai Tu bunker. Within a short time the significance of this action became apparent. Thus, when the 3d Division and Team 155 commanders left, Ai Tu remained the only South Vietnamese field command in Quang Tri Province with operational control of uncommitted RVNAF forces, and contained the only U.S. military facility north of Danang that could control air and naval gunfire assets.

As such, the Ai Tu field command quickly became the collection point for intelligence and tactical information vital to the security of Quang Tri Province. The continued effectiveness of the 3d ARVN Division units depended on it. For five critical days naval gunfire missions, B-52 ARCLIGHT strikes, tactical air support, and Vietnamese fire support coordinations were all controlled from within a single bunker at Ai Tu. It was to become an emergency combat situation unparalleled in the history of the U.S. military involvement in the Vietnam War.

As senior Vietnamese commander in the TOC, Col. Ngo Van Dinh, VNMC Brigade 258, was thrust into the role of coordinating the 3d ARVN Division's supporting arms in addition to his own brigade forces while I was tasked to coordinate all U.S. supporting arms. We started as strangers. Time

---

*Major Neary was later recommended for a Bronze Star medal for his exemplary actions. The citation read in part:

The immediate communications advice which Major Neary rendered to the acting senior advisor, 3d ARVN Division command post (forward) proved indispensable to the successful operation of the forward command post under exceptionally difficult and trying circumstances.

and chance had brought us together to share the next few critical days.

There was no time for formalities, no time to waste. Maj. Jon Easley, Dinh's senior advisor, met the colonel and me, and recommended that we assemble all U.S. and Vietnamese officers in the TOC's large briefing room and collectively brief each other on the situation as we knew it. Until the moment Colonel Murdock directed that I assume the G-3 advisor's role, the visiting U.S. Marines had been operating without any real authority. They had been caught in the TOC bunker as the initial assaults began across the DMZ and during the next seventy-two hours had become progressively more involved. The Marine advisors in the TOC all had extensive experience in fire support coordination and had literally grown up employing close air support aircraft, naval gunfire ships and their own artillery. The officers remaining from Team 155 had less experience with coordinating supporting arms and let the Marines take the lead in coordinating both U.S. and ARVN weapons systems. As the momentum of the Nguyen Hue Offensive pressed south, the primary source of tactical information was coming through the Marine advisor's radio network. Slowly the Team 155 advisors began yielding to the suggestions and recommendations of the Marine advisors as how best to integrate supporting arms firepower. The change in roles became more pronounced during the next few days.

Shortly after 2000 on Saturday, all U.S. Army, Air Force, and Marines in the TOC moved into the division's briefing room. The staff of Brigade 258 was already there along with several liaison personnel from the 3d ARVN Division who had remained to help coordinate ARVN artillery. There were approximately twenty-five to thirty-five officers in the room. We all rose when Colonel Dinh entered. Enemy artillery continued to impact around the bunker.

Major Easley recommended to Dinh that I brief on the situation as then reported to U.S. advisors. At center stage was a well-lighted map of Quang Tri Province. ARVN fire bases had been highlighted. He introduced me as the new assistant senior Marine advisor to the Vietnamese Marine Corps and added that the senior U.S. advisor of Team 155 had placed me in charge of all U.S. personnel in the TOC.

It was a solemn assemblage. Weary eyes looked at me as I moved to the map. Directing my first comments to our senior officer, Colonel Dinh, I said:

"Sir, let me begin by saying we are not leaving. As long as the Vietnamese Marines remain, the Americans in this room will be at your side. Some advisors have departed, but the rest of us are staying." I then introduced the members of the advisory staff.

"Major Brookbank sits just behind you. As the Air Force liaison officer, he and his section personnel will continue to request all of our TAC Air, SKYSPOTS and B-52 ARC-LIGHT strikes.

"Major Parrish, Team 155's B-52 strike planning officer, has remained behind to assist our planning.

"Major Neary, just across from you, is our communications officer. He and his section have maintained solid communications with our headquarters in Danang as well as with every U.S. advisory team out on the fire bases.

"Lieutenant Eisenstein is our Naval Gunfire Officer; you already know him. He will continue to operate out of the G-3 watch area. Right now he has four U.S. destroyers off the mouth of the Cam Lo-Cau Viet River. More ships are on the way."

Using a red grease pencil to cross out all the fire bases that had been lost, I drew a solid red line to show how the 3d Division defensive posture had been reduced to the Cam Lo-Cua Viet River and the western fire support bases, Mai Loc and Camp Carroll. The enemy's attacks were closing in on Carroll and Mai Loc. We discussed the possibility the NVA might attack but felt their forces were too extended to undertake it. Across our northern front it became clear that the Cam Lo-Cua Viet River would become the main battle line before the sun would rise on Easter Sunday.

Dinh, who spoke excellent English, looked to his left and spoke softly to his G-3 operations officer. I waited, because it was critical that we all understood exactly where our front lines were located. He looked back at me in agreement. This was the first clear assessment since the beginning of the offensive.

Together, we explored the possibility of reopening Route 9 to Camp Carroll and FSB Mai Loc. Both fire bases needed a resupply of artillery ammunition. It was doubtful whether any road-clearing action could be undertaken and reliance on emergency resupply sorties from U.S. Chinook helicopters would have to continue. If this effort was unsuccessful, both fire bases with their thirty-four artillery pieces would be more vulnerable. The loss of these artillery positions and their guns would be a colossal military defeat. We quickly dropped this discussion and shifted to the subject of fire support planning.

A weather report had been received indicating the low overcast could be breaking up. By morning the skies would perhaps be clear enough for TAC Air to be employed against the enemy. This forecast had a psychologically beneficial effect on everyone present. With air support maybe, just maybe, the enemy's momentum could be blunted.

The goal of our meeting was to assure that both Vietnamese and Americans who remained were fully aware of the critical combat situation in Quang Tri Province. We achieved this. Our next objective was to develop together a general plan of defense. We Americans led the discussion, but our comments were presented in an advisory manner because the Vietnamese commanded their units; we did not. As COVANs, our recommendations were always presented carefully to avoid embarrassment to any Vietnamese officer. That would have negated our function. To be effective, everyone had to understand our proposed concept of defense, but more importantly, how it would work and who should be seen when problems arose. I stressed that the counterpart-advisor relationship must function more closely and effectively now, during a time of stress, than at any other time.

Colonel Dinh approved a general defensive plan to stop the enemy north of the Cam Lo-Cua Viet River and west of Camp Carroll, Mai Loc and southwest of Ai Tu around FB Pedro. He designated several officers to be responsible for in-

suring that all fire support coordination problems were re-
solved or brought to his immediate attention.

During the period when the TOC at Ai Tu was to function
as headquarters of the 3d Division (Forward), the Americans
in the bunker made, or were party to, decisions that were in
reality of a reinforced division level rather than a brigade. Although it was not necessary, Dinh and his staff were always
consulted and their approval was sought prior to any decision
to employ U.S. air and naval gunfire. This not only enhanced
the Vietnamese colonel's position, but directly contributed to
the excellent relationships that developed among the team in
the TOC. Captain O'Toole best described these relationships:

> It seemed everything happened in a hurry and, under the cir-
> cumstances, we could have been excused if we had worked
> around the Vietnamese in an effort to speed decisions which
> were above the brigade level. This was never done and it is to
> the credit of all the U.S. types in the bunker that it was not
> done. I believe that we avoided a human error which cemented
> further U.S. and ARVN relations.[5]

The meeting of counterparts and COVANs had been a
success. The feeling was rekindled that by working together
the North Vietnamese invasion force could be slowed. We could
buy time for the South Vietnamese government to respond to
an invasion across the DMZ. For the first time, the Ai Tu TOC
had a "team" within it; a team whose members knew what was
to be done and who was going to do it. Composed of Vietnamese soldiers and Marines, as well as U.S. Army, Air Force
and Marine personnel, the team set about the demanding task
to develop a defensive fire plan which integrated ARVN and
Vietnamese Marine artillery with U.S. air and naval gunfire.
Over the next few days, personnel on the team changed and
officers were shifted, but the team spirit never changed, and
this was the truly important achievement of that first meeting.
It was a beginning and a source of hope.

Next, U.S. Marine artillery advisors with Brigade 258 had
another fruitful meeting with Major Huah, commanding of-

ficer of the 3d VNMC Artillery Battalion, and with the liaison
personnel, 3d Division. Together they began setting up an integrated fire plan to cover all remaining South Vietnamese positions. Capt. Al Nettleingham, USMC, recalled, "They started
from nothing. There were no targeting records in the vacated
fire support coordination center (FSCC). They could locate no
records on any enemy targets." Captain O'Toole and Captain
(Dai Uy) Chau, S-2 intelligence officer, began collecting and
passing data on enemy movement and troop concentrations.
The two officers also began feeding additional information received through other channels on actual targets and where
enemy contacts were heaviest. On two occasions, diverted
SKYSPOTS ordnance landed atop enemy units preparing to
attack VNMC units.

Targeting information was sent out to the ARVN artillery
batteries at FSB Mai Loc, Camp Carroll and the 3d VNMC
Artillery Battalion located near the TOC. With centralized fire
planning, the batteries began to respond to calls for fire missions. The ARVN's two 175MM batteries also began at long
last to shoot counterbattery fire missions.

Maj. Regan Wright, Capt. Bob Evasick and an ARVN lieutenant colonel unknown but to God, assisted in the development of a division-wide fire support plan. They began their
fire planning by breaking the targets down into those that could
be attacked by air, naval gunfire or artillery. Once identified,
the air targets were fed to Major Brookbank's liaison section.
This officer, a U.S. Air Force reservist, became the air officer
for "everyone in Quang Tri Province."[6] He pursued every possible communications channel to bring air power to bear on
the enemy. The major's personal efforts to get TAC Air on
targets were instrumental in slowing the enemy's advance.
However, the full force of the North Vietnamese invasion soon
challenged his true mettle. He demonstrated that he possessed
the stamina and those special qualities of which heroes are made.

Fire support coordination problems did not evaporate when
the meeting was over. On the contrary, they became more visible and there were many more fire planning situations to resolve.

Brookbank's air liaison section was literally saturated with requests for air support. For his air requests to be approved, a similar request had to originate from and be communicated through Vietnamese channels. Under routine conditions this dual requesting procedure worked. During the first few days of the enemy's offensive, the South Vietnamese Air Force (VNAF) net broke down. Eventually, requests for air support were simply validated by the senior Vietnamese in the TOC and sent by Brookbank's section to the U.S. Air Force Direct Air Support Center 1 (DASC) in Danang. He described the number of SKYSPOT requests submitted by the ARVN personnel during the first few days as "astronomical," with suspected enemy troop locations seeming to be the most frequent target description.

Late on the evening of 1 April, General Giai requested an immediate air strike on the recently abandoned CP bunker at Charlie 1. The NVA had moved their forward headquarters into the large underground bunker. With most of the 57th Regiment's communications system left in operative condition after the withdrawal, the NVA soldiers were using the telephone switchboard to call into the main telephone centers of the 3d ARVN Division. The reports of NVA soldiers using the telephone reminded me of the U.S. Civil War of the 1860s, when Yanks and Rebels also spoke a common language.

The enemy quickly took advantage of the telephone lines by calling whatever South Vietnamese unit would answer their ring. As could be expected, these calls by the enemy created even more confusion among ARVN units.

Adamant about the destruction of Charlie 1's command bunker, Giai said, "It is absolutely first priority." Brookbank relayed the request to the DASC, but hours went by with no action taken. Pressed by Giai and Murdock as to the status of the air strike, and unable to attain any information through the telephone, Brookbank, in violation of U.S. security procedures designed for more tranquil times, went to his radios and contacted the U.S. Air Force airborne command and control (ABCC) aircraft flying somewhere over Hue City. Having made his original request to destroy the target almost eight hours earlier, Major Brookbank, in total frustration, had finally jumped his Air Force command and control channels to obtain critically needed support. He would later have to repeat this procedure to protect his own life and the lives of all the men in the besieged TOC bunker at Ai Tu.*

Earlier in the day Lt. Col. Heath Twichell, Jr., U.S. Army, senior advisor, 57th ARVN Regiment, suggested to his counterpart the advisability of requesting orders to withdraw from Charlie 1 and set up a bridgehead defense north of Dong Ha before the NVA infantry sighted on both flanks could cut off their only route of withdrawal. The regimental commander hesitated and stated, "I can do nothing without orders from the division."[7]

Twichell quietly telephoned the TOC to recommend that Murdock or his deputy discuss such a withdrawal with General Giai. At approximately 1800, the regimental commander received orders to withdraw the 57th further south.

The darkest of nights fell over Quang Tri Province. To the north of the Cam Lo-Cua Viet, the 57th Regiment on Charlie 1 was planning to pull off its fire base at 2400. Trucks were used to move one battery of 155MM howitzers (four guns) and one VNMC battery of 105MM howitzers (six guns) south on Highway 1 across the Dong Ha Bridge to new positions south of the river. The 2d Battalion of the 57th would perform a rearguard role after the truck convoys had cleared the fire base. The 1st Battalion was to fall back into positions both north and south of the Dong Ha Bridge, while the 3d Battalion and the regimental headquarters were to move into assembly areas south of the Cam Lo-Cua Viet River.

At 2200 the TOC received a radio message that two artil-

---

*Major Brookbank was later recommended for a Bronze Star from the U.S. Marine Corps. His citation from the secretary of the navy read in part:

Major Brookbank maintained his post within the 3d ARVN Division tactical operations center at Quang Tri combat base for over ninety-six hours without rest as he processed and coordinated simultaneous requests for close air support, tactical air observation and aerial interdiction of enemy forces by B-52 strategic bombers, and other delivery systems.

lery pieces had to be left in the battery positions on Charlie 1. Not enough trucks arrived to tow the ten guns. One 155MM and one 105MM howitzer had to be destroyed.

Out on the western fire bases, enemy artillery continued to pound Camp Carroll, Charlie 2 and FSB Mai Loc. B-52 ARCLIGHT strikes were requested to strike enemy positions much closer to Mai Loc than those requested the previous day. The 4th VNMC Battalion was now fairly well located; any movement to Brigade 147's west would be enemy. During the night the artillery batteries at FSB Mai Loc continued to fire at the enemy gun flashes and at the 57MM recoilless rifles firing at them from 1,500 yards to the west.

Around 2400 Colonel Murdock called the G-3 watch area from his new location in Quang Tri City. He directed that Major Parrish (B-52 strike officer) come to his location. I protested this decision as we had just begun to develop some semblance of order. I told him bluntly, "To lose him now would interrupt our fire planning."

Murdock listened and deferred his decision, saying he would call back.

Shortly thereafter, Brig. Gen. Thomas Bowen, Jr., USA, Deputy Senior Advisor, FRAC, telephoned me direct from Danang and informed me, "All restrictions are off on U.S. air; continue to request targets for B-52s." I told him, "We have already requested around fifteen ARCLIGHT strikes and forty to fifty SKYSPOTS."

His telephone call said something far more important. Finally, the senior U.S. military officers in Danang and Saigon were aware of how critical the situation was in Quang Tri Province. It would have been unthinkable, just forty-eight hours earlier, for a general officer to tell a U.S. lieutenant colonel, of any U.S. armed service, that he had carte blanche to designate targets for B-52 ARCLIGHT strikes. The killing zone from one ARCLIGHT strike of three B-52s covered an area of 3,000 square meters. Over 250, 750-pound steel bombs could saturate the target area producing devastating physical and psychological effects on any surviving enemy. Bowen's call now placed the decision to employ B-52s against the advancing three North Vietnamese divisions squarely in my hands.

Being unprepared for such blanket authority, I responded, "Yes, sir, I will do as ordered. However, I would ask that the general give me his full name and rank." He did this, and I wrote it down and stuffed it into my pocket.

This was to be the first of many telephone calls from more senior American officers directing that certain actions be taken. Telephone calls were soon being received from Murdock's advisory staff in Quang Tri, FRAC headquarters in Danang, and MACV's main operations center in Saigon.

Before another two hours passed, a U.S. Air Force general would also telephone directly into the G-3 watch area in the TOC. Maj. Regan Wright had walked into the room as a telephone rang. He later recorded:

> I remember picking up a telephone and was surprised to be talking to a U.S. Air Force general in Saigon. He told me that we had all the U.S. air assets in Southeast Asia. This was amazing, and I remember looking around and there were four or five Americans standing there, no one above the rank of major except a lieutenant colonel, and here's an Air Force general telling us we had control of all air assets in Southeast Asia. He said, "At this time we have twenty-five SKYSPOTS and seven B-52 strikes," and we can have them on a daily basis.[8]

It was a confusing night. Every remaining fire base was reeling under artillery or infantry attacks. The withdrawal of the 57th was progressing slowly. At midnight, its 1st Battalion was moving into blocking positions on both sides of the Dong Ha Bridge while the regiment's 2d Battalion, serving as rearguard, was still several miles north of the Dong Ha Bridge.

At 0040, Murdock returned to the TOC bunker. While he was there, a radio message came in from the 57th. "Contrary to their earlier (2130) report, the ARVN's four 155MM howitzers and one 105MM Marine howitzer which were left behind are still capable of being fired. Several stacks of 105 and 155 ammunition are still on position." Another hour went by before we reconfirmed the guns had been left behind. It was an unfortunate report, but the fact that it had been made confirmed that our radio reporting system was improving. The colonel listened to the report and without speaking left the G-3 watch area.

Working together in the TOC bunker, South Vietnamese and U.S. fire support coordinators scheduled naval gunfire to cover the 57th withdrawal. At 0215, U.S.S. *Buchanan* fired fifty high explosive (HE) rounds into Charlie 1 and, later, at 0330, the U.S.S. *Waddell* (DDG-24) moved onto the gunline, sending another fifty rounds of HE into the deserted fire base. Again at 0525 the Waddell began firing on Charlie 1, but after twenty-five rounds had been fired, both of her guns went down. She pulled off the firing line for repairs. Her last radio message was, "We'll return as soon as the guns are up." Two hours later she returned.[9]

The NVA artillery fire on the TOC bunker at Ai Tu had now settled into a scheduled routine. At 0140, 0240, 0420 and 0545 the compound received heavy 130MM artillery attacks. Other enemy shellings were mainly of the interdicting and harassing types. Together, this fire was just enough to keep those personnel who had to move outside the bunker on guard and without sleep.

At 0630, the senior U.S. Navy officer aboard ship, (called the gunfire commander), radioed Lieutenant Eisenstein that "our brothers" were two hours offshore in the Tonkin Gulf. In the running radio dialogues between Eisenstein and the naval gunfire ships, we were informed that a U.S. Marine special landing force (SLF) had been ordered into the area. Over 3,000 U.S. Marines and sailors were embarked on two LPHs, two LSTs and two destroyers.

The word of their arrival swept through the TOC. Both Vietnamese and Americans were exhilarated by the news. It was truly the first good news we had received since the invasion was launched three days earlier.

The fact that an SLF was close by was comforting. My twenty-plus years as a Marine also made me fully aware they would not be recommitted into South Vietnam without a careful decision by the Joint Chiefs of Staff in the Pentagon and the National Security Council. To complicate their recommitment further, if a decision were made to land the Marines, their operational control would pass from commander, U.S. Seventh Fleet to commander, Military Assistance Command, Vietnam (MACV). No amphibious or helicopter landings could be executed until MACV's staff, Maj. Gen. Kroesen at FRAC, and Lieutenant General Lam had developed a joint operation plan for the Marines once they came ashore.

It seemed clear that, all things considered, it was too early for U.S. ground forces to be recommitted ashore. The test for President Nixon's Vietnamization program would have to run its course. South Vietnam's armed forces (RVNAF) would have to fight the NVA without U.S. ground combat troops.

Unknown to the Americans in the bunker, but most significant for General Abrams' headquarters in Saigon, U.S. Navy ships had been monitoring the raging battles ashore by listening on the U.S. advisor's radio nets. With the tactical information they gleaned from listening and from our naval gunfire liaison team, the gunline commander began to radio almost hourly reports to the Commander, Seventh Fleet and Commander-in-Chief, Pacific Fleet in Honolulu. Each of these "flash" messages was readdressed to General Abrams' Saigon headquarters.

Within the MACV headquarters there was deep concern about what was really happening along the DMZ. There had only been sporadic reports from the FRAC headquarters in Danang, and Captain Izenour's radio reports from Captain O'Toole were still not being accepted by the MACV intelligence center watch officers. Yet, the U.S. Navy was reporting an NVA invasion underway. Four U.S. destroyers were now off the Cam Lo-Cua Viet River expending hundreds of rounds of ammunition on "reported" North Vietnamese units. To confuse the situation even more, a U.S. Marine lieutenant colonel was repeatedly cited in naval messages as the senior coordinator of all U.S. supporting arms in the 3d ARVN Division's area of responsibility. In Saigon the MACV staff knew of no Marine lieutenant colonel assigned to duty in MR-1.

Maj. Robert Sheridan, USMC, the senior U.S. Marine at the Marine advisory unit's Saigon headquarters, was located and ordered to report to General Abrams' office.

In general, the Navy's reporting was very accurate. Again,

unknown to us in the TOC, the name Lieutenant Colonel Turley, USMC, began appearing in most messages. The full reverberations of this would be felt in the next twenty-four hours.

At 0645 a Colonel at FRAC called to inform us a decision had been made that "No aircraft will go north of the Cam Lo-Cua Viet River without gunship escorts . . ." This was a confusing telephone call, because all ARVN units were either south of the river or immediately on the other side. When asked to clarify this, he said he would visit our position later in the day and explain the new flight restrictions. He never arrived. There would be many more telephone calls like this. We recorded them in our advisor's G-3 journal, and then turned our attention back to the Nguyen Hue Offensive.

Several hours earlier there had been a lull in the reporting from the fire bases, so activity in the TOC slowed, giving the few of us still awake a rare opportunity to think about what had happened over the last few days. For me, it was a time for reflecting while making a head call and eating a can of "C" rations. I couldn't remember having eaten since the invasion began. There had been no opportunity to shave or even wash our faces. It had been three days now since several of us had last slept. Sitting on the plank decking near the G-3 watch area, I opened a can of ham slices and another can of soda crackers. There wasn't time to heat the ham. I tried to scrape the grease off, then made a sandwich with a cracker. Except for the grease, the ham was tasteless. Even the crackers tasted bad; I couldn't finish it. I was hungry but had no appetite, exhausted but couldn't sleep.

Just sitting there hurt. I was so tired and perplexed at how I ever managed to get myself into such an unbelievable situation. How could all this have happened in four days? It didn't seem real.

Before leaving Saigon—an eternity ago—I had written my wife, Bunny, and told her not to expect any mail for at least a week and that I would write again after my return from places such as Quang Tri, Mai Loc, Sarge and Dong Ha. I wondered if she had heard anything on the evening news about the NVA Easter offensive.

It would soon be daylight. The tempo of the North Vietnamese invasion would increase shortly. The enemy was winning in Quang Tri Province. The Cam Lo-Cua Viet River was the last natural obstacle for the ARVN to use as a defensive line. If they failed to hold along the river, the North Vietnamese could break the back of the 3d ARVN Division and move into Quang Tri City. Time was running out; some way we had to hold.

I remember thinking that we were not going to let those NVA "bastards" win without giving it our best shot.

# CHAPTER NINE

# DAY FOUR: EASTER SUNDAY

Like the lonely sentinel waiting for the dawn, the first light of Easter Sunday was slow to reach down on Quang Tri Province.

While most of the western world prepared to celebrate the joy of a risen Lord, events in this northernmost province of Vietnam would be radically different from the traditional Easter anyone on the advisory team remembered. Indeed, the catastrophic events due to take place in one short day could never have been predicted and would shock both the opposing armies and governments. The course of the war would change unalterably from this date on. The assumptions and plans each army had used to fight the war up to this point would no longer apply. April 2, 1972 could arguably be called the most memorable day of the war.

The morning began under a solid overcast with cloud cover down to 1,000 feet. Aircraft of the U.S. and Vietnamese stood ready and armed at Danang and other airfields but would have to wait before any attack could be launched against the lucrative targets offered by the two infantry divisions and two tank regiments of the North Vietnamese advancing on the Cam Lo-Cua Viet River and the threatened city of Quang Tri.

Throughout the night, the enemy's guns had intensified its bombardment of the retreating South Vietnamese soldiers and civilians. The badly bloodied 3d ARVN Division was hurriedly trying to reposition itself along the Cam Lo-Cua Viet River to forestall the southern thrust of the North Vietnamese Army. Although the ARVN units had made no actual sightings of communist tanks or armored personnel carriers (APCs), their reports of heavy engine noises, the "clacking of track" and even ground vibrations from locations near the recently abandoned Alpha 2 positions on National Highway 1, heightened the anxiety among the commanders and their U.S. advisors in the three ARVN regiments conducting retrograde movements.

The preceding day had been a near disaster for the South Vietnamese forces. Eleven major fire bases had been lost along with fifteen artillery pieces. The last two remaining western fire support bases, Camp Carroll and Mai Loc, were under extremely heavy artillery fire and probing ground attacks. Marginal weather continued to greatly favor the communist invaders. There had been no letup in the viciousness or intensity of the NVA attack across the DMZ. The full force of the NVA's military might was being thrust against one of the newest and worst-trained South Vietnamese divisions. The question to which we in the TOC were seeking to find an answer was, "Could the 3d Division hold on until reinforcements arrived?" The prospect of its doing so was extremely bleak.

The enemy's boldness and methodical execution of its battle plan reaffirmed one of General Giap's predominant principles, "Strike to win; strike only if success is certain; if it is not, then don't strike." A critical day of fighting was about to begin.

Shortly after 0700, Major Joy reported from Mai Loc that his brigade advisory team had reestablished radio contact with the Alpha command group from FB Sarge. Both Major De and Major Boomer were alive; the 4th VNMC Infantry Battalion had broken out of an encirclement during the night and was now moving toward Mai Loc combat base.

Joy indicated that De and Boomer had abandoned FB Sarge, leading the remaining Marines over the perimeter's eastern wire. They left the destroyed fire base at 0340, Friday with only what they could carry on their backs. A moonless night shielded their movements, as the survivors linked up several hundred yards down the slope, closed into a column formation and headed generally east. The column was forced to move slowly, as many were wounded. In his subsequent report, Boomer said:

> Daylight found us moving generally in an easterly direction as quietly as we could, concerned only with survival at this point. It seemed that everywhere we turned there were North Vietnamese. As we moved throughout the day we could hear them below us, to our front and to our rear. But we were able to avoid any confrontation during that day as we moved east.[1]

Sometime during the following day, Boomer became separated from his enlisted Vietnamese radio operator. Later that evening, the operator reappeared but without the advisor's radio. His feeble explanation was simply that it had been lost. Uncharacteristically, Major Boomer became enraged and fought back the urge to beat the young Marine. He thought better of the idea because any loud outcries could reveal the column to the NVA moving all around them.

The jungle terrain, dense undergrowth and ragged slopes made every mile difficult. As the rain finally halted and Saturday evening descended, the column simply stopped in its tracks. No one in the column had any food. No fires could be lit so everyone simply dropped by the trail side and slept until dawn.

Boomer later recalled that no one in the unit had any idea of where he was. Moreover, without his radio Boomer was totally unaware of events elsewhere that day in Quang Tri Province. The only fact both he and his battalion commander really knew was that North Vietnamese soldiers were seemingly everywhere.

By 0900 Sunday morning, the column began to move out of the thick mountain jungle into the more sparsely covered hills. At that point, the 4th Battalion's luck appeared to run out. As they were attempting to move through thick six-foot high elephant grass between two North Vietnamese units, whose voices they could hear very distinctly, the NVA troops discovered the Marines and engaged them with intense small arms and rocket fire.

The discipline of the bloodied 4th Battalion survivors fell apart; they began to break. Prior to this last onslaught, these troops had acquitted themselves bravely. But after two days of constant heavy shelling on FB Sarge and the stress of the march through enemy territory, the unit's members were psychologically exhausted. Their response to the new attack was simply to run headlong to the east. Boomer remembered:

> I tried to stop them by firing over their heads because I knew they were leaving a large column of wounded behind. I can remember clearly the terrified look in their eyes as they streamed past me. My shouts had apparently been heard by the North Vietnamese because I began to hear screams of "COVAN, COVAN." The Vietnamese word for advisor is the same on two sides. At that point I realized that trying to get the battalion to return fire and give our wounded a chance to escape was futile. It was also very clear that if I stayed in that position much longer the North Vietnamese would make a concerted effort to capture me because they knew an American was close by. So I turned and moved with the rest of the battalion heading east. At that point it was every man for himself.[2]

During this confrontation he lost contact with Major De who seemed to have simply picked up what he had and moved out. An artillery lieutenant remained with Boomer. They moved east as quickly as they could for at least an hour before they felt that there was no immediate danger of the North Vietnamese overtaking them. They finally reached a little hamlet to the northwest of FSB Mai Loc. To their great surprise, they discovered Capt. Ray Smith with the remnants of the Bravo command group there. Until that moment each advisor believed the other was dead. Smith had been badly scratched by the barbed wire but was not seriously hurt; he appeared gaunt, but was no worse for the wear. Major De, as well as a significant number of Marines from the 4th Battalion were also there. Someone had made some soup; it was their first food in two days.

While sitting there, they watched the headquarters of Brigade 147 at FSB Mai Loc come under a tremendous artillery attack. Boomer recalled that it was as if they were watching a movie: They sat out in the open receiving no enemy fire, while very clearly within their view another Marine position was under heavy attack only a mile away. However, the remainder of the 4th Battalion was in no condition to help anyone. They could only sit and watch.

Boomer talked with Major Joy on Smith's radio several times during the afternoon. It was very obvious that nothing was to be gained by Brigade 147 remaining in its isolated position. He knew from his earlier heavy enemy contacts that it was only a matter of time before FSB Mai Loc would also be overrun. He and Joy discussed the possibility that the brigade might have to destroy its artillery weapons after dark and then march its units out. If that occurred, the brigade and 4th Battalion could somehow join together and move toward the old 3d Division headquarters at Ai Tu.*

On the far western flank, the 2d ARVN Regiment, commanded by Lt. Col. Huynh Dinh Tung, was still withdrawing toward the Cam Lo Bridge. Although the regiment had also been reinforced by an armored cavalry squadron equipped with U.S.-made M-113 APCs, the .50-caliber machine guns of the vehicles would be no match against Soviet-made armor. The elevated gravel roadway south from Alpha 4 and Charlie 2 was marked with burning and deserted vehicles destroyed earlier by enemy artillery fire.

As had been the case for the other fire bases that had fallen, NVA infantry and sapper units had infiltrated around Charlie 2 and 3. Groups of enemy soldiers had been seen on both sides of the road leading south across the Cam Lo-Cua Viet River. Tung knew he had to cross the river into Cam Lo as quickly as possible because enemy soldiers, observed off to the west, were moving south at the same rate of speed as that of his own regiment.

While the 4th Battalion was closing on the village of Mai Loc, the 7th Battalion was ordered to move two companies approximately 2,000 meters south of FSB Mai Loc. Colonel Bao

---

*Maj. Walter Boomer was later awarded the Silver Star medal for his heroic actions as senior advisor, 4th Vietnamese Marine Infantry Battalion.

directed them to attempt a link-up with the missing infantry company of the 8th Battalion which had been forced off FB Holcomb.

The executive officer of the 7th Battalion, Captain Kim, and his COVAN, Capt. Ronald Rice, moved out from Mai Loc with the 1st and 2d Companies and the Bravo command group. Shortly after leaving their battalion perimeter positions the Bravo group made contact with enemy units due south of FSB Mai Loc.[3] It was apparent that during the night NVA infantry units had moved closer to the southern flanks of Brigade 147's position. The Vietnamese Marines now had confirmed ground contacts with the enemy on three sides of FSB Mai Loc.

During the night, General Giai contacted the headquarters of MR-1 to reposition elements of the regional and popular forces (RF/PF) east of Dong Ha, extending on a line east to the Gulf of Tonkin in order to prepare a unified defensive line on the south side of the Cam Lo-Cua Viet River. Although he still did not have operational control over these regional forces, it was reported to him that they had aligned themselves along the widest portion of the Cam Lo-Cua Viet River as he had requested.

The repositioning of the 3d ARVN Division was almost complete. The RF/PF units near the coastline had fought well against small enemy infiltration and sapper units. As members of regional forces units these soldiers normally had their families located in the areas where they were assigned. There had been no reports that large numbers of civilians were leaving the coastal areas which was further evidence that the regional forces were establishing a line to defend their villages and families.

North of the Cam Lo-Cua Viet River, and on Camp Carroll, south, the 3d ARVN Division's three infantry regiments again suffered more casualties under the enemy's artillery during the night. Directly north of Dong Ha, elements of the 57th Regiment still had not completed their withdrawal across the Dong Ha Bridge to the south bank of the Cam Lo-Cua Viet River.

The 2d Battalion, serving as rearguard, was still approximately two miles north of Dong Ha. Their orders were "to hold the small Touc Khe Bridge until ARVN engineers arrived to blow it."[4]

The G-3 advisors in the TOC at Ai Tu now had steady radio communications with advisors to the 56th and 57th ARVN Infantry Regiments, 20th Tank Battalion and Vietnamese Marine Brigades 147 and 258. The 3d Division's ARVN radio network had improved during the night and every American advisor could be reached by radio. The TOC was beginning to receive almost simultaneous duplicate radio reports confirming enemy activities.

At 0854 the dreaded report was received over both Vietnamese and American tactical radio systems. "Enemy tanks sighted on the high ground at FB Alpha 2." This was the first confirmed sighting of North Vietnamese armor; the word was immediately relayed on to FRAC headquarters in Danang.

At 0910 U.S. Navy destroyers offshore reported seeing tanks in the open north of the Cam Lo-Cua Viet River. Their request to attack the enemy armor with their five-inch guns was quickly approved.

The TOC became a flurry of activity. Colonel Dinh came into the advisors' G-3 watch area, to inform me personally of his report on the enemy tanks. However, he did not know how many or what kind, but it didn't matter. The mere presence of tanks on the battlefield had elevated the seriousness of our precarious situation. In response was a staccato series of questions from Colonel Dinh.

"Should I request B-52 strikes?"

"Yes," I responded.

"Can we get air support?"

"No, sir, the cloud cover is still too low for TAC Air. I'll get with our air folks (U.S. Air Force liaison section) to insure they report the enemy tanks to the DASC (direct air support center) in Danang."

During this dialogue, Capt. Al Nettleingham radioed to Capt. John Ripley, advisor to the 3d VNMC Battalion near Dong Ha, that "enemy heavies" were moving south on Highway 1, between Alpha 2 and Charlie 1.[5] Then, Captains Nettleingham and Evasick began coordinating with ARVN and Marine artillery fire support planners to bring indirect fire down on the tanks.

At 0915, Captain Murray told me in the fire support coordination center (FSCC) that I had a personal phone call. I returned to the G-3 watch area and picked up the telephone.

"Lieutenant Colonel Turley, sir."

"Lieutenant Colonel Turley, this is Colonel Murdock. This telephone call is to order you to take over as Chief Advisor, 3d ARVN Division (Forward). The commanding general, FRAC, directed that I make this call directly to you. This is an operational emergency. Do you understand my order?"

"Yes, sir, Colonel, I do. (Thinking to myself, I'll do my best.) Colonel Murdock, since this is such an extraordinary order at a very confusing time, may I have your social security number?"

He responded immediately to my request, and I wrote it down along with the time of his call. I then directed the G-3 watch officer to make the following official entry into the advisor's G-3 journal:

0915 Lieutenant Colonel Turley, USMC, takes over as chief advisor (CA) 3d Division (Forward) by order of Colonel Murdock, USA.

The colonel's call was completely unexpected. Added to the reports of a column of enemy tanks, I remember thinking "the world around me sure seems to be falling apart." What I had dreaded had happened, and I was now officially in charge of coordinating all U.S. forces and supporting arms assets in northern Quang Tri Province. My first thoughts were not on the war but on the strange premonition I had experienced on the C-130 flight to Phu Bai just a few days before. My mind raced on; "How could this have happened to me? Why me, Lord? What can I possibly do that hasn't already been done?" The weather seemed to be against us; the ARVN infantry units were disappearing; their artillery wouldn't shoot back; Soviet-made tanks were coming straight at us. And not only this, there were also U.S. Army personnel over whom I had theoretically been placed in command, but whom I had never seen. I was now responsible for U.S. nationals with little knowledge of who they were, where they were, the actual numbers involved or any vital data. In the hectic moments when Murdock and I had met beside the tactical map, he had not bothered to provide me a list of personnel or the units to which they were assigned.

With all of these thoughts also came the realization that from that moment on I would have to remain the most calm, unflappable, and steady individual in the TOC bunker. My feelings were ambivalent at this turn of events, but I knew that the other Americans there must not perceive any difference in our working relationship. If we were to remain alive, the team effort which had been working well had to continue as if nothing had changed. However, deep inside me was a sudden sense of loneliness, although I was in the midst of a crowd of gallant young Americans. I was reminded that command is a lonely road.

This level of pressure was something I hadn't experienced before. I couldn't help thinking "Here's the colonel calling me from Danang, eighty kilometers from the battle area. He's the 3d Division's Senior Advisor, not me; he should be here. I'm just a visiting Marine. He and I were in completely different chains of command. He is safe in the rear and we're getting our collective ass blown away.

"That's it. This whole damn thing is falling apart and Murdock has very conveniently, but officially, dumped it on someone else. When it all collapses they'll say there was a Marine in charge; it was his fault. It could have been any Marine lieutenant colonel. Gerry Turley isn't important; it's just important that a U.S. Marine has now been placed in charge."

Because his order had been so specifically directed to me, the weight of it rested heavily on my shoulders.

A voice broke into my thoughts, "Colonel, the monsoon weather is beginning to break up along the coast. Cloud cover is still too low for tactical air strikes but the weather is definitely improving!" I looked up at Major Brookbank, a very tired Air Force officer, who had been talking to me while I was mulling over Colonel Murdock's telephone call.

"Thanks, Dave. Please keep me informed when we do get a break in the weather."

A series of radio reports confirmed that the enemy had launched a two-pronged armored attack with the main thrust moving south on Highway 1. The rearguard of the 57th Regiment, located on a small bridge two miles north of the Dong Ha Bridge, reported observing the enemy's armor.

A second, smaller tank column of PT-76 amphibious tanks was observed traversing the beaches north of the Cam Lo-Cua Viet River's outlet into the Gulf of Tonkin. The U.S. destroyers steaming just off the coast radioed to the TOC that four enemy tanks were visibly moving south across the sand dunes.

Lieutenant Eisenstein's naval gunfire team was actively developing several defensive fire plans to strike these NVA tanks as they approached the Cam Lo-Cua Viet River and the Dong Ha area. Commander Thearle, commanding, USS *Buchanan* (DDG-14) again responded to the call for naval gunfire support as did four other destroyers—the *Strauss*, (DDG-16), *Waddell* (DDG-24), *Anderson* (DD-786), and the *Hamner* (DD-718), which had joined on *Buchanan*.[6] Naval gunfire became the primary supporting arms against North Vietnamese targets moving anywhere along the coastline, inland to Highway 1, and around the city of Dong Ha. Their guns were desperately needed further inland but their limited ten-mile range precluded this support.

Ahead of the larger NVA tank column on Highway 1, terrorized civilians surged onto the roadway in their flight south to cross the Dong Ha Bridge. Most refugees were forced to walk; a few families rode atop trucks, while others jammed into small three-wheeled trucks and clung tightly to their perilous positions. Prized water buffalo were being urged along the shoulders of the roadway.

Meanwhile, back in the TOC, several important events happened in quick succession. First, the South Vietnamese Air Force (VNAF) liaison officer and his tactical air control party (TACP) suddenly picked up their personal gear and left. As an omen of this event earlier in the morning, Major Brookbank had attempted to process an air request with his VNAF counterpart who refused to clear the air strike with the comment, "What's the use?"[7] Now, without notice or authority to leave, the captain and his vital air control party had fled the bunker because they were afraid of the enemy's incoming artillery.

Next, a radio transmission to the senior advisor of the 57th Regiment confirmed that none of the infantry battalions of the regiment had any capability to blow the Dong Ha Bridge. While he had heard that some ARVN engineers were supposed to be at the bridge, he was not sure if this was true.

Finally, based upon my own evaluation of the critical tactical situation confronting the 3d ARVN Division, I decided that the Dong Ha Bridge must be destroyed. Because this was a monumental decision, I personally telephoned the FRAC headquarters in Danang and informed them of our desperate situation and my plan to halt the NVA's advancing tank column by blowing the bridge.

Within minutes a telephone call was returned ordering me not to destroy the bridge. The reason given was, "We have to save it for our counterattack north." Under the circumstances such an unrealistic statement could only have been made by a staff officer isolated from the realities of the battle. I vehemently disagreed with the Army lieutenant colonel who made the call and told him it was our only hope of stopping the North Vietnamese offensive.

He remained adamant as to the necessity to save the bridge from destruction. In spite of my efforts to describe how tenuous our whole defensive posture was and that we were barely holding the lines as it was, the telephone voice from Danang was crystal clear. "Don't destroy the bridge. This is an order, Colonel Turley."

"This is ironic," I thought. "I've been coordinating the advisory team's efforts for three days now and have made seemingly endless decisions involving tactical situations and supporting arms employment which have affected the lives of thousands of ARVN soldiers and several Americans and until this very moment have received absolutely no command guidance on how to perform the duties of chief advisor, 3d ARVN Division (Forward). Major General Kroesen, USA; his deputy, Brigadier General Bowen; Lieutenant General Lam; and Brigadier General Giai have all been in the TOC during the past three days and each has recognized me as the G-3 advisor or, later, as the senior U.S. advisor. I have briefed each of them on the very fluid combat situation as we Americans knew it and have described our advisory actions to support the 3d ARVN Division's defense against the advancing North Vietnamese divisions. Not one of these senior officers had any suggested changes in our hastily developed defensive measures or offered command guidance to enhance our U.S. supportive actions. Now, when I disagree with a lieutenant colonel staff officer on the most critical and time sensitive of tactical decisions he gives me my first order, an order not to act."

I acknowledged the order and again repeated my decision to destroy the Dong Ha Bridge, if there was no other means to halt the enemy's attack. It was our last option.

As an interesting sidelight, I find it intriguing to recall how clearly my mind was functioning then. A series of unprecedented events plus chance had somehow placed me in the center arena of U.S. combat actions to assist the South Vietnamese military in saving their northern provinces from being overrun. My progressive involvement in the chaotic events of the previous three days precluded me from avoiding future professional controversy. The circumstances were too significant, the eventual outcome too important to avoid lengthy investigations by the South Vietnamese government or by General Abrams, our MACV commander.

What was most interesting to me was a strange awareness that once I had made a major decision such as the evacuation of Alpha 2, and had committed myself to the advisory tasks of fending off the NVA, all subsequent decisions were really irrelevant. I knew I would be eventually called forward to explain my actions. The die was being cast each step along the way. Any additional decisions would be unimportant as to the final approval or disapproval of my advisory actions within the TOC. I knew, from that point on, I could not get any deeper into controversy or difficulty than that which already faced me. This awareness lessened the mental strain of the officially ordered "emergency responsibilities" that had been thrust upon me.

# CHAPTER TEN

# COMMIT THE RESERVES

By mid-morning fifteen to twenty enemy tanks were observed in the vicinity of Charlie 1, and at least a company of NVA infantry had moved to the western flank of the 57th's 2d Battalion. The 2d Battalion had been ordered to hold its position until ARVN engineers arrived to destroy a small bridge. However, in the face of the growing enemy strength, and with no sign of the promised engineer support, the 2d Battalion was then ordered to continue to withdraw toward the Cam Lo-Cua Viet River to avoid its being cut off.

Whether it was intended or not, the movements of the North Vietnamese invaders were gradually revealing their tactical plan. The main thrust of the enemy's infantry and armor attacks was straight toward the Dong Ha Bridge and Highway 1 leading to Quang Tri City. The successful capture of the bridge would permit the enemy's invasion forces to move across the Cam Lo-Cua Viet River and on toward the south unhindered by further natural terrain barriers.

The slow pace of the retrograde movement by the 57th Regiment was preventing stabilization of its assigned defensive positions on the south side of the Cam Lo-Cua Viet River in a timely manner. Thus, reinforcements from elsewhere would now have to be committed to the defense of the Dong Ha Bridge and the key road junction of Route 9 and Highway 1. The 3d

Vietnamese Marine Battalion was all that remained to halt the oncoming NVA armor.

When the 3d Battalion arrived at the Dong Ha combat base* on the night of 30 March, it had been assigned the mission of "division reserve" for the 3d Division.[1] Now, based upon our critical situation, the decision had to be made to commit Major Binh's 3d Marine Battalion, as it was the only battalion not totally committed to the battle.

I contacted the newly established headquarters of the 3d ARVN Division in Quang Tri City seeking immediate command guidance. General Giai and Colonel Murdock were away from the CP, leaving Colonel Chung, the division's chief of staff, as the senior Vietnamese officer there. He listened to my explanation on the critical need to hold the Dong Ha Bridge. As the chief of staff, he had full authority to act, but he dithered and replied only that, "We must wait for General Giai to return. I can take no action now. We wait."

With precious minutes ebbing away, I felt we could not wait because the NVA were closing in on Dong Ha.

"Jesus Christ," I thought, "won't someone make a decision?" A sense of desperation overtook me at the prospect of losing the day because of command indecision. It seemed that no ARVN officer wanted to make a major tactical decision.

Finally, I turned to Colonel Dinh, my counterpart, the 258th Brigade commander in the TOC bunker. Observing the amenities attendant in our role as advisors, I requested that we meet privately in the common area between our G-3 operations areas. Moving over to the 1:50,000 map where Murdock and I had stood when he had placed me in charge, we reviewed the situation.

"Colonel Dinh," I began, "we must reinforce the 57th ARVN Regiment at the Dong Ha Bridge. All we have left is your 3d Battalion with its 106MM recoilless rifles, which I realize are pathetically inadequate in the face of such a heavy tank threat."

Pointing to the map, I continued, "You have to move the 3d Battalion into the line. We'll need everything we have to

*Old headquarters, U.S. 3d Marine Division.

stop the enemy's tank column. Sir, there's no other unit left; you must commit the 3d Division's reserve."

Reiterating my earlier efforts to reach higher authority, I said, "General Giai is out somewhere in his helicopter. Colonel Chung, his chief of staff, refuses to make a decision on committing the division's reserve force. Colonel, you've got to act." Again, I pointed to the tactical map, indicating where the NVA tanks were last reported, and commented that time was critical because this day's battle would be decided at the Dong Ha Bridge. Dinh was quiet. I studied his face for some indication of his thoughts. He remained expressionless, looking first at the map and then at me, blinking slowly as he did so. After several long moments of silence, he finally said, "I cannot."

I was absolutely dumbfounded by his decision. "Colonel, we're desperate! You've got to move the 3d Battalion around to the south side of the bridge. If you don't, we're going to lose the God-damn war!"

"I cannot commit my 3d Battalion without first getting approval from our commandant, General Khang, in Saigon."

"Colonel Dinh, you don't have time."

Almost pleading, I continued, "Please, Colonel, we need the 3d Battalion. We advisors have done everything possible to assist the 3d ARVN Division and your two Marine brigades; now, if you don't act, it's all over. We're going to lose at the Dong Ha Bridge."

His continued refusal to act sent my mind spinning. I thought, "God, this is crazy. Here I am saying 'please' to a South Vietnamese commander to deploy one of his battalions to stop an enemy invasion and he's telling me that he must call Saigon. I know this is his country, not mine. We all must be crazy."

Colonel Dinh looked at me and again repeated, "I cannot."*

Shaking my head in disbelief, I was amazed at the extent to which each Vietnamese commander carefully guarded his combat actions lest he be singled out for criticism later.

I was, after all, only the commander's COVAN and as such there was nothing more I could do. I anguished over his in-

---

* In later reflections upon the 1972 Easter invasion, I considered this moment to be my psychological low point.

decision and returned to the G-3 advisors watch area. The other U.S. Army and Marine advisors who had been waiting knew, even before I told them, that Dinh would not commit his 3d Battalion to the defense of the bridge.

Personally hurt by his failure to respond to the immediate tactical situation, I was trying to regain some optimism when a hand came to rest on my shoulder. As I turned, I was surprised to see Colonel Dinh standing behind me. He looked at me and in the most beautiful English said, "The 3d Battalion will take the Dong Ha Bridge. I will give the battalion commander the order to hold Dong Ha. You radio your advisor and tell him of my decision."

"God, maybe there is a chance after all!" I shouted and hugged the colonel in my joy. He was, after all, a true warrior, as somehow I had known. He had proven his mettle.

I turned back toward the Americans in the G-3 watch area, Major Easley, the two Army and one Marine captains, and we got back to work. A report came crackling over the radio and one of them spoke to me. "Colonel Turley, the 2d ARVN Regiment has just reported that their rearguard battalion is almost encircled north of Cam Lo."

"OK, record it in your journal," I said.

Captains Murray and Avery were already busy attempting to locate the 2d Regiment's position on the tactical map. The situation was not encouraging as one battalion was still a thousand meters north of the Cam Lo-Cua Viet River. The regiment's radio reports indicated that their only route south was jammed with refugees all the way into Cam Lo. "They're also taking heavy artillery fire at this time," reported a watch officer. Another officer spoke up, "They want an observation aircraft with a FAC up over their area."

"Be honest with them," I said. "Don't give them false hopes if nothing can be arranged. Tell them we'll try to get a light observation aircraft up, but it's doubtful because of the low cloud cover."

I asked Captain Murray to get Captain Ripley on the radio. He was the advisor nearest the Dong Ha Bridge. Ripley acknowledged our radio call on the first transmission. Using the secure voice cypher, I briefed him on the decision to commit the 3d Marine Battalion to the defense of the Dong Ha Bridge.

John reminded me that the 3d Battalion's Bravo command group and two infantry companies (exactly half the battalion) were operating with the 20th Tank Battalion about five miles to the west of Dong Ha on Route 9; the only forces remaining under Major Binh's command at the Dong Ha combat base were two infantry companies. The thought of such a lightly armed and small force stopping a potential major tank attack seemed laughable; but it was all we had.

Earlier in the morning, the 3d Battalion's Dong Ha positions had undergone a forty-minute artillery attack during which over 500 artillery rounds and rockets were estimated as having impacted within their perimeter. "There was a lot of material damage, but only a few casualties," Ripley noted.[2]

At that point he cut short the radio transmission because his counterpart wanted to see him. Since we both knew our dual radio system was working, the reason was apparent; Major Binh had just received his new mission from Colonel Dinh.

Binh immediately ordered his remaining two infantry companies to assume defensive positions along the river bank on both sides of the Dong Ha Bridge and to prepare for both infantry and armored attacks. He advised both of his company commanders that he was leaving his CP and would drive west on Route 9 in order to make radio contact with his Bravo group which was working with the 20th Tank Battalion near Cam Lo.

While he and Ripley were driving westward toward Cam Lo, the commanders of his 1st and 2d companies assembled their Marines and alerted them to the battalion's new mission. Except for two 106MM recoilless rifles, the only anti-tank weapon the Marines possessed was a shoulder-fired rocket system known as the M-72 LAAW—a Light Anti-Armor Weapon with a small armor-penetrating warhead enclosed in a fiberglass tube. It was a one-time fired weapon with a maximum effective range of 250 yards. Carried by infantry units, the LAAW could best be described as a "last resort" weapon for close-in combat against lightly armored vehicles. It was still untested against Soviet-made T-54 tanks.

The 3d Battalion's 1st Company deployed into defensive positions on the south side of the Dong Ha Bridge, while the

2d Company established its defensive positions to the west of Dong Ha along Route 9 in the vicinity of the abandoned railroad bridge. Each company was stretched out over approximately 400 meters of riverfront.

The damaged railroad bridge itself, just north of 2d Company, had already fallen to the enemy. From the top of the northernmost steel girder, a large North Vietnamese flag taunted observers as the red and blue fields, with a yellow star, fluttered ominously in the light coastal breeze.

Assigned to 1st Company was Sergeant Luom, a rocket squad leader, with three rocket teams. Having been instructed to prepare for an enemy armor attack, Sergeant Luom and his squad moved forward deploying a rocket team on each side of the highway bridge abutment. From these positions, the LAAW anti-tank rockets could be brought to bear on any enemy vehicle that approached the bridge from the north. Then, with one assistant, Luom established a hasty position on the southern tip of the bridge.

To provide themselves at least a minimum amount of protection from enemy fire, the two Marines placed two dirt-filled wooden ammunition boxes across their front and lay down behind twelve inches of dirt protection. There, with five M-72 LAAWS, Luom and his assistant awaited the enemy tanks. All the while, refugees and bands of ARVN soldiers were still attempting to flee across the Dong Ha Bridge in their flight to reach Quang Tri City.[3]

With the 3d Battalion's two infantry companies now deployed along the southern bank of the Cam Lo-Cua Viet River, the stage was set. The last elements of the 3d ARVN Division's reserve were committed; now, no units were available if this thin defensive line was broken. To "commit the reserve" has a special meaning in military parlance far beyond what seems to be simply asking for more help. It means this, obviously, but it also means that the situation has become so severe that in effect you are playing your last card. You are down to your last option; if this doesn't work, the game is usually lost. What's more, you have the additional disadvantage of being without enough protection to evacuate your force if the reserve doesn't work and the enemy is successful. Casualties will be much greater and, of course, the reserve force will suffer the most, if not be lost altogether. Commanders therefore are very reluctant to commit the reserve.

While Sergeant Luom positioned his rocket teams, Major Binh made radio contact with Lieutenant Colonel Ley, commanding officer, 20th Tank Battalion, to inform him of his new mission to hold the Dong Ha Bridge. He then requested that his Bravo command group and two infantry companies be returned to assist in the defense of Dong Ha.

Because the 20th Tank Battalion also had a defensive mission to protect Dong Ha, the two commanders agreed to meet at the western gate of the old Dong Ha combat base. Shortly before 1000, Colonel Ley and his advisor, Major Smock, moved to the rendezvous point and with Major Binh and Captain Ripley planned a coordinated defense of the Dong Ha area. Simultaneous radio messages had come through that an enemy armor column consisting of at least eighteen to twenty tanks was moving south on National Highway 1 and closing on the bridge.

It was now 1015. From their location, on a small hill just off Route 9, the commanders and their COVANs could look across the Cam Lo-Cua Viet River and see the enemy tanks as they moved some 2,800 meters away. Ripley radioed to the TOC and verified the enemy tank sightings. When queried about the type of tanks, Captain Ripley responded, "Twelve T-54s and eight PT-76s."

It was at this time that I ordered Ripley to "somehow blow up the Dong Ha Bridge." With the same degree of calmness in his voice displayed by Major Boomer in abandoning FB Sarge, he acknowledged a seemingly impossible combat order and said he would radio back to us his arrival at the bridge.

As every seasoned officer knows, there is a quantum difference between the issuing of a life-threatening combat order and the execution of that order by the persons to whom it is given. The desperate nature of my order to Captain Ripley clearly made it a "last option" decision and mandate. If he failed, we were all lost. The multitude of difficulties that he thereafter faced in merely getting to the Dong Ha Bridge, much less setting about its destruction, could have easily precluded a hundred lesser men from responding to and carrying out such a dangerous mission.

As was later revealed, Ripley literally had to beg, cajole, persuade and finally set off on foot before Colonel Ley was convinced that he was going to obey his latest order and get to the Dong Ha Bridge any way he could.

Ley agreed to let Ripley lead the 20th Tanks eastward to Highway 1. Major Binh and Ripley climbed onto the lead tank, holding on to the infantry handles along the tank turret as the column moved east on Route 9 toward Dong Ha. The road was littered with the wreckage of war—dead and dying refugees, livestock and burning vehicles—all of which the tanks had to maneuver to avoid. In his after-action report, Captain Ripley described this move as follows:

> Once we began our movement to the bridge, the enemy commenced an artillery attack which was to easily be the most devastating and destructive attack that I had witnessed. It virtually tore up Dong Ha leaving no area untouched, causing many civilian casualties, causing many casualties in livestock and disrupting the entire village. Of course, further movement was virtually impossible.[4]

The intensity of the artillery attack, which continued for about forty-five minutes, destroyed a large part of the city. During this period, at least 1,000 rounds fell on the area, with as many as five to ten rounds impacting simultaneously. Upon seeing the enemy's massive artillery attack, the ARVN tank battalion commander refused to enter what was left of the city.

Being familiar with the side roads around the Dong Ha area, Ripley convinced the armor commander, after a lengthy discussion, that the column could move to the Dong Ha Bridge by another route. After backtracking to the old west gate, they turned southeast and traveled along the southern boundary of the Dong Ha combat base. This allowed them to reach Highway 1 about 1,500 meters south of the bridge. Although several rounds of artillery struck near the tank column before it reached Highway 1 around noon, no damage was experienced and it appeared that the column had not as yet been observed by the enemy. Ripley radioed the TOC of his arrival on the main north-south highway. Refugees had filled the roadway and further movement to close the 1,500 meters to the bridge by vehicle would be agonizingly slow. Undaunted, their tank column turned north and headed toward the Dong Ha Bridge.

Both Ripley and Smock were unaware of dispositions or activities of the 57th Regiment around Dong Ha. The withdrawal of the 57th had proceeded in good order and most of its elements had crossed over the bridge. As the last of the NVA's preparatory fires struck Dong Ha, chaos set in. A radio message received through ARVN channels, and received in the 57th Regimental CP reported that "enemy tanks were crossing the Dong Ha Bridge." Lieutenant Colonel Twichell, the senior advisor, recorded:

> Momentary panic struck the command post. Word of the "enemy tanks" spread rapidly to the troops and many of them left their

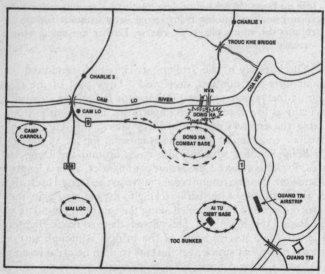

**20TH TANK BATTALION'S MOVEMENT TO
NATIONAL HIGHWAY 1.**

positions and joined the stream of refugees moving toward Quang Tri City.[5]

Although the report of NVA tanks crossing the bridge was soon verified as erroneous, the rumor had spread and the 57th Regiment disintegrated as hundreds of its soldiers deserted their battle positions. All semblance of military order was lost. The regimental commander fled his CP with his staff following closely behind. Colonel Twichell and Maj. Wallace Fajardo were separated from their counterparts. Their advisor's jeep, loaded with classified communications equipment, was stolen by ARVN officers who panicked and impetuously abandoned their men to seek their own safety.

The dismal report that "The 57th Regiment has broken and is in a complete rout" was duly recorded in the G-3 journal at 1215 as once again the TOC bunker became a place of concern. There was a time when the pervasive fear could have carried the day for the NVA.

The tragic stream of refugees fleeing the scene of devastation all along Highway 1 deeply affected the morale of the 57th Regiment's troops; as they saw the panic and disorder among the refugees, among their own families and relatives, the panic was contagious.

Much of the fear that engulfed the refugees sprang from the memories of the 1968 Tet offensives during which more than 3,000 residents in Hue City were mercilessly massacred by the communists. Highway 1 was devoid of any organized defense. Litter marked the route; dead animals, broken-down trucks, push carts, helmets, weapons and full ammunition pouches were the silent discarded "trophies" of the war.

While Dong Ha was undergoing the final NVA preparatory fires, and before the enemy's armor and infantry moved on the city, Sergeant Luom and his rocket team of the 3d Marine Battalion remained in their assigned positions. As the enemy barrages ceased, the first T-54 tanks arrived at the north end of the bridge. The classic confrontation between an Asian "David" and a 40-ton steel "Goliath" was about to begin. At the point where the road rose to meet the bridge on the north side, the NVA tank slowly moved up to the bridge. Sergeant Luom could hear the distinctive click-clack of its steel track as he extended his M-72 LAAW into the firing position. From a prone position on the bridge's roadway, he could not get a clear shot at the tank, but fired anyway. The projectile passed high over the tank's round turret and exploded harmlessly.

The spectacle of this 95-pound Marine lying in the direct path of a 40-ton tank, which had no intention of stopping, was in one respect incredibly mad. In another, more important respect, it was incredibly inspiring to a pathetically thin defensive force and to many refugees, few of whom had ever witnessed such an act of defiance and bravery.

His assistant handed him another LAAW and, taking more careful aim, he fired a second time. The small anti-armor rocket struck the T-54 at the junction where the turret joins the chassis. From his position nearly 250 yards away it appeared to Sergeant Luom and his troops who were desperately watching the explosion of the projectiles that it had damaged the tank's ability to traverse its main gun. Smoke also appeared from the tank commander's hatch.[6]

For several seconds everything remained still. Then, the commander's head appeared at the top of the turret of the NVA tank as he looked across the bridge to see what had attacked their vehicle. Obviously, he could see little and thus hesitated at the unknown. Then, rather than exploit the psychological shock-action, mobility and fire power of his tank and its 100MM gun, he backed the lightly damaged T-54 off the bridge. Incredibly, the enemy's armored column came to a halt with that single non-lethal hit.

Luom's action had temporarily stopped the North Vietnamese main ground attack. The extraordinary bravery of this one South Vietnamese Marine had caused an armored attack, which until that moment had been almost certain of success, to lose its momentum. In performing this heroic act, he provided critically needed time for the two U.S. advisors, who were on their way to the bridge to somehow prepare it for destruction.*

---

*Sergeant Luom was killed several weeks later only a few miles from the Dong Ha Bridge.

On the south side of the river the still-surging tide of refugees and ARVN soldiers swarmed among the vehicles of the 20th Tank's armored column as it moved onto Highway 1. The two commanders and their COVANs were initially shocked by the hundreds of refugees in the roadways and the composition of the fleeing hordes. For instance, they saw a large group clad in ARVN uniforms pass their M-48 tanks and M-113 armored personnel carriers (APCs). There did not seem to be a civilian refugee among them—just a huge mob of men moving south, neatly dressed, wearing no rank or insignia, and only every third man was armed.

The scene overwhelmed Major Binh. He leaped off his tank, grabbed one of the fleeing soldiers and screamed at him, "Where are you going?" The startled soldier replied that it was "No use, no use." At this Major Binh drew his pistol and shot the soldier, thinking it would cause the others to stop their panic retreat. No one in the tide took notice of the incident as they skirted the body of the fallen soldier and continued moving south toward Quang Tri City.[7]

Amid the chaos and general confusion, Colonel Ley informed the two Americans he could not advance his tank force any closer to the Dong Ha Bridge. Major Smock later recorded:

> Throughout the course of events, Colonel Ley was passive and indifferent to the entire situation. If it hadn't been for myself, and repeated reassurances from the 3d Marine Battalion commander, I am sure the 20th would have withdrawn (retreated) as did many of the other ARVN units.[8]

Since Major Binh* had been ordered to hold Dong Ha at all costs that order in his mind had the finality of "stand or die." As the 3d Battalion's Alpha command group was consolidated with the 20th Tank Battalion's staff among a cluster of M-113 APCs, someone in the shattered 57th Regiment sent an incorrect message through ARVN radio channels. This message indicated that Dong Ha had fallen to the enemy. When

---

*Major Binh was one of the South Vietnamese Marine Corps' most decorated heroes. He held almost every combat award authorized by this government, including the National Order of Vietnam (Knight's Class) and seven Crosses of Gallantry.

Major Binh heard an ARVN radio operator report of the fall of Dong Ha, he turned to Ripley and said:

> Captain Ripley, if you please, I am going to send a message on my command net and I want you to send it on your advisor net so there will be no possible opportunity for misunderstanding. Message follows:
> It is rumored that Dong Ha has fallen. There are Vietnamese Marines in Dong Ha. My orders are to hold the enemy in Dong Ha. We will fight in Dong Ha. We will die in Dong Ha. We will not leave. As long as one Marine draws a breath of life, Dong Ha will belong to us.[9]

At that moment, North Vietnamese infantry were poised on the northern bank of the Cam Lo-Cua Viet River and NVA troop leaders could be heard directing their men toward the old French-built railroad bridge, just west of the main Dong Ha Highway Bridge. The enemy's lead squad started to cross the narrow steel-girdered bridge. One span of this bridge had been partially destroyed in 1967, but it was still useable for foot and light vehicle traffic.

Captain Ripley called for a continuous naval gunfire mission. His request was for "danger-close" interdiction fire on the north side of the river and on the old railroad bridge, 300 meters away. There was almost instantaneous response from the five U.S. destroyers off the coast. Lieutenant Eisenstein and Sergeant Swift, although located five miles south of Dong Ha at Ai Tu combat base, could not actually see their targets but worked up a number of defensive fire plans in the vicinity of the main Dong Ha Bridge which would later prove to be highly effective.

For over an hour, continuous naval gunfire interdicted the approaches to both bridges. Captain Ripley requested that fire support boxes* of approximately 1,000 by 2,000 meters be shifted between the bridges. It was an effective and responsive system.

When Ripley observed four enemy PT-76 amphibious tanks

---

*Rectangular areas in which naval gunfire projectiles impact.

moving along the banks of the Cam Lo-Cua Viet River just east of Dong Ha, another naval gunfire mission was sent out to the destroyers. Again, the Navy's guns responded with deadly accurate fire, destroying all four of the NVA tanks. Watching from his vantage point, Ripley later recalled:

> We could see them [tanks] clearly. My counterpart, Major Binh, and the commanding officer, 20th Tanks, were both observing this superb display of naval gunfire (NGF). When the tanks were hit and burning, both COs were surprised and elated in seeing the potential of NGF. I was to receive many requests for NGF after this remarkable demonstration of its rapid, destructive power.[10]

At 1245 Captain Ripley radioed to the TOC bunker that he had reached the intersection of Highway 1 and Route 9. Then, at 1320, he radioed to the G-3 watch officer that the situation was becoming critical in Dong Ha because the main highway bridge had not yet been destroyed. Marines from the 3d Battalion deployed along the Cam Lo-Cua Viet's south bank were engaged in heavy firefights with enemy troops along the north bank. "There is a continuing buildup in NVA infantry and armored vehicles," he reported.

The 1st Troop of the 20th Tank Battalion, which had taken positions from which it could engage the NVA tank column at the north end of the Dong Ha Bridge, opened fire. The 20th's executive officer, Major Kieu, radioed Colonel Ley that he had destroyed two T-54s. Thus, South Vietnam's only battalion of M-48 tanks had undergone its own baptism of fire and had scored against the Soviet-made armor. Colonel Battreall later recorded:

> The regimental executive officer had picked up the enemy armor commander's radio frequency and was monitoring his net when they (ARVN) opened fire and the enemy commander was totally flabbergasted. He knew he was receiving direct fire from a high velocity weapon, but couldn't comprehend where the fire was coming from, because of the long range involved. It never occurred to him that he was being fired on from that ridge south of Dong Ha.[11]

At 1325, Ripley reported the old railroad bridge had been partially destroyed as a result of naval gunfire, but still remained passable. The enemy forces continued to build all across the ARVN front. "Three rifle companies are now on line. We're just barely holding on," Ripley reported.

It was becoming clearer each moment that something had to be done to destroy the highway bridge. With naval gunfire striking the most immediate targets north of the Cam Lo-Cua Viet River, Ripley and Smock made their final dash for the Dong Ha Bridge. Smock, an armored officer, who had had no previous training with demolitions, followed Ripley in a broken-field run across the bullet-swept roadway. They were reported to have made it safely to the concrete base of the bridge but at that point radio communications were lost. We later learned that their Vietnamese radio operators did not accompany them.

In the TOC at Ai Tu, we were not certain whether the two advisors were alive or dead. After repeated attempts to reestablish radio contact, we initiated one final act in a desperate attempt to destroy the highway bridge. I directed Capt. John Thiesen to commandeer a six-by-six military truck and load it with as many explosives as he could locate in the nearby Quang Tri ammunition dump. Captain Thiesen, who had been in-country only two weeks, grabbed his helmet and flak jacket and left the TOC in search of a truck, a brave driver and "some type of demolitions." As he left, the enemy's artillery built up to a crescendo as the incoming artillery rounds were impacting all over the Ai Tu and Quang Tri combat bases. Thiesen was a lonely figure moving through the encampment area seeking assistance from the South Vietnamese. He finally located a six-by-six truck loaded with five or six tons of explosives. He immediately radioed his discovery into the TOC and was told to "remain with the vehicle and be ready to move to the Dong Ha Bridge on order."*

---

*Captain Thiesen later received a Bronze Star for this action.

CHAPTER ELEVEN

# RESPONSIBILITY
# AND DECISION

Easter Sunday's battle between Asian brothers was fast reaching its climax in the battle for Dong Ha Bridge. Even the most optimistic among us had no illusions that we would be able to hold against the mass of the enemy's armor and continuing infantry attacks. Although only twenty tanks had actually been seen and reported, estimates, later confirmed by intelligence reports, put the number at over a hundred. It would also later be confirmed that at least five regiments of North Vietnamese artillery provided the neutralization fires that struck the Dong Ha area. Over a hundred Soviet-made long-range guns orchestrated their pre-assault preparatory fires as the infantry and armored forces massed to execute their river crossing which they expected to be violent and victorious.

The only organized resistance at this stage of the battle that prevented the Nguyen Hue invaders from exploiting three days of nearly complete battlefield successes was an inexperienced ARVN tank battalion and a battered Vietnamese Marine battalion.

NVA soldiers could be seen scurrying all along the north bank of the Cam Lo-Cua Viet River. Two hundred meters across the river from the massing NVA was the South Vietnamese final defensive line, still being hastily emplaced around the strategically important Dong Ha Bridge. As the 57th Regiment "broke and fled in a full rout" earlier, the 3d Marine Battalion now moved forward and deployed along the south bank of the river. Approximately 300 Marines entered the central arena of the battle at a time when every infantryman was needed along the forward battle line. The 3d Division's "reserve" was now committed and engaged in heavy firefights. South Vietnam's final wall of defense along the south side of the Dong Ha Bridge had been reduced to about fourteen inches—the approximate depth of a Marine's chest. In the center of this battle, two Americans—a soldier and a Marine—were attempting to destroy the one bridge that could halt the immediate North Vietnamese Nguyen Hue Offensive. The opposing armies were competing for precious minutes of time. For the attacker, time was needed to assemble its armored force to advance across the Cam Lo-Cua Viet River; for the defender, time was critical to attempt to halt the enemy's passage to the ancient city of Quang Tri, opening the way to Hue and then, perhaps, to the end of the war.

Back in the TOC, other battlefield reports were as ominous as the situation at the Dong Ha Bridge. Out on the western front, the 2d Regiment had completed its withdrawal across the Cam Lo Bridge, but reported that NVA infantry units were so close behind that the bridge could not be destroyed. The Cam Lo Bridge was one that could support T-54 tanks, should the enemy choose to use them.

At Camp Carroll, two miles further south, the largest artillery fire base in Military Region One (MR-1) had undergone two infantry assaults since dawn. General Giai had ordered the commander, 56th Regiment to "hold at all costs,"[1] with no immediate prospect of reinforcements. Radio communications, through ARVN channels, were repeatedly interrupted. Casualties had been reported but for unexplained reasons South Vietnamese Air Force helicopters would not fly med-evac missions.

Further south, FSB Mai Loc remained under NVA long-range artillery fire. Enemy infantry units had moved closer to the fire support base's perimeter during the day and the headquarters of Marine Brigade 147 was under direct fire from 57MM recoilless rifles.[2] The U.S. pilots of CH-47 Chinooks reported receiving increasingly heavier small arms fire on their resupply flights into Mai Loc's landing zones. Even though each flight delivering critically needed pallets of artillery ammunition was becoming progressively more dangerous, they continued.

Quang Tri Province remained covered by a blanket of low clouds. The weather was beginning to show definite signs of clearing, but U.S. and South Vietnamese aircraft were still confined to the airfields.

Naval gunfire had become the only responsive twenty-four-hour weapon for attacking the massing enemy forces. Lieutenant Eisenstein's naval gunfire radio nets were in constant communication with the five destroyers defending the Dong Ha area. Radio transmissions between the U.S. gunline commander and the TOC had developed into an "open line" telephone dialogue. These Navy-Marine Corps discussions unintentionally expanded into situational reports. The Navy frequently reminded the G-3 watch officers and naval gunfire personnel that our "brothers" were off the coast and "If they are needed ashore, where do you want them to land?" The comment was stated in such a way that it begged the question as to whether or not Marines were to be sent ashore. All that was being asked of us was, "If they come, where do you want them?" These radio transmissions eventually resulted in several more "flash—Operational immediate" naval messages.

Unknown to the Americans in the TOC, the senior U.S. Navy officer aboard the destroyers released another radio message which subsequently became known as the "land the landing force" message.* It was composed on one of the destroyers without the full knowledge either of the G-3 watch officers who were ashore or me.

Again, without the knowledge of the advisors in the besieged TOC, this second message was received shortly after its transmission at General Abrams' MACV headquarters in Saigon. His immediate reaction was to find out, "What the hell is this Marine lieutenant colonel doing up in MR-1? Order Turley back to Saigon; I want to see him personally." Despite a multitude of individuals in the chain of command and their op-

---

*For the full text of this message see Appendix B.

portunities to take responsibility, the already established pattern was being followed; i.e., say nothing and leave all the responsibility to those in contact with the enemy. We had no choice. Our decisions were made of grave combat necessity. We would have to live, or perhaps die, with the responsibility for these decisions.

At 1451, I had a call from Saigon. At the other end of the line was Maj. Bob Sheridan, USMC, the senior advisor to Marine Brigade 369, which was still located in the Saigon area. His conversation began with a flurry of questions, "Jesus Christ, Colonel! What are you doing up there? The MACV people here in Saigon think you've gone crazy! There are all sorts of Navy messages down here which say World War III is underway! Worse yet, the Army types down here want to know who the hell's Turley?" Sheridan also informed me that General Abrams wanted to see him since he was the senior Marine of the advisory unit in Saigon.

My conversation with Sheridan lasted about fifteen minutes, during which time I recounted the major events of the past several days: the loss of ten fire bases; the sighting of T-54 armor with an attack expected at any moment at Dong Ha; the PT-76 tanks now verified by Captain Ripley and by U.S. destroyers offshore; the panicky flight of the 3d ARVN Division headquarters back to Quang Tri; and the order from the Army Senior Advisor which resulted in my assuming the position of chief advisor, 3d ARVN Division (Forward). The telephone call came as a most welcome relief. Bob Sheridan's humorous responses to my summary of the four days of the Easter offensive would have done justice to the "Johnny Carson" television show. Before we broke off our call, Bob went over the notes he had written. On an earlier Vietnam War tour in 1967, he had served with the 3d Marine Division in the Dong Ha area and was familiar with all the fire bases and areas we discussed. He closed off by saying his Marine brigade would be coming our way in the morning. This was my first knowledge of reinforcements on the way to MR-1. I shared this new information with my counterpart, Colonel Dinh.

Our advisory activities were so intense at this time that the G-3 journal simply could not contain all the events being reported which otherwise should have been recorded. General Giai's plan to reposition all his forces on the south side of the Cam Lo-Cua Viet River was noted. Unfortunately, that plan was not completed before the NVA began its dawn attacks which kept the ARVN Division in a reacting posture.

Because of the NVA's armor threat along Highway 1, our primary area of focus at this time was on the activities around the Dong Ha Bridge. However, an unusual radio message from the senior advisor of the 56th ARVN Regiment quickly shifted our attention out to Camp Carroll.

Colonel Camper's radio transmission reported he had been trying for some time during the day to meet with his counterpart. However, the regimental executive officer stood in his way and physically prevented such a meeting with the commander.

By chance, Bill Camper had discovered that the ARVN officers of the 56th Regiment at Camp Carroll were having a meeting. He insisted that if the officers of the regiment were having a meeting, he should be there.[3] Again, the 56th's executive officer refused to let him in, a most extraordinary circumstance. Returning to his bunker Camper related this incident to Maj. Joe Brown. Both were uneasy; they sensed something was wrong.

In their three short weeks as advisors to the 56th Regiment, the two Americans and the ARVN commander were still not completely assimilated into a well-functioning counterpart-COVAN team. Camper had worked hard to cement a strong working relationship with his counterpart, Lt. Col. Pham Van Dinh. He was aware, however, from his previous advisory tour that it takes time for a Vietnamese to accept an American advisor and to integrate him into ARVN operational planning. Camper and Brown had done everything possible to assist the 56th Regiment. They now discovered that at the moment when the closest cooperation was needed to repel continuous attacks, they had been isolated from the regiment's officers. As a result, Camper's rich talents and extensive combat experience were not being utilized.

The regiment's tactical situation had progressively worsened during the last twenty-four hours. Camper expressed his own frustrations to Brown. The two Americans sat alone in their underground bunker for the remainder of Easter Sunday morning unaware of the major drama unfolding around them, and unaware of the unique role they would soon play in it. As advisors, they had no alternative but to wait until their Vietnamese commander chose to meet with them. Time seemed to be working against everyone at Camp Carroll.

Simultaneously with the tank attack moving toward the Dong Ha Bridge, the North Vietnamese increased the tempo of their shellings of Camp Carroll and FSB Mai Loc. The 1,800 South Vietnamese soldiers and two Americans at Camp Carroll came under yet another withering artillery bombardment and a third major ground attack. Capt. David Randall, with Brigade 147 at Mai Loc, recorded:

> At approximately 1200, Camp Carroll to our north and our position came under an intensive artillery attack. In fact, at one time we were able to monitor some of the North Vietnamese artillery observer's radio commands back to the 130MM battery. His corrections to the guns were given in commands of right ten (meters), drop twenty and left five, add ten. So it was obvious that what he was working on was a precision destruction mission.[4]

At approximately 1400, one of the most bizarre and demoralizing incidents of the Vietnam War began to take place at Camp Carroll. Because of their continuing uneasiness following the morning's confrontation with the 56th's regimental executive officer, Camper and Brown decided to leave the safety of their bunker and move around the perimeter of the fire base to see what had developed. As they moved together they could see that morale was very low. The troops reported that they had not seen any of their officers, and there were numerous wounded who remained unattended. The artillery batteries still had stocks of 105MM and 175MM ammunition, but food supplies were getting very low.

As the two COVANs returned to their bunker, something very strange began to happen. It was suddenly very still and, for the first time since the Nguyen Hue Offensive began, the two officers were shocked by the fact that there was no incoming artillery, no ground attacks; nothing. In his debriefing, Camper later noted:

> It just got quiet all of a sudden. It was real scary. Colonel Dinh came over to our bunker and told us he was going to surrender Camp Carroll. He said the men refused to fight any longer.
> He had received an order from General Giai 'to hold at all costs.' There was no possibility of reinforcements so his officers had had extensive negotiations by radio with the North Vietnamese forces prior to his decision to surrender. This was one of the reasons Colonel Dinh wouldn't see me earlier.
> Colonel Dinh offered me the choice of surrendering. I said I would not surrender, that we would find some other way to get out. He said that we (myself and Major Brown) could hide among his troops when they went out the gate to surrender to the North Vietnamese and once we were outside the perimeter, we could fall down in the grass and crawl away. I dismissed this as ridiculous.[5]

Dinh then proposed that he and Camper commit suicide "in order to save us from embarrassment."

He responded by saying, "That's not what Americans do," and attempted to dissuade Colonel Dinh from surrendering by suggesting a plan for the entire unit to break out of the enemy's encirclement by using the two M-41 tanks and three other tracked vehicles. These latter vehicles had twin 40MM guns. He proposed that the regiment plan to break out to the southeast where they could join up with the Marine elements in the village of Mai Loc and at the fire support base. Dinh would not even discuss the plan, and dismissed Camper's proposal by saying, "It would not work."

Dinh's reaction was more than Colonel Camper, a gentlemanly, professional soldier, could bear. For a fleeting second he harbored the thought of killing his counterpart. He was both angry and scared enough at that moment to have given in to the urge, driven as he was by frustrations and disappointments. Then he thought, "What good would it do? What would it accomplish?" As he later said, "First, it wasn't my nature to take advantage of any unsuspecting person, and second, it would not have let me or Joe Brown off the hook."[6]

For several moments the two colonels stood looking at each other, as what little rapport had ever existed between the two men was forever broken. On the one hand was a determined American advisor who believed that the 56th Regiment could still fight if properly led; on the other, a South Vietnamese commander who was about to betray his country.

Camper extended his right hand to his counterpart and they shook hands, for whatever reason. He wished Dinh well and told him that he and Major Brown would take care of themselves. He told Dinh, "I will do as I think best." Camper said later, "I could no longer advise him and told him we no longer had any responsibility toward each other."

When Camper told Dinh of his intentions to notify his senior advisor of the situation, Dinh became very concerned but did not attempt to prevent the transmission. Camper's radio report revealed some of Dinh's concerns:

> He asked me not to tell General Giai that he was surrendering. I told him I wasn't concerned about General Giai, I was concerned about me and Joe Brown. He left the bunker and I did not see him again.[7]

At 1502, the G-3 advisor's journal noted Colonel Camper's radioed message to the TOC. To prevent the enemy from possibly intercepting his messages he simply stated, "Yeoman Echo [call-sign of the advisor, 56th Regiment] requests to leave this position. He and his assistant are no longer needed. He has reasons but cannot explain now."

At the time Camper's radio call came in, I was in the G-3 area. Because the two of us had never met, I did not fully appreciate the subtlety of his radio message, just as he was unaware of the rapidly deteriorating and critical situation that was taking place in the Dong Ha area and along the Cam Lo-Cua Viet River. At that moment, I violated the unwritten "advisor's code," which had originated when the first Americans entered combat operations with South Vietnamese forces eighteen years earlier. It was a simple code, namely that the advisor in the field, the "man in the arena," must always call the shots, because as the professional soldier under enemy fire only he can fully appraise the combat situation.

Before fully thinking about Camper's peculiar request and its strange wording, I reacted with a curt radio response.

"No, Colonel, stay where you are and do your damn job!"

Under the circumstances, my response was unfair and unprofessional, and in retrospect can only be explained in terms of the personal pressures on me at that moment. However, as soon as I made the transmission, I knew I was wrong. Disappointed with myself at losing my composure with a field advisor who had by that time been under ninety-six hours of continuous enemy artillery fire and ground attacks, I ached inside. There was a short silence, then came his reply.

"Roger, out."

Approximately twenty minutes later, around 1520, Bill Camper again radioed the TOC, and this time his message was explicit. "The base commander wants to surrender. The white flag is going up in ten minutes." There was no more time for us to question the import of the message, only to act.

Captain Avery and the four or five other officers in the G-3 watch area responded immediately without knowing at exactly what time the surrender at Camp Carroll was supposed to take place. The two field advisors had precious little time to decide what they were going to do and get ready to do it. The only positive thing in their favor at this time was that the artillery and ground attacks had stopped and they were no longer under a constant artillery bombardment. It was safe to get out of their bunkers and move around.

Camper and Brown took their radios, codes and classified cypher (secure voice) equipment and remaining "C" rations and piled everything in the middle of the floor of their bunker. Opening the kerosene lantern and placing incendiary (heat) grenades on the top of their classified materials, they then poured kerosene on the wooden plank floor up to the doorway.

With their rucksacks packed with a few personal items and one backpack radio, Camper followed Brown up the bunker steps. Once outside they used more kerosene as a fuse to set everything off. In a few seconds, the bunker exploded into a ball of flame and black smoke billowed from the doorway. Standing among 1,800 silent observers, the two Americans were committed to fight on, alone except for two enlisted Vietnamese radio operators who had agreed to remain with them. Shouldering their packs and moving away from the burning underground bunker, the two Americans could not believe what was happening. Camper remembered:

> By this time the regiment was stacking its weapons. It reminded me of an old movie about the island of Corregidor when the Americans surrendered in 1942. They were stacking their weapons, ready for the enemy to accept their surrender.[8]

In one last conversation with a Vietnamese officer, Bill Camper spoke briefly to the 56th Regiment's operations officer, a major who was one of the few who could speak good English. Deeply hurt that his counterparts had deceived him, Camper told the S-3 officer, "You don't know what you are doing. You are a coward and should come with us and we will fight our way out." There was no response to Camper's remarks from the Vietnamese because his last resort to "save face," was silence.[9]

At the southeastern corner of the fire support base perimeter, the lonely foursome began cutting their way through the barbed wire. Camper planned to head toward the Marine positions at FSB Mai Loc, hoping to avoid encountering any North Vietnamese units. Their luck did not hold, as shortly after passing through the barbed wire of the perimeter they were confronted by an enemy company-sized unit which started firing its small arms and moving directly at them.

With Major Brown and the two Vietnamese soldiers returning fire, Camper used the backpack radio to call the G-3 advisors at the TOC for help.

As frequently happened in this phase of the Vietnam War, chance and unusual circumstances placed the two Americans and their radio operators in a unique situation. At the moment they were reporting the imminent surrender of Camp Carroll, a single U.S. CH-47 helicopter was braving the enemy's small arms fire to deliver a critically needed load of 105MM artillery shells to FSB Mai Loc, approximately two miles away. Captain

Avery, U.S. Army, miraculously was able to make radio contact with the pilots as they were approaching the Mai Loc landing zone.

Avery, aware of the critical time factors involved, carefully briefed the pilots on the urgency of attempting a rescue of the two Americans. The pilots acknowledged their new mission, but heroically continued their effort to supply Mai Loc with the ammunition. The advisors to the 147th Brigade heard the helicopter approaching and attempted to make radio contact. Unknown to them, however, the pilots had already switched radio frequency in an attempt to contact Colonel Camper. Even as the external pallets of ammunition were being placed in the landing zone at Mai Loc, Captain Avery was radioing Camper to switch frequencies, "Call Coachman 005, it's a helicopter."

Camper had no idea that "Coachman 005" was a large troop-carrying CH-47 helicopter flying into the Mai Loc combat base. Hearing intense enemy antiaircraft fire to the south, Camper switched frequencies and called, "Coachman 005." He received an immediate response. The pilots who responded had never flown into Camp Carroll, some 3,000 meters to their northwest, and Camper recalled telling them to "Look for the windsock. We are just outside the perimeter by the helicopter landing pad. There is no artillery incoming, everything is calm."

The two advisors and their radio operators began to fall back through the barbed wire and away from the pursuing NVA. Moving toward the heli-pad, they heard the largest troop-carrying helicopter in the U.S. Army coming straight at them over a small hill. Enemy infantry on the hill immediately began firing at it. Camper radioed, "Watch out, that's the enemy there." At the same moment, two Cobra helicopter gunships appeared and dove toward muzzle flashes from the NVA, spraying the area with their machine guns. The CH-47 flew on and landed at the heli-pad, as Camper's group arrived. He recalled that:

> Joe Brown and our two Vietnamese got on, then a bunch of Vietnamese tried to get on. A lot of the Vietnamese that had decided to surrender tried to get on. I had a little problem; I kind of went beserk. I threw some people off. Everyone who did not have a weapon was not allowed on the plane. Joe Brown kept yelling at me, "Colonel, for God's sake get on here."[10]

The North Vietnamese infantry closing in on the fire support base were now shooting at the helicopter's tail rotors, trying to knock out the aircraft's hydraulic system. Camper jumped aboard the chopper, moving off the tailgate into a canvas seat. There were about thirty Vietnamese, all armed, clutching handholds as the pilots lifted off, tilted the aircraft over and headed eastward. Colonel Camper looked back as the helicopter lifted off. Later he said, expressing his great relief: "We took off from there, never to see Camp Carroll again. It was a good feeling."

Minutes after the CH-47 lifted off, a large white flag was raised over the main gate at Camp Carroll. This done, all radio communication with the 3d Division TOC at Ai Tu was severed. The largest artillery assemblage in MR-1 was silent under an array of white flags. The 56th ARVN Regiment and five batteries of artillery no longer existed.

Camper requested that the CH-47 pilots take them back to Quang Tri. However, the aircraft's hydraulic lines had been damaged and the pilots had to land in the first safe area to survey and report the damage. When the helicopter reached Highway 1, it landed on the road in the middle of a 122MM rocket attack, dropped off the survivors from Camp Carroll and limped south. Meeting a jeep with several Americans, the advisors used their radio to report their arrival along the national highway. Later, another helicopter picked up Camper, Brown and their two faithful Vietnamese radio operators, returning them at last to Quang Tri.

Upon arriving at the 3d Division's headquarters, Colonel Camper made a personal report to both General Giai and Colonel Murdock. The division commander refused at first to believe the report that Lt. Col. Pham Van Dinh had surrendered the 56th Regiment and the five batteries of artillery at Camp Carroll. Camper had the distinct feeling that the general was calling him a liar and a coward for leaving the fire base, and he was deeply hurt by Giai's accusations. Murdock calmed the scene, however, and shortly thereafter arranged to place the two COVANs on a helicopter that carried them to the landing pad of the FRAC headquarters. They had lost everything but the clothes on their backs. Camper confirmed to the FRAC operations center that Camp Carroll had indeed surrendered and this helped restore some credibility to those of us U.S. officers still in the TOC bunker.

There is a saying about military men: "One must prepare for a moment that may never come; to thrust oneself into the uncharted arena of battle and lead should the need arise." In the case of Lieutenant Colonel Camper and Major Brown, these two officers demonstrated far above and beyond the call of duty that they possessed those extraordinary qualities of which heroes are made. While they were there on watch fate placed them under the enemy's guns. When thousands chose to quit, and to surrender, these two American soldiers showed the resolve to fight on. Faithful to their code as American fighting men, they had climbed their mountain.

Although the Camp Carroll debacle was over, the war continued at such an intensive pace that the next morning Bill Camper and Joe Brown would be called upon to return to U.S. advisor roles with the 3d ARVN Division. On 3 April they assumed the duties as senior and deputy senior advisor, respectively, to the 2d Regiment.

Later that day General Giai requested that Camper visit him. It was apparent the general had spoken to some of the soldiers who had flown out of Camp Carroll on the Chinook helicopter. These ARVN soldiers, rescued by the fortuitous appearance of the aircraft sent to extract the advisors, confirmed Camper's and Brown's report. General Giai ended their visit by apologizing to Camper for his earlier unkind comments.

In what has often been called a "war without heroes" the individual heroism of Col. William Camper* and Maj. Joseph Brown, Jr., U.S. Army officers, must not go unrecorded. While both officers were recommended for Meritorious Bronze Star medals based upon their entire Vietnam combat tour, neither officer was ever cited for his personal heroism while at Camp Carroll. The reasons for such an oversight are unknown; perhaps one day the omission will be rectified.

Our emotions ran high. None of us could even contem-

---

*On 27 April Lt. Col. William Camper was seriously wounded near the Quang Tri Bridge, and medically evacuated to the U.S.

plate surrender. Furthermore, many of us Marine advisors had known and served with Capt. J. J. Carroll, a brave Marine for whom the fire support base had been named.* It pained us to realize that the honor of his name would now be associated with an ignominious defeat and act of treachery.

The Camp Carroll disaster must have been one of the most emotional battle scenes ever recorded in Vietnamese history. The two COVANS, Camper and Brown, were in total disbelief that a viable fighting force of nearly 2,000 men was irretrievably preparing to surrender; to willingly, almost eagerly, betray their country during a time of national emergency; to quit without attempting to break through the enemy's fragile encirclement such as had been done under more devastating conditions in the breakout from FSB Sarge and Nui Ba Ho only two days previously.

Conversely, Camper and Brown decided to fight on; to be killed in battle if need be, but never to stop fighting. The thought of such an act was repugnant to their soldierly ethics.

Both men knew how desperate the situation was. FSB Mai Loc was under heavy attack and Brigade 147 could not come to their rescue. The nearest possible assistance was at Ai Tu, but the urgency and the fifteen-mile distance through scrub and jungle would preclude help from arriving in time.

They made the separation from their former counterparts showing what respect they could muster. Neither advisor wavered from his intent to leave the battlefield honorably. With a thorough awareness of the imminent dangers of an escape attempt, they moved toward the perimeter wire. The silent eyes of hundreds of alert, unarmed soldiers watched their dramatic gesture of defiance. They were heroes among cowards, separated from ordinary men by their courage. As Camper led the way, he epitomized the code of the fighting man—"I shall never cease to resist my enemy."

The surrender at Camp Carroll created a catastrophic void in the shrinking defensive line which the 3d ARVN Division was struggling so desperately to maintain. Lieutenant Colonel

*Capt. J. J. Carroll was killed in action in 1966 near the present camp.

Dinh's treacherous act in the surrender of his regiment en masse had an enormous adverse psychological impact on the remainder of the besieged South Vietnamese units. Losses such as that of the 1,800 soldiers and the artillery batteries at Camp Carroll simply could not be absorbed without making further troop withdrawals.

The Americans in the TOC were also stunned by these events. Our hearts were heavy at the news and what it portended for the ultimate outcome of the battle. None of us could even contemplate surrender. It boggled the mind to witness such a colossal collapse. Because events happened so quickly, we did not have time, once we were aware of the intended capitulation, even to report the surrender to FRAC headquarters before the white flags had actually gone up. Our most immediate and paramount concern was to save the two COVANs before they were seized by the conquering North Vietnamese. It was only after the Chinook had lifted from the heli-pad at Camp Carroll and was flying to Quang Tri that we found time to report the fall of the fire support base to FRAC's operation center.

Because of the significance of the event I telephoned the FRAC operations center personally. Our relationship with their operations center had become very strained after I told them I intended to ignore their order not to destroy the Dong Ha Bridge. When I made the unpleasant report that Camp Carroll surrendered at 1530, the G-3 watch officer who received it was at first unbelieving, and snapped back, "Wait one." The next voice on the line was that of the lieutenant colonel I had confronted earlier. As I began to recount the sketchy series of events leading to Camp Carroll's surrender, he surprised me by interrupting my report saying, "Colonel, you're crazy. General Lam's MR-1 staff doesn't know about any such surrender. Camp Carroll has twenty-two guns, 2,000 ARVN soldiers; it would never surrender. I think you've flipped. Let me speak to one of the U.S. Army officers in the TOC."

His demeaning request, which challenged my professional integrity as a Marine officer, came at the wrong time. Checking my wrath, I repeated the events leading to the surrender and told him that Colonel Camper and Major Brown were in the air after being extracted by us and once they were located, a more detailed report would be provided. I hung up, seething.

The next task was to meet with my counterpart, the Brigade 258 commander, and confirm his awareness of the surrender. I found that he had already received a report through ARVN channels. Col. Ngo Van Dinh, VNMC Marine Corps, seemed to be psychologically overwhelmed because he had known Lt. Col. Pham Van Dinh since the 1968 Tet Offensive when Pham Van Dinh assisted in the raising of the South Vietnamese national colors over the ancient Citadel at Hue. At that time, then a captain, Pham Van Dinh became a national hero. Now, as a senior commander, he had chosen to surrender his regiment and the largest artillery fire base in MR-1. To Marine Colonel Dinh it seemed almost impossible to comprehend; but it was a fact—the 56th ARVN Regiment no longer existed as a South Vietnamese fighting force.

Colonel Dinh, a quiet man, though obviously taken aback by the surrender, appeared more resolute than ever. He had been among those who had chosen to leave North Vietnam in 1954, and had been fighting the communists ever since. As a warrior he had experienced nearly two decades of combat victories and setbacks, so the surrender of Camp Carroll would somehow be overcome.

"We must destroy the communists," he said. When he repeatedly chose the word "communists" instead of "North Vietnamese," I was reminded that the South Vietnamese military referred to their enemy only as communists because they could not perceive that their North Vietnamese brothers were really attacking the South. "The enemy is the communists and they must be killed," was the declaration the South Vietnamese Marines would make.

While the advisors had been concentrating on extracting the Americans from Camp Carroll, Dinh had been monitoring the increasingly critical situation around the Dong Ha Bridge. Through his brigade radio nets he had been receiving steady reports from Major Binh's 3d Battalion. Binh's 1st Company, deployed on both sides of Highway 1, on the south end of the bridge, had reported seeing Captain Ripley and Major Smock under the bridge itself, planting explosives. This was our first confirmation that actions were underway to destroy the crucial highway bridge.

Returning to the G-3 watch area to share this information with the watch officers, I was again asked to take a telephone call from FRAC. This time it was from a fellow Marine officer, Lt. Col. D'Wayne Gray, the commanding officer of 1st AN-GLICO's Sub Unit One, who had arrived at FRAC headquarters earlier in the day. He had obviously been briefed by the FRAC staff on the confusing events in northern MR-1.

He was blunt, "Gerry, cool it up there. You are to return to Saigon and report to General Abrams."

It was a direct order from a senior Marine officer, and I acknowledged it.

To say I was completely stunned by the impact of his telephone call would be the classic understatement, for I had known D'Wayne Gray for almost ten years. However, he obviously was carrying out instructions from a higher headquarters to order me so abruptly out of the immediate battle area in the middle of this critical period. I told him I would go to the Phu Bai airfield and catch a flight south as soon as possible.

Before our conversation ended, I briefed D'Wayne on the number of ARVN fire bases that had fallen, the retreat of the 57th Regiment, and our employment of naval gunfire around Dong Ha. D'Wayne's responses were polite, but I had the distinct feeling he didn't believe me. I could understand his skepticism. The rapidity with which the NVA's Nguyen Hue Offensive had overrun most of Quang Tri Province was even difficult for us on the scene to accept, so the situation could very well seem unreal to those far from the fighting, looking at situation maps.

Because our advisory efforts had to continue, I told D'Wayne that I would inform Colonel Murdock of his order, then make my way back to Saigon. I told the Americans in the TOC bunker of the telephone call and my order. Looking at the weary faces of the U.S. Army, Air Force and Marine officers standing around me, I thought, "God, I am so proud of them." They had jelled into a team and had, of combat necessity, performed superbly under the most trying and traumatic conditions. Most of them had assumed responsibilities far greater than men of their rank would normally be called upon to accept. No one spoke when I told them of the circumstances causing me to report to General Abrams, but simply acknowledged the fact of my leaving.

Just before they left to return to their duties, I said, "It's too late to catch a plane today. I'll go tomorrow, and until I leave, nothing has changed. I'm in charge. Let's continue to support the Vietnamese as if nothing has happened."

I felt a deep embarrassment at knowing that I had been ordered to leave my position at such a critical moment. The rebuke seemed unfair because so many others had sought refuge while I stayed to help my counterpart. The circuitous manner in which D'Wayne Gray had been ordered to make contact and order me back to Saigon was even more cutting. Obviously, neither Colonel Murdock nor the staff officers at FRAC had informed D'Wayne that General Kroesen himself had ordered me to assume the role of chief advisor of the 3d ARVN Division. Instead, they remained silent, thereby expressing amazement at the seemingly erratic actions that emanated from the forward headquarters where I was the senior American present. The issue of taking responsibility was again raising its head. I had known that the "time to stand tall and report" would someday arrive but was mentally unprepared for it at this critical point in the battle. For awhile I felt tainted and professionally discredited by the FRAC staff, but then I realized that I was only feeling sorry for myself. Also, I was certain that when the full story was known, my Army, Navy, and Marine seniors would understand my actions. As I returned to the task of coordinating the U.S. advisory efforts, it was impossible to resist mumbling to myself that "those dirty bastards at FRAC are going to try to hang me." It may seem a small thing but I felt a little better for saying it.

# CHAPTER TWELVE

# ACTION AT THE DONG HA BRIDGE

Far from the relative security of our TOC bunker and my personal problems, Captain Ripley and Major Smock had been under the Dong Ha Bridge for over an hour. Their extraordinary actions to destroy the only direct approach to Quang Tri and Hue City by the NVA's armored columns were later recognized as an epic example of fortitude, extraordinary bravery and personal resolve to defeat the enemy by fulfilling the last order given, even if it meant losing their own lives.

They knew the gravity and utter desperation of their seemingly impossible mission—the destruction of the bridge. What they didn't know was the catastrophic events that had taken place around them: e.g., the loss of Camp Carroll that had the effect of now focusing all the enemy's effort—the entire invasion—on capturing Dong Ha with its strategic bridge.

The story, which was later fully documented, revealed that after a dash across the bullet-swept ground, the two officers made it to relative safety under the bridge. Once there they found five ARVN engineers huddled together. Captain Ripley's later statement noted:

> They seemed to be wondering if we were sent to kill them or if they should save us the trouble and kill themselves. No humans . . . ever looked more hopeless or helpless.[1]

Ripley looked over the 500 pounds of TNT and plastic explosives that the engineers had prepositioned beside the bridge anticipating its possible destruction whenever such an order were given. He recalled, "Smock and I would never have been able to do this under the circumstances originally facing us." However, while he quickly discovered there was an abundance of explosives, the blasting caps necessary to detonate the explosives once set were nowhere to be found. From his Army ranger course classes on field expedients, John remembered that a hand grenade could be used as a detonator. The problem in resorting to such an extreme measure was that it would leave him only four seconds to drop the twenty feet from the structure to the ground and move away from the bridge before the 500 pounds of demolitions exploded.

The ARVN engineers had begun to place explosives under the bridge. Looking over the charges that the Vietnamese had set, Ripley concluded that had the explosives been detonated, they probably would not have destroyed the bridge. Rather, their emplacement of the explosives may have dropped a span; but only enough so that the span would have contacted the embankment, permitting the enemy's tanks to cross the bridge, drive down the remaining span onto the embankment and still make it ashore on the south side of the Cam Lo-Cua Viet River.

Realizing that the explosives had to be reset, Ripley and Smock began exploring the understructure of the bridge. As they did so the ARVN engineers melted away, leaving the two Americans with the job of placing the twenty-five to thirty boxes of explosives needed to do the job properly throughout the bridge. This meant the two of them would have to haul each box onto the bridge's abutment and place them in a staggered alignment between the steel girders. A high chain link fence, topped with protective wire—German steel tape consisting of razor-sharp edges rather than the more common barbs—crowned the anti-sapper fence.

After a quick conference, it was agreed that after Ripley cleared the fence Smock would push the boxes of TNT over it, leaving Ripley the task of emplacing each box beneath the spans (the girders or stringers). In Ripley's haste to get them over the anti-sapper fence, he forgot to remove his field webbing, full canteens, magazines and CAR-15 rifle with full magazine; a mistake he would pay for as the explosives became heavier and his muscles wearier. Although the adrenalin was pumping through his veins, Ripley could feel the fatigue from two sleepless nights, little nourishment and incessant enemy small arms fire, artillery and infantry attacks. Even before his Herculean task began, John was near exhaustion.

In plain view of the enemy infantrymen on the north bank of the river, Ripley scaled the anti-sapper fence, slicing his legs and back on the steel tape in the process. He began hand-walking out over the river along the first "I" beam girder. As he swung hand over hand, carrying two fifteen-pound C-4 satchel charges over his shoulders, he suddenly became aware of the heavy burden he had undertaken. About halfway out over the flowing river Ripley tried to swing his body and hook his heels on the steel girders. He ached with pain; the load seemed unbearable. After several attempts to swing up, his heels finally lodged securely on the "I" beam, after which he worked his way up on to the steel bridge. Once there, John discovered that the support girders were separated horizontally by approximately the same width as the wooden artillery ammunition crates in which the ARVN engineers had packed the TNT. This at least made the task a bit easier.

Crawling back and forth in a channel formed by adjacent "I" beams, Ripley placed the demolitions in a staggered alignment between the seven beams (six channels). His next challenge was to systematically pack the boxes of explosives into the channel formed by two adjacent stringers. Each beam was large enough and had a horizontal piece at the bottom upon which he was able to crouch over inside the channel. With his knees on the bottom of the beam, he was able to arm each channel. It was, however, necessary for Ripley to drop down from one beam and swing over to the next as in turn he placed and armed each set of charges. This was a feat very similar to a high-wire act in a circus.

Occasionally Ripley could observe the enemy on the far bank. In his report he remembered:

Rather than concentrating their fire on me—and I certainly couldn't have made it through had they done so—they seemed

CUT AWAY
I" BEAM

TNT
C—4

## CAPTAIN RIPLEY UNDER DONG HA BRIDGE

to be watching incredulously as my body would appear, then
disappear hanging above the river. The enemy watched with a
mixture of what seemed to be humor and amazement. In my
judgment, they knew their massive assault would be successful
and whatever I happened to be doing was relatively inconse-
quential; besides, I was providing them amusement.[2]

While Ripley was moving around on the structure of the
bridge itself, Major Smock remained on the ground shuffling
the crates of demolitions over the chain link fence and up onto
the steel girders where Ripley could then get them. This required Smock repeatedly to expose himself to the enemy on
the north bank. Small arms fire struck the steel and concrete
above him and bullets ricocheted down around him.

What appeared to be the most ominous threat, the T-54
tank damaged by Sergeant Luom, never materialized. The remaining tanks in the column stopped alongside the road. After
being struck by Luom's LAAW, the NVA tank backed into a
defiladed position off the ramp of the bridge, almost at water

level. From that position, the lead NVA tank commander was able to get a clear view of Ripley as he worked under the bridge. Although he was not able to rotate his main gun because of the damage from the hit by Luom's LAAW, he maneuvered his tank by neutral steering (reversing his treads), pointed the 100MM gun in Ripley's direction and fired several rounds at him. All of these missed because of the low angle of fire, with the rounds simply skipping off the "I" beam and impacting behind the dangling Marine. Ripley's report recalls:

> Successful or not, a 100MM round slamming into a steel stringer beside you pumps up your adrenalin, cleans out your ears and motivates you to a greater speed and efficiency.[3]

Having lost all awareness of time, Ripley and Smock were totally engrossed in their desperate task. In actual time the stowing of the demolitions on the bridge went faster than anyone could have expected. The entire exercise of scaling the fence, dragging and packing explosives, swinging under the beams and hand-walking back and forth, and ultimately arming the charges took approximately two hours.

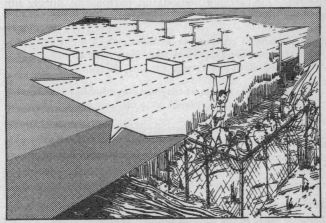

**MAJOR SMOCK LIFTING UP EXPLOSIVES
DONG HA BRIDGE**

Once the explosives were in place, the two American COVANs felt a tremendous sense of relief. However, a critical function still remained to be accomplished: a way to detonate the explosives in the absence of detonators (blasting caps).

Dropping off the bridge, Ripley once again scaled the anti-sapper fence hoping to find some electric detonating caps but had no luck. He finally located some time fuse detonators which left him with the complicated task of cutting lengths of fuse, attaching it to the detonators—hoping that his estimate was correct (length of fuse equals time of burn) and, of course, getting the individual detonators back out to the charges over the river.

Under normal circumstances a special pair of "crimper" pliers is required as the standard tool for preparing demolitions. With none available, Captain Ripley's only field expedient method to measure the fuse consisted of using an arms-length estimate and then applying an old western miner's technique of "jawbone crimping." Thus, once he had secured the detonator to the fuse, his task became much trickier, as he put the blasting cap in his mouth and the fuse into the open end and *very carefully* bit down to crimp the detonating cap to the fuse. John's report reflects his nervousness during this process:

> All the while I recalled the demonstration of the destructive power of a blasting cap I had seen. When inserted into a softball it had blown it to shreds.
>
> My mouth didn't seem as tough as the softball. I could just imagine what a mistake would do to me.[4]

Once the detonators were prepared, Ripley hand-walked and swung back out along the bridge girders to place them in the charges. Again, without the missing crimpers, Ripley found it necessary to use his K-Bar fighting knife to cut a recess in the explosives for the detonators. Without the standard fuse starters John would have to use a series of matches to ignite the six time fuses when the time came to blow the bridge.

Returning to the abutment for what he thought would be his last trip, Ripley felt completely exhausted. Enemy small arms fire had prompted his movement over the anti-sapper fence. Landing on the ground beside Major Smock, who was by that time equally tired, the two began a tension-releasing, light-hearted running patter that bordered on the ridiculous. As the bullets richocheted around them Smock said, "How in the hell did I get myself in such a mess with a ranger-trained Jar-head?"[*] Never at a loss for words, Ripley responded in kind, "How in the hell should I know? Consider yourself lucky for hauling explosives and learning something useful from a Ma-rine. You God-damn tankers never get your hands dirty or your asses muddy anyway!"

This interchange continued while the fuses Ripley had lit were burning.[5] Suddenly, Ripley's eyes caught sight of a box of electric detonators a mere five feet away. A sense of des-peration came over him as he realized that if he relied on the time fuses already in place and left the area of the bridge, (as-suming they evaded enemy fire in the process) it would be impossible to return if for some reason the fused detonators malfunctioned. Ripley felt compelled to go back out on the bridge and place the electric caps alongside those already fused and burning.

Rescaling the anti-sapper fence with a handful of electric detonators, Ripley moved back into the bridge's understruc-ture with an overriding thought, "God, don't let my strength fail me now." Only by drawing upon hidden reserves did he make it to the structure. There, working swiftly, he primed the stacks of explosives and quickly returned to Smock's side. At that point, their final task was to connect the wire leads from the individual blasting caps to a length of communications wire. Once assembled the communications wire could be trailed back to a protected position from which the charges could be det-onated.

Smock later recalled Ripley's actions:

I was convinced that there were sufficient demolitions present to destroy all of Dong Ha, let alone a silly damn bridge, but I

---

[*]Jarhead is an "endearing term of respect" used by other services when referring to Marines.

acquired the company of a "dumb jarhead, ranger school-trained Marine." Not only were we going to destroy the bridge, but we were going to do it by the numbers, IAW* ranger school doctrine.[6]

A few minutes later Ripley moved out from under the bridge and prepared to hook up the detonators. With that, their "impossible mission" would be almost completed. However, at that moment Smock glanced at the old railroad bridge of which one ten- to twenty-foot span had been partially destroyed. Suddenly he realized that with the highway bridge down, any armor or engineer unit could easily repair the railroad bridge. Smock said later:

> According to my training, tanks and truck vehicles could cross that bridge with minimum effort. We would have to destroy the damaged trestle as well. John told me to take a look at it and do whatever I felt was required and that as soon as he had finished wiring the first bridge he would be over to give me a hand.[7]

Proceeding to the railroad trestle Smock emplaced crates of explosives strategically along the undamaged portion of the bridge. When this was done, Ripley ran another wire from the detonator to permit both bridges to be blown simultaneously.

The two Americans, still under NVA small arms fire, made one last inspection of their electrical wiring arrangement because both bridges had to be blown on the first try. There would be no time for a second attempt as the enemy became more alert to the significance of their efforts during this last phase. More fire was concentrated on the two Americans as they completed their preparations. The 3d Battalion's Marines were firing back defiantly and not giving the enemy a free hand. Leaving the underside of the bridge, Ripley carefully played out the communications wire so as not to lose or confuse it with other wire lying about, and he and Smock prepared for their final dash to a protected area about two hundred yards to the south.

From his crouched position, Ripley could see a Marine squad

---

*IAW—In Accordance With.

leader directing the fire of his men. By arm and hand signals and the fact that the squad leader appeared to have anticipated their predicament, John indicated that they were about to leave the bridge for the dash back to safety.

He responded and managed to communicate this to all the defenders along the south bank and the crescendo of their fire peaked as the Marine captain and Army major made their move. Although caught off guard, the NVA on the opposite shore still managed to react.

As they ran towards the squad position, what looked like grim-faced Marines in fighting holes, trenches and buildings all began jumping to their feet, shouting: *Dai uy, Dai uy, dee dau, dee dau!*[8]

The vernacular translation is simply, "Captain, Captain, move your ass, run, run!" Move they did, somehow surviving a run through a hail of enemy fire. They were safe.

Once under cover, Ripley stripped the insulation away from the ends of the communications wire and began looking for a battery that would have to do as there was no "hell-box" (a hand-cranked device that provides a surge of electrical current to charge the electric detonators). Finding one in a shattered jeep lying on its side on the road, Ripley remembered:

When I touched the wire to the battery, my head was as nearly as charged with emotion as the bridge was with explosives.

Nothing happened! I tried a second, third, a tenth time, switched the wires, scraped the terminals—still nothing.[9]

By this time the NVA were increasing their fire on the bridge, so there was no way Captain Ripley could survive another trip underneath the bridge to reconnect the fuses. Suddenly his knees buckled, his helmet was slammed against his head, and he was thrown to the ground. Dazed, he looked skyward to see great chunks of the highway bridge flying through the air. The southern span was wrenched from the midstream pier and fell into the river. As the broken span sank into the Cam Lo-Cua Viet River, the NVA's gateway to Quang Tri was closed. The bridge's remaining roadway, made up of twelve-inch wooden timbers, erupted into flames and would burn through the night and five more days.

The open space between the north and south banks was a beautiful sight for the two Americans to see. At 1630, Captain Ripley reported to me, "The Dong Ha Bridge has been destroyed." An entry noting the exact time of the bridge destruction was entered into the G-3 journal. At the same time I telephoned the FRAC operations center and reported the southern-most spans had been destroyed on the Dong Ha Highway and the adjacent railroad bridge. My report was acknowledged without further comment.

That was it: a simple, terse report; nothing more. I knew this officer was physically and emotionally drained, and so was I. In the brotherhood of arms there is an inexplicable phenomenon, particularly when men are under stress. Far more was transmitted through the tone, inflection, and emotion of one's voice than from the actual words of the message. Here was a brother Marine I had earlier sent to near certain death, and he had somehow survived. His brief report said everything that needed to be said. No elaboration on how he accomplished his task, or of the great difficulties involved; simply, it was done. We both knew all the rest.

As Captain Ripley and Major Smock were in the final phase of preparing the Cam Lo-Cua Viet River bridges for destruction, Major Brookbank informed me that the cloud cover had finally lifted over Dong Ha. A VNAF light observation aircraft was soon overhead and spotted the stalled enemy tank column north of the Dong Ha Bridge. The airborne observer had earlier requested close air support aircraft with iron bombs. Within a few minutes Brookbank had received a report from the USAF Direct Air Support Center (DASC) in Danang that a flight of four VNAF A-1 aircraft had been launched and would be on-station shortly to respond to the request.

This was the first real break in the weather in four long days of heavy combat. Brookbank's announcement helped raise the morale of everyone in the TOC. To the valiant Marines of the 3d Battalion dug in along the south bank of the Cam Lo-Cua Viet River, the long overdue sight of their own airplanes attacking the enemy across the river would be far more exhilarating.

At 1640 the first flight of propeller-driven A-1s began attacking the T-54 and PT-76 tanks. It was the largest concentration of North Vietnamese armor ever confronted by the pilots, and they attacked vigorously, flying dangerously low as they bombed and strafed the Soviet tanks, destroying eleven. More enemy armor was discovered and the South Vietnamese pilots requested that additional flights be launched to strike the armor parked along Highway 1.[10]

The South Vietnamese air armada grew in size and intensity as the day passed. However, the enemy antiaircraft fire began to seek out the low-flying A-1s. Late in the day, around 1751, one A-1 aircraft was struck by an SA-7 Strella heat-seeking missile. Capt. Thu Vo Than was able to turn his burning aircraft straight up to permit him to bail out. Forces on both sides of the Cam Lo-Cua Viet River stopped firing and all watched as the parachute drifted to earth. Wind carried the pilot away from the South Vietnamese Marines, and he landed 300 meters north of the burning Dong Ha Bridge where he was observed being captured by NVA infantry.

Within ten minutes after the destruction of the two bridges over the river, the NVA artillery regiments ceased their daylong attacks by fire on the Dong Ha area.

Except for light small arms fire it was now possible for the defenders of Dong Ha to leave their fighting holes. Major Binh immediately began to reinforce and consolidate his positions along the south bank. Wounded Marines were evacuated and he saw to it that critically needed ammunition was redistributed along the line. Tanks from the 20th battalion moved their M-48s onto the high ground overlooking the north bank. The ARVN tankers continued to fire on the enemy tank column even as the Air Force A-1s ran their air strikes, to assist in suppressing antiaircraft fire from the target area.

The late afternoon skies continued to clear, allowing the long rays of the sun to cast grotesque shadows created by the burning highway bridge and billowing black smoke from the enemy tanks. With the coming of night, a B-52 strike rumbled across Camp Carroll. This bombing mission was our last measure available to prevent the enemy from employing the captured twenty-two artillery pieces against the ARVN Division. "J.J." Carroll would have understood this, I thought.

As Easter Sunday came to a close, the momentum of the Nguyen Hue Offensive slackened. For the first time in four days the enemy's artillery attacks were reduced to scattered interdiction fires. In this single day, however, the 3d ARVN Division had suffered its largest one-day losses since the NVA crossed the DMZ.

On the battlefields the division's three infantry regiments had all suffered badly. The 56th Regiment no longer existed as a South Vietnamese fighting force. So it was for the five batteries of artillery that were at Camp Carroll. The 57th Regiment, including its commander, had broken under the enemy pressure and, in complete rout, had retreated. Its future as a viable fighting force was at best questionable. The 2d Regiment, in battle order, completed its withdrawal across the Cam Lo Bridge and was in the process of establishing a new defensive line nine miles west of Dong Ha. However, one of the 2d Regiment's three infantry battalions still remained unaccounted for. The 3d ARVN Division began the fierce fighting on Easter Sunday with nine infantry battalions; just twelve hours later the division could count only two remaining viable and on the defensive battle line.

The two Marine brigades, the 147th and 258th, remained almost intact and fully operational. The heroic effort of the 3d Marine Battalion had held the river's edge against the rising communist tide, and had bought the time needed for the two Americans successfully to destroy the enemy's bridgehead. Not since the Army's epic World War II battle for the Remagen Bridge over the Rhine River had such a structure played so pivotal a role in a battle. The destruction of the Dong Ha Bridge brought the NVA's armored thrust to an abrupt halt. To renew their offensive would require the NVA to re-route their heavy T-54 tanks some nine miles west to cross the Cam Lo-Cua Viet River Bridge. To completely halt the enemy's armor attack, the bridge would now have to be destroyed.

In addition to the defeats inflicted by the NVA upon the three ARVN infantry regiments, the 3d Division suffered severe material and equipment losses. Huge quantities of radio and telephone communications equipment, vehicles and supplies were left behind when the ARVN FBs were abandoned.

During the four days of the offensive the division had lost, abandoned or surrendered an unprecedented quantity of artillery weapons: thirty-six 105MM howitzers; eighteen 155MM howitzers and four 175MM guns.[11] Over 80 percent of the 3d ARVN Division's artillery weapons was in the hands of the enemy. For the division to remain a marginally operational fighting force, immediate replacement of guns and trained crews was necessary and would become a priority task for JGS headquarters in Saigon.

As Easter Sunday drew to a close, the MACV staff in Saigon was drafting General Abrams' daily operational summary report to the Chairman, JCS, Pentagon. As it had been during the four previous days of battle, the flow of information from MR-1 remained slow, and this fact again resulted in another inaccurate OPSUM being submitted to Washington, D.C. The recently declassified personal appraisal of the Commander, U.S. Military Advisory Command, Vietnam, on the friendly and enemy situation reported in part:

> 1. (S) The overall situation in Quang Tri Province is fluid and enemy pressure continues at a high level against RVNAF. Highly accurate and heavy artillery fire remains the mainstay of the enemy's offensive. During the past three days the enemy has forced the evacuation of FSBs A-2, A-4, C-1 and C-2 in northern Quang Tri Province and FSBs Holcomb, Sarge, Nui Ba Ho, Khe Gio (YD0255) and Fuller along the western crescent. Control of these areas will facilitate his use of observed fire into ARVN positions.
> 2. Enemy forces continue to press their attack in the Quang Tri lowlands. Installations remaining in friendly hands continue to receive accurate and heavy ABFs of mixed artillery, rocket and mortar rounds. Cam Lo (YD1359), Pedro (YD2548), Mai Loc (YD1051) and Carroll (YD0654) have been under extensive ABFs with Cam Lo and Pedro also receiving heavy ground attacks. Carroll is reported surrounded and late reports indicate it has surrendered. . . . Initial reports indicate U.S. aircraft had sixteen to twenty SA-2 missiles launched against them while operating over South Vietnam. One EB-66 and one VNAF 0-1 were downed. As a result, a new SAM confirmed operating area centered just north of the western DMZ has been established with a radius of twenty-four nautical miles.

3. (S) ARVN forces are now deployed generally south of the Song Mieu Giang—Cua Viet as far west as Carroll with the 57th Regt. and 2d Regt. located in the vicinity of Dong Ha, the 56th Regt. at Carroll, the 147th VNMC BDE and 3d Div. Hq. at Quang Tri City. Territorial forces are assisting in the security of routes and key bridges. Resupply of Mai Loc and Carroll remain critical. Mai Loc received some resupply by CH-47 yesterday. The aircraft received extensive damage and were unable to resupply Carroll. Resupply drops were scheduled to both bases today. The 20th ARVN tank BN was reported in contact with enemy tanks in the vicinity of the Dong Ha Bridge. Results of this action are not yet available. It is reported that refugees are moving south into Quang Tri City. Movement appears orderly. Activity in the remainder of MR-1 remains on a low level. Redistribution of combat assets to reinforce the 3d Div. is expected to detract from friendly operations in the remainder of the MR. . . .

4. (S) A U.S. air cavalry troop is moving from MR-3 to MR-1 today. A VNMC brigade of three BNs will be moved to MR-1 from the Saigon area starting tomorrow. Twenty-two combat skyspot and 71 LORAN sorties have been flown and eleven ARC-LIGHT strikes have been delivered during the past thirty-six hours. Three destroyers have thus far fired over 1,400 rounds in support of ARVN operations. A fourth destroyer is scheduled on station today.

5. (S) Enemy-initiated activity has increased slightly in MR-2. In NW Kontum Province several FSBs in the rocket ridge area received ABFs with strong probes in the southern portion of the ridge. . . .

6. (S) In MR-3, enemy activity has increased during the past few days. Action was highlighted by the appearance of enemy armor for the first time in that area . . .

7. (S) Activity in MR-4 remains at a low level.

8. (S) In summary, the situation in MR-1 remains serious. Weather continues to hamper air support. Increased pressure in MRs 2 and 3 continue to indicate a well-planned, coordinated enemy offensive is in progress. GP-4.4.[12]

Once again MACV's daily OPSUM contained some incorrect information, but for the first time the message portrayed the fact that the NVA had launched a series of successful attacks against ARVN and Marine forces along the DMZ. The ineffective flow of information from the battlefields to MACV and the South Vietnamese JGS would be attributed to Lieutenant General Lam. Gen. Cao Van Vien, chairman of the JGS, later recorded:

> General Lam had a characteristic that should be avoided by leaders at every level. He would not report bad news or was very slow to do so. When the enemy offensive first started, he failed to report accurately on the DMZ situation and as a result, the JGS had no way of knowing that it was a large-scale invasion. As chief of the JGS, I did not fully grasp the real situation until General Abrams, COMUSMACV, informed me what was happening.[13]

# CHAPTER THIRTEEN

# EVACUATION OF FIRE SUPPORT BASE MAI LOC

The loss of Camp Carroll made the last remaining fire base on the western flank untenable. FSB Mai Loc had been under artillery attacks over the past three days, equally as heavy as those inflicted on Camp Carroll before its surrender. NVA infantry had been sighted on three sides as they began an effort to encircle the Marines of Brigade 147 on the fire support base. The ARVN 155MM battery (four guns) and Marine 105MM battery (six guns) continued to fire at the approaching enemy. Colonel Bao met with his unit commanders to review the combat effectiveness and identify the remaining stocks of ammunition and food. His commanders all reported that their stocks of small arms and rifle, machine gun and artillery ammunition had dwindled to critical levels.

Several hours before Camp Carroll surrendered, Colonel Bao and Maj. Jim Joy, his Senior Advisor, met to discuss the possibility that FSB Mai Loc and the airstrip might have to be evacuated. They recognized the danger to their position if Camp Carroll fell. Bao made no decision at that time. Now, however, with artillery ammunition almost exhausted, the remaining supply of small arms dangerously low—and with little chance of resupply of either commodity—the fall of Camp Carroll imminent, and bad weather, he wanted the advisors to be aware such a course of action might be dictated.

After reviewing the situation with his commanders, Bao then asked Joy for his recommendations on the best method for evacuating the position, a withdrawal route and a time of departure. He immediately advised that it was imperative that the east gate be held open by the 7th Battalion. Their mission should be to keep the enemy far enough back to permit the position to be evacuated quickly once the withdrawal itself had begun. He further recommended no attempt be made to evacuate the position until after dark, which would preclude enemy artillery from placing accurate fire on the exposed Marines as they moved out of position.

Together the Vietnamese colonel and his American advisor studied a tactical map searching for the best possible route eastward to the Quang Tri combat base. Joy later recommended a withdrawal route out of their position northwest to the village of Mai Loc where Brigade 147 would link up with the survivors of the 4th VNMC Battalion. Once the link-up was made, the column would turn due east and march toward Highway 1. The 7th Battalion, which had its three companies on the southern and eastern perimeter of the base, would withdraw last and assume the mission of rearguard to the brigade.

In sharp contrast to the near-tragic situation at Camp Carroll, where the two army advisors were isolated from their counterparts, Bao openly shared his thoughts and plans with his senior Marine advisor. Together the two leaders discussed a most difficult combat decision. They were soliciting each other's counsel to develop an operational plan which, if executed, would abandon the last South Vietnamese fire base on the western defense line. Over 1,500 lives would depend upon the selection of a correct course of action.

Before the meeting ended, Joy asked Bao to give him sufficient advance notice of the move, in order to permit time for the advisors to destroy a sizeable amount of classified code materials and some radio equipment. The colonel agreed and recommended that everything be made ready in the event that it was necessary to evacuate FSB Mai Loc that day.

Calling his assistant advisors together, Joy told them of the meeting with the brigade commander and the proposed action that they had discussed. They began their own preparation to destroy everything that could not be carried, as Joy radioed the advisors with the 4th and 7th Battalions. To avoid compromising the plan, he attempted an improvised code of BENT (beginning of evening nautical twilight or dusk) to pass the anticipated time of execution. Both of the advisors to the 4th Battalion, Major DeBona with the 7th Battalion, and Major Boomer, he called acknowledged the message in code.

During the afternoon Mai Loc's last thread of communication with the 3d Division TOC was lost. The incoming NVA artillery fire had repeatedly destroyed or disabled the last RC-292 antenna poles and guide cables available to the advisors. On six earlier occasions, a team of advisors had braved the unrelenting incoming artillery fire to replace or repair antennas or cables, but after losing the last antenna, the advisors were limited to communicating with Major Boomer, using backpack radios. Thus, whenever Joy needed to contact DeBona with the 7th Battalion, Boomer had to relay the message.

At 1730 the G-3 journal entry noted the loss of communications between Brigade 147 and the advisors. The last message Major Joy received from the TOC had been sent through the Vietnamese radio net. That message requested the COVANs with Brigade 147 to change their radio channels to the emergency air-ground frequency and contact "Ramrod," the U.S. Air Force air borne command center (ABCC). Despite repeated attempts to establish such a communications link, no contact could be made with "Ramrod" and communications remained poor.

At 1815 on Sunday evening, Colonel Bao informed Major Joy that he had made the decision to abandon the Mai Loc combat base. He had been in radio contact with General Giai, and had been instructed to make his own decision on remaining at Mai Loc. Giai told him, "Remain if possible, but if the situation becomes untenable, leave."

Fortunately, all foreseeable preparation for evacuation had already been made following the earlier conversations between the brigade commander and his advisor. Joy immediately requested Bao's permission for him and several of his Marines to leave the underground command bunker and begin the destruction of the advisor's equipment that would be left behind. Bao concurred. As Joy was putting on his helmet and flak jacket, he heard Bao speaking to his Marines in the brigade's TOC, advising them:

> The decision has been made to leave, but it will be an orderly departure. The brigade command post, 2d Artillery Battalion and detachments will move out to link up with the 4th Battalion to plan the final move eastward toward the Quang Tri combat base and the 7th Battalion will bring up the rear. We will begin our march as soon as it is dark.[1]

At 1800, Mai Loc's two artillery batteries had depleted the last of its 105MM ammunition and only forty rounds of 155MM ammunition remained. Because the withdrawal would be on foot, the ten howitzers would have to be left behind. Meeting with the artillery commanders, Maj. Tom Gnibus and Captain Randall reviewed the procedures for destroying ("spiking") the guns to render them inoperable. The firing lock had to be removed and an incendiary grenade placed in the breech.

When the last 155MM rounds were fired the cannoneers began to spike their guns. Although the procedure was simple, this was psychologically the most onerous task any artilleryman could ever perceive happening and in itself signalled defeat. With time running out the brigade headquarters assembled to begin the march out. Grenades were ignited, inserted into each artillery piece and the breech closed in a locked position. The 4,500 degree "burn" of the incendiary grenades raised the temperature within the breech to a white-hot level causing the machined parts to melt and then, when cooled, form into a mass of useless metal.

While the advisors were searching through their destroyed tent area for things to be thrown on the pile of burning classified materials, the headquarters personnel of the brigade, loaded heavily with packs, radios and other equipment, were the first to move through the east gate. Other units formed into long twin columns and began to move out in the order of march prescribed earlier. Darkness shielded their withdrawal and except for the shuffling sound of marching feet, rattle of canteens and the occasional banging of rifles, the long columns of South Vietnamese were silent. They each knew the fifteen-plus miles march to safety could erupt at any moment into a fight for their lives.

As soon as the COVANs were certain their pile of papers and equipment was engulfed in flames, they also joined the column. Major Joy later reported:

> The withdrawal of the Mai Loc combat base was conducted under extremely heavy enemy artillery fire. As the column came out the East gate, it was engaged by small arms fire from the east. The 7th Battalion, which had been in contact all day, had held the enemy far enough off to make the NVA's small arms fire generally ineffective. Also, as the column exited the gate, it crossed the airstrip and entered the trash dump depression and this caused it to be out of visual sight of the enemy to the east.[2]

The column remained under artillery fire until it reached Mai Loc Village, when it temporarily lifted as the Marines passed through the village, then began striking around them once again as they emerged on the other side. Although the enemy's 130MM guns bracketed the road, none of the eighty-five-pound projectiles fell on the column of Marines. Moving in the center of the column, the advisors commented upon the general ineffectiveness of the enemy's fire because their withdrawal made them, as massed troops in the open, the ideal target for artillery. They concluded from the pattern of the impacting shells that the NVA was shifting its fire over the area, as if searching for the escaping South Vietnamese. The NVA would fire two rounds into an area and then shift to another grid square (1,000 meters) and fire another two rounds. It appeared that the brigade's luck was holding, as a light rain swept in across the area, further reducing the visibility to a few feet.

As the last companies of the 8th Battalion passed through the east gate, the 7th Battalion, with three companies in steady contact with the enemy, began to try to disengage and assume its rearguard mission. The 1st Company was in contact with enemy units to the south. Just before dark about sixty Marines from FB Holcomb struggled through the 1st Company's lines and moved into FSB Mai Loc. However, over half of a rifle company from the 8th Battalion was still unaccounted for.[3]

The 2d Company disengaged from the west side of FSB Mai Loc and passed through the east gate in good order. The 3d Company, which had been positioned around the 7th Battalion Alpha command group, became intermingled during its move with the rear of the column and remained separated until the battalion passed Mai Loc Village.

There was confusion as to which units were actually in the column and where they were located. This was to have the biggest impact upon the 7th Battalion. Major DeBona recorded:

> It took a rather "monumental" effort for the battalion to disengage since two of its three rifle companies were in contact.[4]

The 3d Company of the 7th Battalion became intermingled with elements of the 8th Battalion and would not rejoin its parent unit for twenty-four hours. As the 7th Battalion assembled to link up with the rear of the column, the battalion's Alpha command group, with Major Hue, overran an enemy 82MM mortar position which had been firing at Mai Loc. The NVA crew was killed and the mortar destroyed. The march continued. Major DeBona and Captain Rice remained at the point of the rearguard and did not rejoin Major Hue until 1900.

The distance from Mai Loc Village to Quang Tri combat base was approximately twenty kilometers. The terrain along the route had long been known to be some of the most difficult terrain in Quang Tri Province. Dense undergrowth, low hills with sheer slopes and the meandering Song Dinh River prevented any roads from being built in the area. The brigade commander had purposely selected the most difficult route because he felt it would provide their best opportunity to reach Highway 1 without encountering the enemy.

Turning eastward after passing through Mai Loc, the 7th Battalion became separated from Brigade 147 in the darkness and rain, and Major Joy lost radio contact. Colonel Bao decided not to wait any longer and continued on. His leading elements moved slowly but steadily until around 2300. At that time they encountered a stream where the heavy underbrush hid the stream bank. This delayed the column over three hours as individuals inched across a waist-deep stream with vertical banks nearly ten feet high.

During the halt for the stream crossing, Major Joy contacted a U.S. FAC and also a Stringer aircraft. Both were requested to notify the 3d ARVN Division headquarters of their location and did so. This was the first radio contact between the TOC and Major Joy's advisors since mid-afternoon.

Joy had positioned himself in the center of the brigade column, and Maj. Tom Gnibus, as well as Captains Kruger, Randall, and Evasick, remained grouped with him. Radio communications were maintained with Major Boomer, Captains Smith and Rice, all with the 4th Battalion, which was at the head of the column, and Major DeBona with the rearguard battalion.

When the time came for Joy's advisors to cross the stream they found themselves further separated from the brigade's lead elements of the column. Radio contact with the 7th Battalion became intermittent. Through radio communications with the 4th Battalion advisors, Major Joy was able to determine the general route taken by the head of the column.

As the night passed, the psychological strain on Colonel Bao and the personnel of his brigade was beginning to take its toll as the units in the center of the column became intermingled and tactical integrity was lost. The units groped through a drizzling rain, dense gnarled underbrush and rugged terrain, all the while in the dark. Major Joy later reflected that his advisors were not sure a U.S. unit would not have reacted any differently.

The epic trek of Brigade 147 toward Highway 1 became almost too much for Major Boomer. Nearing a state of total physical and mental exhaustion, he became disoriented. He knew that lying down to rest would have meant abandonment. As a last desperate act, he located a loose strap hanging from Captain Smith's battered rucksack. Boomer tied the strap tightly around his wrist and, with his arm stretched out, staggered along behind Smith. In the darkness he drifted into brief periods of sleep and delirium as he was yanked along the trail by an understanding Smith. There were no words spoken between the COVANs; the bond of unity was so much greater than a canvas strap. Smith knew they would somehow make it to safety.

At 1930 the 7th Battalion left Mai Loc Village and began to move eastward following the trail of the brigade's columns. Majors Hue and DeBona soon discovered the trail was littered with the wounded and exhausted Marines of the 4th and 8th VNMC Battalions. These survivors of FBs Sarge and Nui Ba Ho and the few stragglers from FB Holcomb had simply run out of stamina and collapsed along the trail.

Throughout the night the 7th Battalion picked up and somehow carried every exhausted or wounded Marine they encountered. Major DeBona reported that to the best of his knowledge the battalion did not leave one Vietnamese Marine behind.

Major Hue had planned to march due east on a compass azimuth, believing this would keep the battalion from becoming lost in the dense foliage. This decision, however, eventually required the column to cross and recross the unfordable Song Dinh River four times. When the river was first encountered, the battalion was able to locate ten serviceable air mattresses. Using these, DeBona, Rice and a few South Vietnamese Marines ferried the battalion, including the wounded, across the river.

Once on the other side, vertical cliffs covered with thick underbrush further hindered the column's progress. DeBona remembered:

> We had no more than cleared the column when we immediately ran into the river again. We once again pulled our amphibious assault with the air mattresses.[5]

By 1200 the 7th Battalion had lost its physical link with the brigade column. The Song Dinh River had now been recrossed three times. Too exhausted to move on, the column of drenched Marines stopped, lay down along their newly blazed trail and slept.

The historic events of Easter Sunday in Quang Tri Province had not completely run their course. Two more unexpected situations occurred, both involving U.S. aircraft. The first tragic event happened when a North Vietnamese SAM-2 missile downed an EB-66 electronic warfare (EW) aircraft with the loss of five of its American crew. The second situation arose when a B-52 ARCLIGHT strike was erroneously programmed to bomb the Ai Tu TOC bunker while it was still occupied by U.S. advisory personnel and the headquarters of Colonel Dinh's Brigade 258.

As the South Vietnamese A-1 aircraft were completing their air strikes on the burning tank column north of the Cam Lo-Cua Viet River, U.S. aircraft were also entering the air space just south of the DMZ. Two EB-66s (callsigns BAT-21 and 22) flying out of Thailand were escorting a cell of B-52s, bombing targets on missions requested earlier by the Americans operating the Ai Tu TOC bunker.

One Soviet SAM-2 missile struck the BAT-21 aircraft directly in the electronic counter measures (ECM) compartment. The aircraft disintegrated and went down. Only one survival radio was activated, later determined to be that of Lt. Col. Iceal Hambleton, which began sending out an audible "beeping" signal on emergency frequencies.[6]

Coincidentally, an airborne search and rescue (SAR) task force* was operating nearby. It had been launched from Danang to evacuate some advisors from Quang Tri but that mission had been cancelled. The two A-1 aircraft from the SAR heard the emergency calls and headed toward Hambleton's position. Amid intense ground fire the U.S. A-1 Skyraider pilots orbited Hambleton's position, talking with him and trying desperately to keep the NVA from capturing him.

Meanwhile, contact had been made with four U.S. Army helicopters—two Cobra gunships and two passenger-carrying Hueys. Approaching Hambleton's position, two of the four helicopters were shot down. One Huey was completely destroyed with no survivors. The Cobra gunship was able to limp out to the coastline, where it landed on a beach.[7]

To prevent the enemy from approaching Hambleton's position, the OV-10's airborne FAC coordinated the placement of a ring of area-denial ordnance surrounding Hambleton's

---

*A typical SAR task force included one or two HH-53 "Super Jolly Green" rescue helicopters and four to eight A-1 propeller-driven attack aircraft.

position. Once the "gravel"* type munitions had been seeded, the OV-10 crew flew to Danang. There they met with U.S. Army advisors, exchanged target information and established a zone of operation north of the river. It was decided that in the no fire zone around Hambleton, the U.S. Air Force would control all air strikes and artillery fire.[8]

At first glance this unilateral rear area arrangement of giving the USAF control of all TAC Air, naval gunfire and artillery fire probably seemed like a rational decision to officers eighty kilometers from the battle lines. However, it was a near-tragic decision for the 3d ARVN Division, which at that time was near collapse from the unrelenting pressure of the North Vietnamese divisions.

When viewed in relation to all the events of the day, a worse decision could not have been made. Of equal significance, the USAF did not coordinate the activation of their "no fire zone" with the 3d ARVN Division. General Giai, as the ground commander, was the only person who could properly authorize any restrictions on supporting arms weapons in his area of responsibility. There is no record that his approval was ever sought and when the overall desperate circumstances of the South Vietnamese forces are taken into consideration, it is highly doubtful he would have authorized such a large no fire zone.

Around 2115 a telephone call was received in the TOC informing the G-3 watch officer that a massive SAR was initiated in the Cam Lo area by the 7th Air Force. The first thing the USAF did was to set up a no fire zone twenty-seven kilometers in radius around Hambleton's position. The radius virtually encompassed the 3d ARVN Division's remaining area of operations, extending east almost to the ocean and south to include the Ai Tu combat base. One brief bit of guidance from the Air Force's Direct Air Support Center (DASC) in Danang was to the effect that "Because of the pending rescue mission no air strikes, artillery or naval gunfire can be fired anywhere in northern Quang Tri Province without first receiving approval from the DASC."[9]

In essence, this restrictive fire plan would have put the 3d

---

*An antipersonnel munition, which has the appearance of gravel and explodes when disturbed.

Division's few remaining artillery batteries in a stand-down posture at a time when the NVA was attacking and winning all across the battlefield. Our immediate reaction was to protest the imposition of such a large and unrealistic no fire zone. Frantic telephone calls were made back to the DASC and to the FRAC operations center but to no avail. The standard response from both facilities in Danang was "Hey, there is an American pilot down and everything possible has to be done to rescue him." In a manner similar to the lieutenant colonel's earlier guidance, "Don't blow the Dong Ha Bridge," our repeated attempts to either lift or reduce the size of the no fire zone were overridden.

Major Brookbank best summed up the frustrations of the Americans in the TOC when he submitted his after-action report:

> In my opinion this (no fire zone) gave the enemy an opportunity unprecedented in the annals of warfare to advance at will. With three enemy divisions plus heavy artillery striking the AO, the 3d ARVN Division was unable to return fire or request TAC Air in the area. Some specific targets were struck after considerable delays in obtaining clearance. It was five days later before it was known that 100 to 150 TAC Air support sorties were flown in this area and no intelligence was passed as to what was being accomplished. This SAR operation cost the 3d ARVN dearly in not being able to fire at known targets of urgent tactical importance. Although the no fire zone was later reduced to 5,000 meters and then to 2,700 meters until the rescue was completed around 12 April, this particular area covered the main NVA offensive thrust from the north at the Cam Lo Bridge crossing.*[10]

In the TOC bunker Colonel Dinh came over to the G-3 watch area seeking an explanation as to why the ARVN artil-

---

*The "BAT-21" SAR was the most extensive rescue ever attempted by the USAF in Southeast Asia. As many as ninety TAC Air strikes per day were required to suppress enemy fire. Despite the USAF's heroic efforts, a SAR rescue was not possible and Colonel Hambleton was eventually rescued in a daring venture by a U.S. Marine team. On the night of 13 April, Lt. Col. Andy Anderson moved through NVA forces, made a rendezvous and then recrossed the Cam Lo-Cua Viet River in a sampan and passed through South Vietnamese lines. Colonel Hambleton's ordeal is set out in detail in the book *BAT-21* by William C. Anderson.

lery batteries and naval gunfire were not permitted to fire on the enemy on the north side of the Cam Lo-Cua Viet River. Several of the Americans tried to explain the no fire zone imposed by the USAF and that we were in the process of trying to get the restriction lifted. When Dinh heard the rescue mission was for one survivor, he held up his finger, and, meaning no disrespect said, "Just one?" We all understood his remark as he turned, shook his head in disbelief, and went back to his active operations center.

Though our efforts to get the no fire zone eliminated were fruitless, in the many telephone calls to the DASC and FRAC the watch officers were able to pinpoint the downed flyer's location (at this time we did not know his name). This information was passed to Colonel Dinh. He immediately turned to me and said, "We must shoot our artillery on enemy targets around Dong Ha. If we do not, the enemy will be able to mass his forces freely for more attacks at dawn."

Fate now presented me with a situation almost identical to Dinh's decision to commit the 3d Marine Battalion. I requested a few minutes to review the situation. He nodded understandingly and returned to his side of the G-3 area. Once again I explained to the FRAC operations center the critical need to allow the South Vietnamese artillery batteries to attack NVA targets. Knowing the location of the downed crewman we could fire safely to within 1,000 meters of his position. My request was denied.

Fully realizing the fragile defensive posture of the 3d Division and the seriousness of again violating a direct order, I met with the U.S. Marine artillery advisors. We all agreed the ARVN artillery could fire in many other areas and not endanger the downed flyer, and that to prevent the total collapse of the 3d ARVN Division the artillery would have to attack NVA targets throughout the night. Captains Nettleingham and Evasick and Maj. Regan Wright felt confident they could monitor all the artillery batteries and preempt any fire missions near Cam Lo. With this information we unilaterally placed a six-kilometer circle around Colonel Hambleton's location and I authorized the advisors to commence their pending fire missions.

At the same time I directed Lieutenant Eisenstein to co-ordinate with the U.S. destroyers and bring naval gunfire to bear on NVA positions. Because the naval guns had a range limitation of ten miles inland there was no possibility their fire could endanger Hambleton. After taking these actions I personally reported them to the FRAC operations center, stating that I accepted the responsibility if anything happened to the downed pilot. I informed Colonel Dinh of my decision and he responded by saying, "Good, we must shoot. I understand the problem."

The intensity of the NVA's SAM missile and antiaircraft fire around Cam Lo reconfirmed the high threat area just south of the DMZ. A 7th Air Force report on the Easter invasion stated:

> Because of the enemy (air defense) environment, the normal SAR team could not operate effectively. As demonstrated in the BAT-21 mission, enemy artillery and weapon fire were a serious threat to slow-moving Jolly Green HH-53 helicopters, A-1 Sandy escort aircraft, and the OV-10 FACs. During the eleven-day SAR effort (2 April to 13 April) SA-2 missiles downed two OV-10 FACs and ground fire caused the loss of a Jolly Green and its entire crew. The enemy in the area numbered in the thousands. High-caliber automatic weapons and even artillery replaced the normal ground fire. Consequently, the enemy threat dictated several changes in tactics. The suppression of enemy fire, previously handled by A-1 aircraft in a matter of hours, now required fast-moving F-4 (jet) aircraft.[11]

Darkness had set in, and the tempo of activity slackened. For the South Vietnamese it was a critically needed opportunity to reposition and replenish their depleted forces. The night enabled the North Vietnamese to conceal the rerouting of their armor and mechanized vehicles westward toward Cam Lo. Also, as critical a target as the Cam Lo Bridge was, with a downed U.S. pilot so close to it, there would be no USAF support to destroy this last passage across the Cam Lo-Cua Viet River. Our plan to destroy the bridge would have to wait until the downed crewman was rescued.

Around 2100 Captain Ripley radioed to report that a new

enemy tank column had come down Highway 1 and turned west on the gravel side road just north of the Cam Lo-Cua Viet River. Although it was dark he reported that "from the engine noises and fires burning in the area, approximately twenty tanks were moving west." He felt "They are making a dash for the Cam Lo area where they probably hope to cross the river."

Naval gunfire was requested to interdict the road. Ripley and Eisenstein coordinated on a fire mission. Within two or three minutes the destroyers steaming offshore had rounds falling on the elongated NVA column. It was an ideal target for naval guns. One tank was hit on the first salvo and remained burning, illuminating the other T-54 and T-55 tanks as they passed alongside.

Before the naval gunfire mission was completed the NVA tank column was hit by a B-52 strike. It was an area destruction mission that had been requested hours earlier when the NVA were moving toward the Dong Ha bridges. Fate and circumstances had placed the enemy tanks in the ARCLIGHT's kill zone at just the right moment. When the thundering noise and the violent shock waves of the 250 or more bombs dropped by the flight had finally subsided, Ripley reported "hearing the cries of the survivors, but no more engine noises."[12]

When dawn broke on 3 April, he reported the hulks were distinctly visible in a moonscape-like scene of craters and mud. He felt the NVA tank column had been completely neutralized.

Within the TOC bunker the team of Americans had responded exceptionally well under the circumstances. As Colonel Dinh's counterpart, Major Jon Easley in Brigade 258, performed his expanding advisory duties in a nearly flawless manner. In addition, he became my principal assistant in the coordination of U.S. and ARVN supporting arms. Jon was a tireless individual who repeatedly demonstrated that rare ability to remain calm when the unpredictable happened. He was quick to develop plans to overcome difficult coordination problems. His personal contribution to the 3d ARVN Division was not to be in a single heroic act but that of sustained exceptional performance.

He quietly assumed a greater role during the two days he had been in the TOC. He established scheduled watch hours for the advisors, verified coordinates and radio frequencies, and maintained a location on the American advisors. He willingly assumed additional responsibilities and thus became the most logical person to replace me during my pending trip to Saigon.

Earlier I had suggested to Colonel Murdock that he assume my chief advisor's role in the TOC. He accepted this recommendation and directed me to insure Easley was fully briefed on the 3d Division's defensive posture before I left for the Phu Bai airfield.

With the slackening of enemy activity, we in the bunker began to take our first real break in days. For me it was a time to gather together my rucksack and weapon for an early morning departure. It was also the unfortunate time to experience a severe case of diarrhea, which seemed to drain off the little stamina remaining in my body.

By 2300 I was extremely weak, sleepy and perhaps nearing mental exhaustion. I requested Easley to take over in the TOC. With my field jacket as a pillow I moved over to one corner of the G-3 common area and lay down to sleep. It did not come easily, for my thoughts were on how I could accurately explain to General Abrams my unusual involvement with the 3d ARVN Division. As the radio traffic emanating from the G-3 watch area seemed to fade away I began a fitful and restless sleep. Little did I realize then that there would be one more crisis to contend with before my morning departure.

Around 0240 I was shaken awake by Maj. Regan Wright with the unbelievable comment, "Get up, Colonel, we're about to be bombed!" After scrambling to my feet, I entered the G-3 watch area. There I was briefed that a telephone call had just been received from a watch officer in Saigon that a B-52 ARCLIGHT mission was scheduled to bomb the Ai Tu and Quang Tri combat bases within the next thirty minutes. Apparently, a USAF officer had called to pass along the information on what then appeared to be just another ARCLIGHT target. The watch officer was jolted into action when the caller said, "Hey, you guys better get your heads down because we're going to be rippling (bombing) the old 3d Division headquarters at Ai Tu in about thirty minutes."

As I listened, Majors Easley, Brookbank and Wright came rushing into the G-3 watch area. We quickly agreed to explore all radio and telephone channels to first verify the validity of the planned B-52 bombing and then get the strike cancelled. Brookbank's task was to contact the 7th Air Force controlled DASC in Danang. Easley and I would telephone the operations centers at FRAC and MACV in Saigon. In a matter of minutes it was verified that a B-52 strike had somehow been approved to bomb the Ai Tu combat base complex.

What apparently happened was that when the 3d ARVN Division and Team 155 reported the relocation of their respective headquarters back to Quang Tri City, it was perceived by these rear headquarters that the Ai Tu complex had been abandoned. Someone in Saigon had approved an ARCLIGHT strike to destroy the ARVN and U.S. command and control systems to prevent them from falling into enemy hands.

Once again, reaction time became critical. The reason why this was happening was irrelevant; only the ability to somehow divert the high flying bombers was important. The bunker had withstood repeated hits from NVA's 130MM artillery. The explosions from the enemy's eighty-pound projectiles had been mostly absorbed by the thousands of sandbags covering the heavy timbered frame, but it had been weakened. If B-52s were to drop their 300 or more 750-pound bombs on the Ai Tu/Quang Tri bases, huge fuel tanks, ammunition dumps, its airstrip and the bunker would undoubtedly erupt into one gigantic fireball. In addition to the loss of U.S. and ARVN lives, the vital U.S. command and control center would be destroyed. Even if the bunker did not receive a direct hit the explosive blast effects would collapse it. Somehow, some way, the planned ARCLIGHT strike must be aborted.

Precious minutes had been expended, confirming and then explaining that we were still at Ai Tu but neither the watch officers in Danang nor Saigon could or would divert the B-52s that were approaching Quang Tri Province. With indecision from MACV, FRAC, and the DASC, Major Brookbank became our last hope to abort the strike and save us. To do so he would again have to violate Air Force radio security procedures.

With his air-to-ground communication systems he was capable of entering USAF emergency radio frequencies. There was no other alternative because we understood that the B-52s were fast approaching their bomb release point. We didn't know if even now we were doomed to be struck by our own bombs.

There had been many unusual incidents in the TOC, but this scene with Dave Brookbank was one of the most vivid. Switching his radio to the emergency frequency, better known as GUARD, and in a dialogue such as no one had ever heard before, he began roughly as follows: "This is Maj. David Brookbank, USAF. I've entered this GUARD frequency to request an emergency abort of a B-52 ARCLIGHT strike which is about to bomb the Ai Tu combat base. For God's sakes don't drop! There are a number of Americans still in the main operations bunker. Someone erroneously requested Ai Tu be bombed, because they thought it was evacuated—we're still here. You've got to abort the mission, this is an emergency. I repeat, emergency. Don't drop, we're still here at Ai Tu."

After Dave Brookbank made his pleading transmissions on GUARD there was no radio response. We really did not expect one for security reasons. So Brookbank tried to authenticate his desperate request by broadcasting that he was also a B-52 pilot, had been stationed at Plattsburgh, New York, and gave the date when he completed flight training. He repeated his name several times, then added that his wife's name was Evelyn and was living in Mississippi.

As he talked into the radio handset the five or six of us around him were watching him and then looking at the timber ceiling above us. Major Wright was standing beside Dave, holding him by the arm and encouraging him to keep talking. "Say anything, just keep talking, keep repeating we're still here at Ai Tu."

No one remembers how long we stood around Brookbank as his radio message was, hopefully, transmitted to every U.S. aircraft then flying in Southeast Asia. It was a desperate message to the B-52 pilots somewhere high above South Vietnam to use "pilots discretion" and not bomb the Ai Tu/Quang Tri bases.

In one last burst of emotion Dave repeated his full name, rank and pilot qualifications and quit broadcasting. Again, there was no response. The suspense was almost unbearable. We waited. If the bombs had been released at 50,000 feet it would take five or six minutes for them to strike the ground. We waited some more. Five minutes passed, then ten, and twenty. As each moment clicked off, our confidence grew in the success of Brookbank's emergency radio call.* After about thirty minutes we felt the threat of being bombed was over. Although still feeling some apprehension, we dispersed back to our work areas.

Easley and I re-entered the G-3 watch area where we reviewed the location of ARVN and the RF and PF forces. The worst of the NVA's Nguyen Hue Offensive seemed to be behind us. We had bought some time and reinforcements were on the way. In the TOC a group of strangers had welded together into a professional team to assist the South Vietnamese Army and Marines halt an enemy invasion. I was reminded of the dictum that

> A military man prepares all his career for a moment that may never come. And if he is a true leader of men, he has trained them so well that should he become a casualty his unit will operate effectively without him.

It was almost morning and I had a mandate to return to Saigon. I knew the U.S. team effort would continue.

---

*Major Brookbank was later able to confirm that a B-52 flight was diverted while en route to Quang Tri Province.

# CHAPTER FOURTEEN

# THE BATTLE CONTINUES

For the officers and men entrenched along the forward battle lines of this savagely fought campaign, the days and nights seemed to melt together. Maj. Jon Easley and I reviewed the known position of ARVN and Marine units as I prepared to go to Saigon.

After four days of arduous combat, the situation still remained critical. The destruction of the Dong Ha Highway bridge had halted the NVA's main attack at the Cam Lo-Cua Viet River, but the invaders were reinforcing their forces along the northern bank of the river. This welcome breathing spell permitted the defenders to consolidate, redistribute forces and ammunition, and make some sense of what had been harrowing combat. However, enemy infantry still crossed the river at night. Fighting continued. The enemy attacks by fire from its long-range 130MM and 152MM guns had slackened. Large enemy movements had been reported all along the battle lines; however, there was no heavy contact. Near Cam Lo the rescue mission to recover the downed American pilot had become the focal point of the U.S. Air Force activity just below the DMZ. The ARVN officers in the TOC surmised the NVA were regrouping and for a day or two there would be only sporadic fighting.

As the fifth day of the offensive began, the 3d ARVN Division's northwestern flank was falling back toward Dong Ha.

The 2d ARVN Regiment was withdrawing its rearguard along Route 9. Elements of the 20th Tank Battalion and a squadron of APCs from the 17th Armored Cavalry were hastily scattered in firing positions along the narrow highway and on the immediate high ground. There were only light encounters with small probes and reconnaissance patrols of NVA infantry which had sneaked across the Cam Lo-Cua Viet River. It was a time of prepositioning and replenishment.

Advisors in the TOC bunker still anguished over just how close the North Vietnamese had almost come to crossing the river. Had their main attack broken through the 3d Marine Battalion and the NVA armored column exploited their tank's mobility and psychological shock effect upon the frenzied mob of deserting ARVN soldiers and civilians, the human tragedy would have been even more devastating. The ARVN's flickering will to fight on might have been snuffed out, the battle, and war lost then.

Colonel Dinh was also devastated by what might have happened. Sometime during the night he directed his logistics officer to locate as many anti-tank mines as he could find and deliver them to the Ai Tu combat base. He viewed the location of his two infantry battalions in the rolling hills directly west to be excellent tank country and the most likely area for an enemy armor threat. His 6th Battalion was positioned around both the Ai Tu and Quang Tri Combat bases. The 1st VNMC Battalion was located on FB Pedro. Since Brigade 147's evacuation from Mai Loc, FB Pedro would have to become the new defensive line directly west of Ai Tu.

During the first days of the offensive FB Pedro had received only occasional 122MM rocket fire and on 1 April NVA infantry began to probe for the locations of the 1st Battalion's four Marine infantry companies. On 2 April, Pedro received its first artillery attack from the 130MM guns. Because the fire base had almost no overhead cover, Major Wong, the battalion commander, made the decision to move his unit off Pedro, leaving only a minimum force behind to protect the fire base's perimeter. Maj. Bob Cockell, Marine senior battalion advisor, positioned himself with Wong in the Alpha command group as Capt. Larry Livingston, USMC, joined the executive officer and the Bravo group. The 1st Battalion deployed in the hills surrounding and overlooking Pedro and they prepared for battle. Located only seven miles from National Highway 1, their mission was to hold Pedro, and block off Route 557 to prevent the NVA from encircling the remnants of the 3d ARVN Division still holding along the Cam Lo-Cua Viet River.

Other Marine units also completed their moves around Ai Tu. Shortly after dawn, Brigade 147's lead elements had resumed their withdrawal from Mai Loc. At about 0800, Colonel Bao's main column reached Highway 1, just south of the old Dong Ha combat base.

Brigade 147's rearguard, the 7th VNMC Battalion column with the wounded and stragglers, had also begun moving around 0500. Their withdrawal went very slowly. At 0700 a light observation aircraft flew over. Maj. Andy DeBona was able to make radio contact with the American pilot who assisted in fixing the 7th Battalion's position and relayed their location back to the G-3 advisors in the Ai Tu TOC.

Around 1030 the battalion came across a woodcutter's trail and the column's movement picked up. Just before the 7th Battalion reached National Highway 1, the lead elements came under a mortar attack. It was later discovered that an ARVN unit, with an American advisor, thought they were a North Vietnamese unit. Major DeBona later recorded:

> After some screaming, hollering and doing all sorts of obnoxious things, I managed to contact the American advisor only 300 yards away, who apologized. Thank God there were no casualties![1]

It would be afternoon before the two COVANs from the 7th Marine Battalion reached Highway 1. Once the wounded were taken care of they located a jeep and drove into the Ai Tu combat base now heavily pockmarked from enemy artillery fire. Ten years later Major DeBona recalled:

> It is difficult to express emotions in words, difficult to express fear, hopes. One thing was for sure, it was good to be alive![2]

They remained in the bunker for several hours. Andy DeBona had arrived without any trousers; they had literally been ripped off during the previous night's four river crossings. John Theisen came forth with another pair while DeBona and Rice were given some "C" rations—their first food in two days. Fortified, they located a jeep and headed north on Highway 1 to rejoin their counterparts. Despite NVA artillery fire around their jeep, they rejoined the Marines of the 7th Battalion.

All Vietnamese Marine units were now accounted for. Hundreds of Marines had become casualties, and several battalions were nearing total exhaustion. The four battalions of Brigade 147 had finally completed their withdrawal and their will to fight the enemy remained strong. With rest and food they would recover to fight again.

It was now time to go to Saigon. In a room adjoining the G-3 watch officer area there was a tactical map of Quang Tri Province neatly framed on the wall. Maps were scarce, but this particular map was not needed now, so I took my K-Bar and cut it out. The 3d ARVN Division's twelve major fire bases had already been highlighted. With a red grease pencil Jon and I crossed out the ten fire bases that had fallen to the NVA. Jon had made arrangements for a jeep and a Vietnamese Marine driver to take me south to Phu Bai, the airfield near Hue. Colonel Dinh shook my hand as I left the G-3 watch area and my besieged brothers.

Outside the bunker we looked at the near total destruction of the Ai Tu complex. The ARVN fuel dump was still burning, belching heavy black smoke skyward. Only a few of the hundred or so Ely huts had survived the enemy's 130MM artillery attacks. The advisors' sensor bunker had received several direct hits, the north side had collapsed. The interior walls were partially burned.

An assortment of military vehicles was moving through the Ai Tu compound. Mostly ARVN trucks, they appeared to be hastily loaded with equipment and personnel from the remaining segments of the 3d Division's headquarters. Again, there was little order in the scramble for a place to ride on the trip back to Quang Tri City.

A truck convoy filled with about 100 men stopped near the

bunker. An ARVN captain had dismounted and was inquiring about the location of Brigade 258's CP.

Out of curiosity we stood and watched as the captain spoke with a Marine officer. We learned he was from an engineer battalion and had arrived with anti-tank mines and a company of men to build a minefield Colonel Dinh had requested.

A VNMC jeep was waiting. Jon had assigned a Marine who frequently drove for the advisors. There was nothing more to be said. He waited as I threw my rucksack in behind the front seat and settled in beside the driver. I cradled my M-16 across my lap, wished Jon well, then tapped the driver on the shoulder as a signal for him to begin our drive down Highway 1. My position of authority at the 3d ARVN Division's forward CP automatically passed to Maj. Jon Easley.

Refugees, thousands of terrified civilians, were everywhere. It was difficult not to become emotionally overwhelmed by their plight. Our jeep moved slowly, carefully weaving around small groups which clung together, probably families or village neighbors.

There was a short delay crossing over the highway bridge spanning the Thach Han River into the west side of Quang Tri City. Thousands of Vietnamese and wandering unarmed ARVN soldiers filled the narrow dirt streets. The ambulances carrying wounded were also halted by the disorganized milling of nearly hysterical people.

After an hour of creeping through the streets the driver cleared the south side of the city and was able to pick up speed on the National Highway 1 to Hue. An unending flow of confused refugees filled the raised shoulders along the flat black-topped roadway.

As we moved along I remembered Bernard Fall's classic book about the first Indo-China War. The coastal highway where our jeep and these pathetic refugees were now moving down had been nicknamed the "Street Without Joy" because of the repeated ambushes of French convoys.[3] It seemed to me history was again repeating itself. The scenario was the same; only the participants were different. I wondered what the final outcome of this battle would be.

Hue City was also filled with refugees. Every conceivable

type of civilian bus, truck, ox carts and ARVN trucks filled with families was moving into or parked alongside of the city's streets. It appeared that thirty to forty thousand disillusioned civilians had arrived, all seeking assistance, food and shelter. Finding nothing, they squatted alongside the streets. South of Hue City there were thousands more refugees along the highway moving toward Danang forty miles away.

As our jeep neared the village of Phu Bai we watched several C-130 aircraft descending toward the single black runway on which I had landed only a week earlier. The high whine of the turbo-prop aircraft engines was clearly distinguishable as the driver turned his jeep off Highway 1 and drove down a potholed road toward the airfield's control tower and loading area.

I was astonished at the difference in the field's appearance from when I had arrived. Where before it seemed isolated and abandoned, now it was alive with aircraft and troop movement. At least eight olive-drab C-130s were landing, taxiing or unloading troops. Aircraft carrying troops never stopped moving. The rear ramps were lowered and embarked troops carrying their rucksacks and weapons stepped off as the aircraft regurgitating its load ebbed forward. Once the last passenger cleared, the aircraft's engines shrieked a new pitch, ramp doors were closed and the pilot steered his aircraft toward the black runway for a take off. They lost no time in leaving.

The hundreds of dark green and black tiger-striped uniforms told me that Brigade 369 of the Vietnamese Marines was arriving. It appeared that Bob Sheridan was correct in his prophecy that reinforcements would soon be on the way to Quang Tri Province. I was later to learn that over 4,000 Marines and ARVN soldiers landed at Phu Bai the next day.

In this scene there was no time to waste. Swinging my rucksack over one shoulder and carrying my rifle, I bade goodbye to my driver, walked out toward the troop unloading area, stuck out my thumb at the first passing C-130 and motioned to the cockpit that I wanted a ride. The co-pilot responded with a friendly wave signaling me to get on board. The rear ramp had not been raised so I ran behind the aircraft and leaped on.

In my anticipation of the impending meeting with General Abrams my mind searched over the hundreds of events that had happened since the beginning of the invasion. Where did I err? What had been reported to Saigon that I didn't know about? What particular incident or event was of such alarming proportions that the commander of all U.S. forces in Vietnam bypassed one of his subordinate commanders to order a lieutenant colonel out of the battle zone? Worry gnawed at me.

Over the past several desperate days, Major General Kroesen had visited the Ai Tu TOC every day. He and General Lam had been in the TOC bunker early on Easter Sunday morning. Both generals made favorable comments as to the fine supporting efforts that the U.S. advisors were providing their counterparts. Obviously, General Kroesen was aware of my recall, yet why hadn't he said something about this to me? Since he had directed that I be placed in charge, why hadn't he arranged to relieve me with one of his own officers? Why had I been singled out to report back to Saigon? It all defied logic.

The whine of the C-130's four engines and the warm air circulating through the aircraft heaters into the otherwise empty cargo compartment caused me to doze. It was an uneasy sleep.

Some thirty minutes flight time before arriving at Tan Son Nhut airfield, the C-130 pilot radioed my initials ahead, requesting that they be forwarded to the Marine advisory unit headquarters, which was the customary way for the MAU to have a jeep waiting when the aircraft landed.

A different kind of personal dilemma was about to begin for me. Immediately after the aircraft landed, Ha Si Chow appeared beside the runway and drove me over to the MACV compound. Once there, my first action was to call the MAU headquarters some ten miles away in downtown Saigon. Over the telephone, Warrant Officer Francis told me that Colonel Dorsey was back from the Philippines. After reporting to General Abrams, he and Abrams had tried to develop some understanding as to why Lieutenant Colonel Turley appeared at these critical times to be in charge in Quang Tri Province sending frequent situational reports through Navy channels and finally requesting the landing of U.S. Marines from the amphibious ships offshore. Gunner* Francis also related how the five or six "operational immediate" messages (which had emanated from the naval gunfire ships offshore) portrayed a desperate situation while the ARVN command channels in Danang were reporting only "minor enemy activity," thus creating all the more confusion as to the true state of affairs. In view of all this, Dorsey had been directed to find out two things: What did Turley actually say? Why didn't he go through normal command channels?[4]

Warrant Officer Francis also related that Brigade 369 was deploying to MR-1, as General Khang alerted his Marine Corps headquarters for movement to Quang Tri Province. Before we finished our telephone call, I gave Francis a status report on all our Marine advisors, namely, that while several had been wounded all were safe. It indeed seemed miraculous to me that no one else had been killed or captured.

That call completed, my next stop was to locate Marine Lt. Col. Pete Hilgartner who was assigned to MACV's J-3 operations section. Until I entered his office, I had not thought about my pathetically grubby appearance. However, it was apparent the filthy, torn uniform and six-day growth of whiskers had startled him. Pete and I had been rifle company commanders together in 1959, which kindled a long friendship. However, recovering from the shock of my appearance, Pete, ever the professional, initially challenged me for writing and sending a series of messages through Navy channels, messages for which General Abrams was personally embarrassed. By sending them through the Navy ships offshore I had jumped his MACV chain of command. I denied doing this, whereupon Pete reached into a stack of papers on his desk and handed me three of the "flash" priority naval messages.

Looking through messages which I now saw for the first time, and staggered by their impact, I groped mentally for a simple way to describe the bizarre set of circumstances which had occurred to convert my "observer" status into that of the role of chief advisor, 3d ARVN Division (Forward). Pete lis-

---

*Marine Corps warrant officers are called gunners.

tened, but obviously remained skeptical, since the events were so far out of the ordinary as to be accepted without some reservation. As I relived and retold the chain of events, a week's pent-up emotions began to unravel. Pete still remained doubtful and said, "General Abrams definitely wants to see you. First, however, you are to report to Admiral Salzer at NAVFORV headquarters. You are to go straight over. Don't stop to get cleaned up; he wants to see you right now."

During the jeep ride into Saigon and to NAVFORV I reviewed the naval messages Pete had given me. Two of them were basically combat situational reports, while the third was an amazing document, setting forth a request as follows:

> Lt. Col. Turley, USMC, Quang Tri reports situation critical and requests immediate USMC assistance to reinforce, fight and hold position. Situation passed via SPOT (NGF net) as follows: position is being heavily shelled. NVA and ARVN tanks engaged at Quang Tri airfield. Request immediate landing BLT southern end Quang Tri airfield. Will have USMC personnel in area with smoke. This is urgent repeat urgent.[5]

Although I had not sent this message, my mind nevertheless flashed back to those hectic moments when the gunline commander's radio inquiries had begged for answers. "God, I can't believe it, but now it's easy to see why General Abrams and Admiral Salzer 'wished' to see me." I again studied what later came to be called the "land the landing force" message, and saw that it was an erroneous report because with the destruction of the Dong Ha Bridge all NVA armor had been halted north of the Cam Lo-Cua Viet River and there had never been enemy tanks at the Quang Tri airfield.

Driving into the NAVFORV compound, Ha Si Chow neared the main entrance. Filled with apprehension about what was about to happen, I lifted out my rucksack and rifle and entered the stately old French colonial mansion.

Looking up from behind his chief of staff's desk as I entered his office, Captain Paddock indicated that Colonel Hilgartner had called to say I had arrived in Saigon and was on my way.

"Just put your weapon and gear down there beside the chair.

The admiral wants to see you," he said curtly. It was apparent that he purposely left me standing and alone, as he wrote something on a memo pad and disappeared into Admiral Salzer's office. Several moments later he reappeared to say "The admiral will see you now," and motioned me toward the door.

It seemed to be a long walk to a position "front and center," in front of the admiral's desk. He stood up as I stopped and seemed as tense as I was. For a long moment he looked me over very carefully, then began by first holding up a similar stack of naval messages, and facetiously asking "Have you been writing any messages lately, Colonel?"

My earlier encounter with Pete and his continued skepticism despite my explanation alerted me to choose my words carefully, very carefully. My answer, simple and direct, was, "No, sir, I have not written or released any messages." He gave me a puzzled look. He looked so impeccable in his all-white uniform, and I felt even dirtier in my disheveled utilities than before. This was obviously a bad situation in which to find myself but I remained at attention until he placed me at ease.

I requested permission to explain the combat situation and the background of my actions while in Quang Tri Province. He sat down as I reached in my trouser leg pocket and brought out the tactical map cut off the wall of the TOC bunker just prior to my departure. I moved closer, around to the left side of his desk, and tried to hold up my map to point out location, positions and somehow relate to him the first five days of the NVA invasion. This was an awkward arrangement so I finally stretched out the crumpled map on the polished tile floor. I relived the situation as I explained the surprise invasion, the loss of the ARVN fire bases, the fact that naval gunfire from the U.S. ships offshore was the only reliable supporting arm, the death of Lieutenant Bruggeman, the appearance of NVA armor, the destruction of Dong Ha Bridge, my gradual involvement in the operations of the TOC at the 3d Division, Colonel Murdock's order that I take over, and General Bowen's blanket authority given to me to designate ARCLIGHT targets. On my hands and knees, stretched out over the map, I pointed out the red x's representing the lost fire bases. Listening intently, Admiral Salzer moved his chair, leaned forward until he was almost on top of me, yet showed no expression.

Although I tried my best to remain calm and professionally cool, the emotions held in check over the past week burst from me. I found myself cursing, speaking too fast and too loud as I described what had occurred, and in so doing I suddenly came to the full realization that I, Gerry Turley, really didn't matter. Time and fate had made me just another casualty of the war. The deteriorating situation in Quang Tri Province had to be fully understood by the senior U.S. commanders before the NVA broke through the remaining ARVN defenses and attacked Hue City. Admiral Salzer needed to know not only the desperate nature of the situation but also how a few Americans—Army, Navy, Air Force and Marines—had together contributed to stopping the massive invasion by the NVA across the DMZ.

Obviously shocked, the admiral expressed surprise upon learning how much of Quang Tri Province had already fallen. Recounting the particular events leading up to the colonel's emergency order for me to take charge, I stood up and pulled from my pocket the scrap of yellow tablet paper upon which I had written Colonel Murdock's social security number and also the time of Brigadier General Bowen's telephone call giving me the unprecedented authority to designate any target for destruction by B-52s.

"Repeat that again," he said. "What did the Army colonel order you to do?"

Again I repeated the unique order and the circumstances under which I had been placed in charge of the 3d Division's forward command post. Sitting back in his swivel chair, the admiral was silent.

Suddenly, another attack of diarrhea struck me and hurriedly explaining this to the admiral, I ran for the nearest head. When I returned, Captain Paddock stopped me, and asked that I wait in his office until the admiral called.

Feeling weak, lightheaded, physically drained and mentally spent, I stood in the outer office uncertain as to whether the admiral believed me. I was almost too exhausted to care. Captain Paddock, perhaps sensing my condition, invited me to sit down and have some coffee as I waited. As I sat in his office it felt too warm, and the warmth seemed to heighten the stench of my filthy clothes.

I had time to reflect on my present situation and surroundings compared with where I had been less than twenty-four hours earlier. Seated in immaculate surroundings with naval officers in crisp, white uniforms, totally removed from the shock of raw and continuous combat, it seemed like another world. It was no wonder my emotions were snapping. I could not imagine how these officers in this pristine Saigon setting could ever comprehend the violence, the desperation, the pathos—and, more importantly—the tremendous horror those fighting in the north were experiencing.

The questions I had been asked more than anything else revealed the lack of understanding by almost everyone in Saigon as to what was happening 300 miles away. It was as if I had been sent to Saigon from the moon. My personal appearance alone was evidence that something had gone wrong which no one wanted to accept. The war was supposed to be over! I represented a visible contradiction to the Vietnamization program. American servicemen were once again directly involved in the war against the North Vietnamese. Several had been killed, others still trapped. A time of crisis was at hand.

When the call came to return to Admiral Salzer's office I discovered two other admirals had joined us. My map with its ragged edges had been moved to a coffee table fronted by three large brown leather chairs. He introduced me to Rear Admirals J. B. Wilson and A. W. Price, Jr., and asked that I brief them on the situation in MR-1. Salzer nodded as I spoke and asked several more questions as I pointed out the location of U.S. destroyers, Dong Ha Bridge and ARVN fire bases on the map. The three senior naval officers were all very interested in my appraisal of the effect of naval gunfire support which I described to them. When I reached the part about asking for and getting the social security number of Colonel Murdock as I received his order to take over I could see that their reserved attitude toward me was visibly changing to one of tacit understanding. Relating the tragic series of events which had happened below the DMZ in the early days of the offensive, I sat in a chair a steward had placed beside me. My story had now been told and I could only hope they believed me. Although I had no perception of what the eventual outcome would be, I felt relieved and tired. I obviously smelled to high heaven, which was personally embarrassing. I longed for this session to end and the opportunity for a hot shower and a long sleep.

The admirals posed a few more questions and expressed astonishment that an Army colonel had placed a Marine junior in rank in charge under such desperate circumstances. Finally, Salzer said: "You'll need to see General Abrams right away. Brig. Gen. John Lanigan is the senior U.S. Marine in Vietnam. He is on the MACV, J-3 staff. We'll meet with him first, then arrange to see General Abrams."

I stood up at attention and automatically responded with as firm an "Aye, aye, sir," as I could muster and then requested permission to get a fast shower and change my clothes before our meeting with General Abrams.

"No, Turley," he said, "I want you to go the way you are. I'll meet you at General Lanigan's office in thirty minutes."

Ha Si Chow was waiting outside and drove me back out to the MACV compound located adjacent to the Tan Son Nhut Airport. I waited as the admiral and General Lanigan first talked privately then motioned me in. As I entered the general's office I was surprised to find four or five Navy and Marine officers there. Among them, Pete Hilgartner's six-feet, six-inch frame stood out among the onlookers. Throughout my briefing only Salzer and Lanigan spoke; the others listened. Again, the events of five days came forth, followed by more questions to clarify the specific situations.

In the middle of my briefing, my diarrhea again returned, necessitating another embarrassing dash for the nearest head. When I returned, the admiral and general led the way down a long passageway to Deputy Commander Gen. Fred Weyand's office. The door adjoining his office to that of General Abrams was partially open but he did not appear. Feeling almost like a puppet on a string I once again told the events which had taken place along the DMZ, while pointing out locations on my tactical map. Spread around the room were six or eight other Army generals and one or two full colonels.

When I reached the circumstances under which Colonel Murdock had placed me in charge, I brought out the crumpled piece of paper, reading the exact time of his telephone call and also the time of Brigadier General Bowen's "carte blanche" authority to designate B-52 ARCLIGHT strikes. When an Army lieutenant colonel on the general's staff requested that I hand over the scrap of paper, I refused. He explained that he merely wanted to reproduce a copy of it but I shook my head no. The room suddenly became quiet. Admiral Salzer took the lead and indicated it would be all right to hand it over. However, I felt it was the only proof to substantiate my claim of being placed in command and, once again, I hesitated. How else could I have obtained the colonel's number, I thought. Another Marine officer stepped forward and said "I'll take it, Gerry. I'll make him a copy and bring the paper back to you."

I agreed to this because, although I felt that at this moment I couldn't trust just anyone, I would trust Pete. Pete and the colonel left together and when they returned he handed the scrap of paper back to me and I placed it back in my pocket.

When the inevitable barrage of questions ended, General Weyand, Admiral Salzer, and the other five or six Army generals indicated that they wished to talk privately, so I stepped into the aide's office. Before I left, General Weyand acknowledged, "Until this moment I was not aware that the commanding general FRAC, the team commander, had placed Lieutenant Colonel Turley in any U.S. Army advisory command position."

Several moments later I was called into General Weyand's inner office and asked once again to point out where the 3d ARVN Division's front lines had been when I left the Ai Tu bunker. His last question surprised me: "Colonel Turley, what do you want to do now?" I was still so emotionally wrapped up in the war I responded even before I had thought through the question, "Sir, they need me back up north."

For a moment none of the generals spoke. Finally, General Lanigan looked at me and said, "I have an Air Force T-39 scheduled to depart for Danang at 1800. If you can get your things together in time you can fly north with me. We'll drive over to FRAC headquarters together and you can catch a helicopter on to Quang Tri from there."

General Lanigan's comments ended the meeting at MACV headquarters. Admiral Salzer shook my hand, reminding me, "Be careful up there, Turley." I nodded to General Weyand. I felt he had been kind and fair with me. His questions were sharp and relevant to the critical situation in MR-1.

There was only an hour and a half before flight time. Once back in my jeep, Ha Si Chow drove almost recklessly back to my hotel. There was only time to shower and shave. God, it felt great! I was rejuvenated, ready to go again.

My personal time of challenge had passed. However, an interesting dilemma continued to stir around me. Unknown to me at that time, there was a series of meetings between general officers and admirals on "the Turley situation." A number of messages were sent between Military Assistance Command Vietnam (MACV); Naval Forces, Vietnam; and the Commander, U.S. Pacific Fleet, which reviewed my individual actions.

Even the Assistant Commandant of the U.S. Marine Corps became involved and subsequently fully supported my actions during these early days. That I was in hot water was obvious. I knew it and indeed saw it on the faces of those in the Quang Tri TOC bunker when I subsequently visited there again. By their looks I could feel not just surprise, but a certain fear, perhaps, that I was still around and could bear witness to the events of the past month. I had been in the pivotal position throughout this entire tumultuous period. I was the one person who could accurately and unimpeachably state which units, and which individuals, had done what from the very beginning of the offensive. I knew the units, the participants, the helpers, the non-helpers, those who came to fight, those who disappeared when their help was needed and, most importantly, those who had no choice in the matter yet remained with their units during an overwhelming enemy onslaught.

To leap ahead for a moment in my personal story, I had this latter fact brought home to me vividly and emotionally on a September morning many months later. We were visited in the field by a few generals during the battle to retake Quang Tri City. They were given a thorough briefing on the actions to date in this violent battle. Following the briefing, the generals were introduced to the assembled staff. Maj. Gen. Joe Fegan, a Marine and the Commanding General of the 3d Marine Division on Okinawa, asked General Lan, the new Vietnamese Marine commandant, "Where is Lieutenant Colonel Turley," in his Texas drawl. Suddenly all eyes focused on me standing in the back of the assembled group. The tall, highly respected Marine moved toward me. Still operating somewhat under a cloud of apprehension and despair because of the so-called "Turley affair," I could not help wondering if the moment had come when my superiors had finally decided what to do with me. I could only hope that I had brought no embarrassment to the Marine Corps, the Vietnamese Marines or certainly to my fellow COVANs who had been fighting so long and hard. I stood motionless, looking in the general's eyes as he arrived in front of me. As a Marine I knew no matter what he said to me there would be no questions, no pleas and no need for explanation. If the general told me to get on his plane and fly back with him to Okinawa in disgrace, my only choice would be to do so, and silently. However, this was not to be. Instead, "Big Joe" Fegan, as he was less formally called, stuck out his hand and said, "Turley, you're the one person I came here to meet. The whole Marine Corps is proud of you. It's an honor for me to finally shake your hand."

I was dumbfounded and reduced to tears. In the many months that passed after the beginning of the Easter invasion, Major General Fegan was the first senior official to openly express strong support for the actions I took during those early days when I had to act alone.* He made a few more polite comments and then hugged me as a brother in arms. It was too much. I wept openly and never felt more proud—before or since.

Maj. Gen. Joe Fegan will never realize what his simple,

---

*In total contrast to this encounter, when U.S. Commandant General Cushman visited Hue City during June 1972, he purposely avoided speaking or shaking hands with the author. It was a singular affront witnessed by the other Marine advisors in the formation.

brotherly act did for an insignificant Marine who was uncertain and weary after six months of nearly continuous battle. Several days later I was to receive both U.S. and Vietnamese decorations but the approving hug of this particular general will always mean the most to me.

My return to the forward battle area again placed me in an entirely new role. Where before I had been directed to assume the emergency position of responsibility within the U.S. Army's advisory chain of command, Colonel Dorsey's presence at Ai Tu dictated that I revert back to my normally assigned billet as his deputy, the Assistant Senior Advisor, Vietnamese Marine Corps. It was from this position that I continued to observe the defense of Quang Tri Province conducted by the South Vietnamese forces during the remaining days of the offensive.

Upon arriving at the Ai Tu TOC, my first priority was to locate Dorsey and brief him on the unexpected series of meetings in Saigon and later at General Abrams' MACV headquarters. Dorsey's characteristically stoic expression showed just a trace of surprise at my fast return from Saigon. He and I moved to an unoccupied room where, undisturbed, I related how the noon meeting with Admiral Salzer had expanded to include NAVFORV's two other admirals and that it was with the admirals that I first learned the numerous naval messages emanating from the U.S. destroyers offshore had been the cause of my hurried recall to Saigon. Once I assured Admiral Salzer I had never written or released any of the radio messages that caused the concern, and that an Army general had placed me in complete charge at the forward command post, the admirals appeared more relaxed and spoke favorably on how well the Marine advisors had performed under such difficult combat conditions. As Dorsey had expected, the admirals were immensely interested in the effectiveness of naval gunfire.

Sitting quietly, he listened to my account of the meeting with General Weyand and his MACV staff officers in which questions focused heavily on the actions of the U.S. Army's Advisory Team 155. He found a cigarette and lit up as I related to him that at no time were any of my tactical decisions questioned. I concluded my briefing by saying that "Admiral Salzer has requested that I prepare a statement on my role in combat situation for the period 30 March through 3 April 1972, which, of course, I shall first submit to the colonel for his review." He nodded in agreement as smoke billowed around his head.

At that point Jon Easley entered the room to provide Dorsey with an update on the 1st Battalion's actions on FB Pedro where the NVA were steadily building up pressure on the western flank. Several more Marines had been seriously wounded by incoming artillery fire.

With Dorsey's encouragement, Jon began to brief me on the activities of the NVA since my departure. He began by saying that Advisory Team 155 continued to move its personnel and communications equipment out of the TOC bunker to reestablish its operations center beside the 3d ARVN Division headquarters in the Citadel. With this movement, about all that remained in the Ai Tu bunker were the headquarters personnel of Brigade 258, several officers from the Vietnamese Marine Division headquarters and the U.S. Marine advisors. Both Majors Neary and Brookbank and their Army and Air Force personnel had already been moved back to Quang Tri City.

The defense line of the 3d ARVN Division along the south bank of the Cam Lo-Cua Viet River continued to be under steady enemy pressure but was holding. Enemy activity had decreased on the morning after the destruction of the Dong Ha bridges. Although contacts were reported all along the front from Dong Ha to Cam Lo, no large-scale attempts were being made by the NVA to overrun any ARVN positions. However, incoming artillery attacks by the NVA continued at a heavy rate.

Jon looked exhausted as he pointed to different locations on a map. His stubby beard showed a touch of grey. He and Colonel Dinh had had little sleep in the past seven days. When he pointed toward Dong Ha he mentioned that the 3d Battalion had captured a number of enemy prisoners, one of whom was a T-54 tank crewman, from the NVA's 203d Tank Regiment, who on initial interrogation reported:

We were totally unprepared for losing the Dong Ha Bridge. We were not prepared to be halted in Dong Ha. Dong Ha would be no problem. The shock-action of our tanks was to have panicked the ARVN soldiers and civilians and the rapid speed of our attack would insure the capture of Quang Tri City in seven days.[6]

At this, Jon's weary eyes seemed to sparkle as he began to tell about the many reinforcing units that were being flown into Phu Bai. It was obvious that the "good news" in the 3d Division was that ARVN reinforcements had finally begun to arrive, with Marine Brigade 369 being the first unit to be flown into Phu Bai, followed shortly thereafter by three ARVN ranger groups.

With its one artillery and three infantry battalions, Brigade 369 was positioned south of Quang Tri City on FSB Nancy. The Marine commandant, General Khang, had also arrived on 3 April, but for some unexplained reason he was not placed in command of his three Marine brigades. However, General Khang moved his field headquarters into Hue and awaited orders from General Lam concerning his participation in the coming battles.

Completing its withdrawal from Mai Loc, Brigade 147 had been transported south to Hue City to rest and replenish the remnants of the 4th and 8th Battalions. All the U.S. Marine advisors to the brigade had also moved down to Hue.

Weather conditions continued to hamper flight operations, as the U.S. Air Force still attempted to rescue the downed American flyer north of Cam Lo. The "no fire circle" placed around him was still in effect, but it had been reduced to approximately 4,000 meters. The Cam Lo Bridge remained in the Air Force "no fire zone" and could not be destroyed.

On the western flank, enemy troops were reported moving through FSB Mai Loc toward FB Pedro. Enemy pressure was beginning to build up around this fire support base from the west and southwest.

Jon went on to describe how the brigade's 1st Battalion around Pedro had already been probed on three sides. The only road from Ai Tu, which extended some six miles out to FB Pedro, had been under attack by artillery and mortar fire. Around noon on 3 April, Bob Cockell reported that the ARVN engineer company had arrived at the 1st Battalion's CP with over 500 anti-tank mines.[7] A Marine infantry company provided security as the engineers dug holes and buried the mines, creating an elongated minefield along both sides of the old colonial road leading from the Ba Long Valley into Quang Tri City. This defensive barrier was some 800 meters wide then camouflaged to blend in with the low green scrub brush. Both Cockell and his assistant advisor, Capt. Larry Livingston, reported that the Vietnamese engineers had done a good job installing the minefield.

The overview presented by Easley on the dispositions of the 3d Division's units and its newly assigned reinforcements was excellent. He concluded his briefing by indicating that although Colonel Murdock had not formally notified him he was no longer in charge of the advisory team's forward TOC, almost all the ARVN's fire support coordination activity had, in fact, taken place back in the Citadel.

With the massive collapse of ARVN defenses, the South Vietnamese JGS located in Saigon had finally directed that actions be taken to strengthen MR-1's defenses. By 5 April the 3d ARVN Division found itself in command of its two remaining infantry regiments, two brigades of Vietnamese Marines, four ranger groups, one armored brigade, and the territorial forces in Quang Tri Province. Although General Giai's 3d ARVN Division had, by these additions, more than doubled in size, neither the ranger commander nor the Marine commandant, who had been sent to MR-1 by the JGS to assist General Lam, were utilized or given a mission.[8] Two days had passed while both tactical commanders and their staffs waited for a combat mission.

It was at this juncture that the American advisors became aware of a long-festering bitterness which existed between General Lam and General Khang stemming from an incident in February 1971. South Vietnamese forces had conducted Operation Lam Son 719, which was South Vietnam's largest military operation to date and was designed to disrupt the flow of supplies by the North Vietnamese down the Ho Chi Minh Trail. As part of this, a multi-division ground attack was launched from Khe Sanh in Quang Tri Province, across the Laotian border, with substantial fire power support being provided by U.S. forces. However, American advisors were, for political reasons, precluded from deploying with ARVN units fighting in Laos.

The operation achieved only limited success, with both forces declaring victories in the two-month campaign, although combat losses were heavy on both sides. During the latter phase of the operation, General Lam, the senior Vietnamese commander, directed General Khang's Marine division to undertake an attack beyond the range of his artillery. The Marine commandant felt it was a poorly devised plan, hesitated, and then failed to comply with the order to attack. Events would later substantiate that Khang's apprehensions were correct, for the NVA had laid a clever trap and were well entrenched to defend the area. His Marine division came out of the operation bloodied but basically unscathed.

To Lam, however, it was an unforgivable incident and one of great personal embarrassment, thus becoming an event he would remember. Now, with Khang again in MR-1 seeking to command his Marines, Lam chose to ignore the commandant's presence. It was a face-saving situation so, instead of taking advantage of the obviously capable staff with Khang, Lam chose to leave the heavily burdened 3d ARVN Division in control of the Marine brigades, rangers, and other reinforcing units.

General Lam was now under heavy pressure from President Thieu and the JGS to halt the massive enemy invasion. While the ARVN defense lines had held, and with more reinforcements arriving in MR-1, he gave serious consideration to a counterattack which would be launched as soon as tactical air could apply its full combat power to support his ground forces.[9] Around 7 April the weather showed signs of improvement.

However, his preoccupation with plans for a counterattack diverted his staff in MR-1 from fully stabilizing the battlefield and organizing a new defense in depth. Lam apparently perceived he could recover his damaged self-esteem by launching a counteroffensive to retake the lost territory below the DMZ.

In sharp contrast to an effort to take offensive action, General Giai sought control of the arriving fresh units in order to consolidate the hastily established defense of Quang Tri Province. Initially, Lam refused Giai's request for the ranger groups. They would be held under Lam's control for the counteroffensive. The MR-1 commander had seldom visited the forward Quang Tri battle areas and seemed oblivious to Giai's defense problems. Lam's mood was optimistic. He repeatedly expressed to his Danang-based staff his conviction that enough forces were now in the Quang Tri area to first halt and then expel the communists.

General Giai was insistent in his request for reinforcements and finally Lam acceded by reluctantly sending him one ranger group, then another. Eventually the four ranger groups, with their twelve battalions deployed in northern MR-1, were attached to the 3d Division. These attachments were to be under the full operational control of General Giai.

With the 3d Division fast increasing in size, its span of control over its units became increasingly more difficult, as Giai now controlled over twenty-four battalions of infantry or rangers and eighteen battalions of artillery. As more combat units arrived, the 3d Division never received additional support in the logistics and signal communication units so essential for the effective exercise of command and control. Logistical support became all the more cumbersome as each major command had to sustain itself, the rangers, Marines, armored and cavalry units all having separate supply systems.[10]

Giai and his division staff recognized their deteriorating ability to control such an uncommonly large force and recommended to General Lam that the control burden be reduced. However, for reasons known only to Lam, these recommendations were never acted upon. The impasse that existed was thus allowed to remain and, as a result, the ranger commander and his staff were left to their own devices in Danang while the Marine commandant sat idly in Hue City. Despite this idleness, both generals discreetly monitored the dispositions of their forces, covertly approving every move their units were tasked to accomplish.

As time passed, the indecision that persisted reflected the split in plans within the command as the 3d ARVN Division pressed for developing a defense-in-depth while General Lam chose to plan a counteroffensive.

North of the Cam Lo-Cua Viet River the NVA continued to reposition and strengthen its forces to achieve the Nguyen Hue Offensive's initial objective, the capture of Quang Tri City. On 6 April elements of the ARVN 20th Tank Battalion and the 3d Marine Battalion positioned along the Cam Lo-Cua Viet River underwent another heavy artillery attack. At 1315 Major Smock, and his assistant advisor Captain Harmon were wounded by shrapnel and evacuated.* Both would be severely missed during the immediate days to follow.

Whenever the monsoon overcast broke, U.S. and VNAF airborne observers flew above the ARVN defense lines reporting NVA enemy infantry, tank columns and large caliber artillery pieces crossing over the Cam Lo Bridge. The enemy's principal routes of movement from Cam Lo were south toward Mai Loc and eastward on Route 9 toward Dong Ha.

Having completed their push to move through the Ba Long Valley on the south side of the Thach Han River, NVA units from observation posts in the Annamite mountains began to place accurate artillery fire on FB Anne. Small numbers of infiltration teams moved eastward into the flat piedmont toward the vital artery known as Highway 1. NVA troops would be within rifle fire range of the "Street Without Joy" by dawn on 7 April.

At 1600 FSB Anne, located four miles south west of Quang Tri City, was evacuated. Inexplicably, under the pressure of heavy artillery fire four 105MM howitzers were left behind.

All ARVN and U.S. intelligence sources indicated the NVA's next battle initiative was about to be unleashed. SAM missiles were taking a daily toll of U.S. aircraft. Antiaircraft guns were emplaced close behind their infantry and armored forces.

---

*Captain Ripley evacuated Major Smock and Captain Harmon and placed them on the APC (which later was the source of a *Life* magazine picture).

# CHAPTER FIFTEEN

# THE BATTLE FOR FIRE BASE PEDRO

On 8 April Colonel Dinh ordered his 3d Battalion back to the Ai Tu Combat Base to relieve the 6th Battalion of the responsibility for the perimeter's security. The gallant defenders of Dong Ha had suffered heavy casualties and were being withdrawn for much needed replacements and rest.

Of the 700 Marines in the 3d Battalion who had entered the city of Dong Ha a week earlier, just over 200 would remain to march out from what had become a Vietnamese Alamo. Their enormous casualty rate occurred because the intensive and continuous combat had killed many outright and had left others to die of wounds as evacuation was not possible. Less seriously wounded Marines returned to the battle lines along the river where they were wounded again, or eventually killed.

Captain Ripley told a story of the unbelievable fortitude of a young Marine private who had been wounded seven times in four days:

He was the same marine I had seen two days before with a serious shrapnel wound in the upper back. Now he was hobbling along with his arm around a wounded comrade attempting to move his friend to safety. Both would be dead at day's end.[1]

In their place, a ranger battalion assumed the responsibility for security of a part of Dong Ha City and the area around the bridges. Relieved of its responsibility at Ai Tu, the 6th Battalion vacated its perimeter positions and moved the six miles southwest to relieve a ranger battalion on FB Pedro.

Colonel Dinh told Major Easley of an intelligence report he had received to the effect that on the morning of 9 April the enemy would strike from the southwest. "There will be tanks," he was told, so the colonel elected to position one of his best battalions, the 6th, as yet unbloodied during the NVA invasion, across the primary approach route into the old 3d ARVN Division.

During the afternoon of the 8th, the 6th Battalion, commanded by Major Tung, moved on foot to FB Pedro. Its route of march followed the old colonial stone road leading into the Ba Long Valley, historically an area where the people were sympathetic to the Viet Minh and Viet Cong.

Making the march alongside their counterparts were Advisors Maj. Bill Warren and Capt. Bill Wischmeyer. Both Marines had arrived in Vietnam on 21 June 1971 and had spent their entire tours with the 6th Battalion. Warren was a bantam weight professional with a fine reputation as a field advisor.

Warren's assistant, Captain Wischmeyer, a tall, sandy-haired officer from Sioux City, Iowa, was one of the MAU's most experienced advisors. He had experienced a situation almost identical to Ray Smith's when the 6th Battalion was positioned on FBs Sarge and Nui Ba Ho. In August 1971 the two outposts were attacked by North Vietnamese forces. Sarge withstood several heavy enemy assaults while Nui Ba Ho was overrun. Wischmeyer was inside a bunker when this happened. NVA soldiers were heard walking on the roof searching in the darkness for the COVAN. After several minutes they moved on, then Wischmeyer and several other members of the 6th Battalion escaped and came back to FB Sarge.

The assignment with the 6th Battalion had been an especially difficult one for the two COVANs because their counterpart repeatedly showed an open dislike for Americans. Partly as a result of this relationship the advisors gave Major Tung the nickname of "Fast Eddy." The COVANs didn't know why; it just seemed to fit him. The two advisors handled the unpleasant and difficult situation very well and as a result were able to contribute frequently to the effectiveness of the 6th Battalion's combat operations.

Major Warren had been out at FB Pedro in late 1971 when it was first being constructed. He recalled:

> Pedro was in the middle of nowhere on terrain that afforded good observation of the southwest approaches into Ai Tu and Quang Tri City. In the fall of 1971 the 6th Battalion was ordered to construct a strong-point to block any approach toward Ai Tu, which was then the 3d Division CP. A dozer was brought out to construct a berm about eight feet tall and sixty meters on each side. For the CP bunker, a large trench was dug and three CONEX boxes were buried in that trench. A covered porch was constructed, making a tunnel out of the bunker with two entrances.
>
> The troops lived and fought from a series of fighting holes and trench lines over which they would put ponchos for shelter from the rains. It was a pretty basic existence. There were no tents, no strong backs; we just lived in the dirt or mud.[2]

Major Tung moved his Alpha command group onto high ground located about one mile northeast of FB Pedro. Two infantry companies were positioned around the hilltop which provided an unobstructed view of the berms around FB Pedro. The Bravo command group, with another rifle company, located itself along Route 557 and about 1,000 meters eastward from the fire base. The remaining fourth rifle company was positioned inside the perimeter of Pedro with one of its platoons being directed to establish a blocking position about 600 meters west. The platoon, consisting of about thirty Marines, dug in on a small hilltop, deploying along both sides of Route 557, a red clay and gravel road that bisected the hilltop. This road was narrow and began its curving path some fifteen miles away at the village of Cam Lo and wound its way through the recently abandoned fire support base at Mai Loc toward Ai Tu and Quang Tri City. As they settled into their blocking position, the platoon was told to "Dig in and be on the alert for enemy tanks," since they were the westernmost defensive position of the South Vietnamese lines.

After reviewing the dispositions that Tung had made of his 6th Battalion around Pedro, Warren felt it best that he and

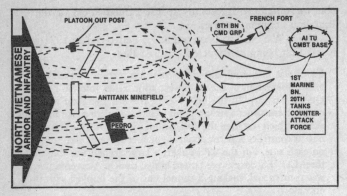

**THE TANK BATTLE AT FIRE BASE PEDRO
AND ACTIVITIES ON 9, 10, 11 APRIL**

Wischmeyer remain together in the Alpha group. The advisors placed themselves beside their counterpart and established radio contact with Major Easley at Ai Tu.

As darkness came, the 6th Battalion was still busily digging in. A heavy overcast blotted out the half moon and the night grew cold, bringing a chill that crept into the bones of the waiting Marines. With contact imminent, no fires were allowed. Major Tung's 6th Battalion was watchful and ready.

Throughout the night Pedro and the hills surrounding the fire base were repeatedly shelled by NVA artillery. The incoming fire was intense and the few bunkers inside the fire base were soon reduced to rubble. Toward dawn the battalion's four different positions began to receive fire from direct-fire weapons. Both Warren and Wischmeyer initially thought the flat trajectory fire they were receiving was from recoilless rifles, because of the very loud report and then the almost instantaneous impact which followed as the projectiles struck into the Marine positions. Bill Warren recalled:

> Come dawn it was like something right out of the movies. At dawn we heard tank engines start up. Wischmeyer and I looked at each other, our jaws fell open and we hit the ground. It was fire from tanks, not recoilless rifles, that had been firing on us.[3]

The battle for FB Pedro began at approximately 0645. The first two enemy tanks were seen moving rapidly toward Pedro from the west. Several minutes later seven more were spotted east along Route 557 approaching at about fifteen miles an hour. This was the NVA's first large armor attack against the western flank; also, it was the first time the 6th Battalion had ever confronted enemy tanks.

The platoon outpost was alerted to the approaching tank column, but was nearly helpless to protect itself since its only immediate tank killing capabilities consisted of the M-72 LAAWs carried by the infantrymen.

During the night, Colonel Dinh and Easley had developed a fire support plan for the defense of Pedro. When Major Tung and his COVANs radioed their initial reports to the brigade of the on-rushing enemy armor, Marine artillery was prepared to respond. Because of the size of the NVA attack immediate requests were also made for close air and tank support.

As the two lead tanks closed in on the platoon position, Pedro NVA infantry could be seen deployed around the other tanks. Eight to ten more enemy tanks began to close up behind the two lead tanks. The rifle company on Pedro identified the armor as "all T-54s and T-55s and closing fast."

The artillery FOs with the Alpha command group quickly called for fire on the attacking formations. Almost immediately accurate artillery fire struck and decimated the unprotected enemy infantry caught in the open. The NVA infantry, now estimated to be at least of regimental strength, was forced to break away from the tanks and take refuge and concealment in a nearby wooded area.

Approximately twenty tanks were now involved in the battle and pressed on with their attack. Their hatches had been closed as protection from the artillery. At 0715 two enemy tanks breached the wire at Pedro and began methodically to crush the hasty defensive positions and rout the 150 Marines occupying the fire base. Withdrawing under this onslaught, the Marines scattered with only their weapons and sought shelter in the rolling hills and brush. Wischmeyer later recalled:

At this point Captain Su, acting battalion executive officer, came running down the road toward our position. About 100 meters to his rear was a tank roaring after him firing its machine gun with bullets dusting off his heels. All of a sudden the tank hit a mine and came to a sudden stop. Captain Su, a reserve officer, later smiled and said, "I am very lucky."[4]

From their higher elevated position Warren and Wischmeyer observed the NVA tanks which were moving against the platoon strong point. Helplessly they watched as the T-54s first overran the outpost, then killed every Marine by gunfire or by the crushing action of their steel tracks.

Bill Warren recalled:

The day was very overcast, very low ceiling, misting, and air support seemed out of the question. But we asked for it anyway. Moments later a hole literally opened up in the overcast and several VNAF A-1 Skyraiders came right down through it. They were flying on the deck and started making bombing runs. Enemy antiaircraft guns opened up on the old propeller driven aircraft. One aircraft was shot down and the pilot killed. They were only on station about five or six minutes but they sure helped break up the enemy attack.[5]

The two tanks that were inside Pedro, however, were not stopped by the air strike and continued to move through the fire base, turning northeast along the trace of the road and proceeding toward the location of the Alpha command group. The high rate of speed of the tanks' advance initially stunned the CP group but as they approached to within 300 meters of the position the lead tank exploded into a fireball. The track on one side separated and pieces flew in all directions. It had apparently struck an anti-tank mine emplaced earlier by the 1st Battalion. Undeterred, the second tank bypassed its burning mate and continued straight on toward the CP group. Warren and Wischmeyer stayed with the Alpha group as it began to seek cover from the tanks. Wischmeyer later reported:

The lead tank was coming straight at us. There was nothing physically being done in the battalion to knock out that approaching tank. The damn thing looked about three stories wide and moving at seventy knots. It was coming very fast. I'd have to say that we were probably in a controlled state of panic, if there is such a thing.

We moved off the hill into defilade. The tank approached to within twenty meters of us, rotated his turret and main gun and machine gun straight at us, but for some reason never fired. He stayed there a few moments, then pivoted around and drove off.[6]

Other enemy tanks, unescorted by infantry moved past Pedro, continuing their attack northeast toward Ai Tu. Several more tanks struck mines and were disabled or destroyed. The Marines had begun to recover from the shock of armor and began to fire at the tanks with LAAWs. The armor attack stalled with tanks turning in different directions to escape the minefield. While the artillery did little more than keep the enemy tanks buttoned up, it was most effective in keeping the NVA infantry pinned down, unable to assist the tanks. The momentum of the battle was shifting away from the enemy tankers and back in favor of the 6th Battalion.

In the brigade TOC, Colonel Dinh and Jon Easley had been closely monitoring the staccato of radio messages flashing between the 6th Battalion, its artillery FOs and the two U.S. advisors. When the enemy's infantry and armor attack began, Dinh alerted the 1st Battalion to assemble a counterattack force. Major Wong directed his Bravo command group and two infantry companies to join with twelve APCs and eight M-48 tanks. Capt. Larry Livingston joined his counterpart, Captain Ne, on the lead APC as the mechanized force moved out of the Ai Tu combat base and into its predetermined attack position.

Capt. Al Nettleingham observed the planning actions in the brigade and TOC. He later said:

I think the whole credit for repulsing the attack belongs to Colonel Dinh. He had his finger on the situation at all times. He knew what assets he had available and then committed them at the crucial moments.

He's a commander in the full sense of the word. His subordinate commanders had great confidence in him, in his judgment. The man presented the best example of decisiveness and military skill that I've seen.[7]

By the time the 6th Battalion and its advisors radioed the brigade about the attack, the enemy had struck the minefield and Dinh ordered the counterattack force to move. The rolling hills leading toward Pedro enabled the Bravo task force to deploy its tanks and APCs on-line while concealing the approach of their force until the last critical moment. As the Marine counterattack force crested the hill overlooking the minefield, the 2d Troop of the 20th Tank Battalion opened fire and began scoring first round hits on the enemy tanks. Three T-54s began to burn immediately and several others in the minefield wheeled around as if to withdraw; several exploded after running over anti-tank mines.

The momentum of the counterattack continued. Major Tung quickly reassembled his two companies, mounted them on his few APCs and joined the 1st Battalion in the attack. As the force approached to within 800 meters of Pedro the heavy artillery of the Marine bombardment forced the NVA infantry to withdraw to the southwest. This left the enemy tanks in an exposed and untenable position where they were destroyed systematically by another sortie of VNAF air, tank fire and LAAWs. Not a single tank escaped destruction or capture. Two tanks abandoned by their crews had received only light damage and would later be driven to Quang Tri City and Hue and placed on display. Several tank crewmen were also taken prisoner.

As in all battles, several unusual incidents occurred during the battle for Pedro. The first of these involved an Advisor, Major Warren, while the second involved a South Vietnamese Marine rifleman.

Shortly after the NVA tanks launched their attack on Pedro, Major Warren noticed that all the enemy tanks were flying bright red over white cavalry pennants from their radio antennas. Bill radioed this information over the advisors' net. In an uncyphered transmission to Major Easley at the brigade CP, Bill recorded:

> It was three or four minutes after I had radioed that NVA tanks were flying small flags and the advancing tanks opened up, that crewmen bent their whip antennas over and pulled off the pennants. Not only were our suspicions confirmed that the NVA was monitoring our radio frequencies very closely, but its ability to get tactical information to units in contact was superb.[8]

In the second incident, several Marines remained crouched in their holes in order to let the enemy tanks roll over them and then stood up to fire LAAWs at the vulnerable rear side of the tanks. The climax of such dramatic action occurred when an unnamed private in an outpost position held fast in his hole as one of the T-54s came clanking to a stop directly over him. The bow of the tank masked the lone infantryman from the driver who had been driving with his hatch "unbuttoned," or open. The Marine leaped out with his M-16 rifle, motioning for the driver and the three other crewmen to dismount. Surprised and somewhat sheepish, the enemy crewmen cleared the tank, turning it over, unscratched, to the Vietnamese Marines who exploited the bravery of the lone rifleman.

There was great significance to the South Vietnamese victory at FB Pedro where the NVA tanks lay shattered and burning. First, it presented the disillusioned South Vietnamese forces in Quang Tri Province with their first real victory in a knockdown, drag-out battle since the communist invasion began. The North Vietnamese had attacked with a regimental-sized force of infantry and a tank battalion and had been soundly defeated. Twenty-three tanks were destroyed or captured. Over 420 of the enemy had been killed, while the Marines and ARVN mechanized units suffered only sixty-six casualties.

More importantly, although U.S. advisors were present the defense was all planned and a successful counterattack executed by South Vietnamese forces. They did it on their own and the Marine commander proved the NVA could be beaten. For the besieged and demoralized 3d ARVN Division, the tank battle at Pedro provided a tremendous psychological lift. It was a new beginning, but only a beginning.

When General Lam received the report of the enemy armor attack and its subsequent defeat at Pedro, he became even more optimistic that the communist invaders could be driven back across the DMZ and he renewed his planning for a major counteroffensive. With more ARVN units being flown to MR-1, there was a daily buildup in the strength of South Vietnamese forces available to contest the enemy.

Several days later the 6th Battalion and the Bravo group, 1st Battalion received a report that enemy troops had infiltrated between their Pedro position and the Ai Tu combat base. Around 0845 on the 12th, the Marines with their tanks and APCs, organized like a mechanized battalion, had begun to withdraw back toward Ai Tu. The tanks and APCs were literally overflowing with troops as everyone sought a place to ride.

About two miles west of Ai Tu was an old abandoned French blockhouse. As the lead elements of the 1st Battalion approached to within 1,000 meters, troops were sighted running around the blockhouse. The column halted, as the 1st Battalion began to probe its way forward. It was quickly determined that the troops were an NVA unit. By mid-afternoon at least two enemy battalions were reported to be dug in cutting the road back to Ai Tu.

Major Tung directed Marine artillery and tank fire to attack the enemy with heavy preparatory fires. Capt. To Non Ne, the leader of the battalion's Bravo group, led the attack. Captain Livingston moved at his side. Ne was hit by enemy machine gun fire. Major Cockell later stated:

> Captain Livingston had nothing but the highest praise for Capt. To Non Ne. He said he was everywhere that day, and was killed like a Marine up there trying to engage the enemy.

> I think a lot of credit goes to Larry at that particular time because, as you know, when one of the leaders is hit in the VNMC it takes them a while to figure out who is going to take over. I think Larry pretty much ran the show for about thirty to forty-five minutes until such time as one of the other company commanders assumed the role as the Bravo commander. Livingston kept the momentum of their attack going.[9]

The battle was fought until dark at hand grenade range. The enemy died in their holes. Major Warren recorded:

> The NVA unit had very well dug in positions along the road with recoilless rifles and other antitank weapons. It was set to wipe us out as we passed. When the battle was over the ground was covered with dead enemy. I remember the dead had new uniforms, fresh haircuts, good rucksacks, good weapons. Most of the dead had gunshot wounds. So they stood and fought. It

was close quarters, rifles and hand grenades. Our Marines closed with them and they fought a good fight; everybody did a good job and we won.[10]

It took almost three days before the initial details on the scope and intensity of the North Vietnamese invasion reached Washington. President Nixon declared that the communist offensive which crossed the DMZ violated the 1968 agreement. The National Security Council met and decided the U.S. would intensify air and naval support. However, no U.S. combat troops would be committed to the offensive. On the contrary, the scheduled withdrawal of U.S. ground forces would continue. A White House spokesman assured the media that Vietnamization was working and the president had high confidence that South Vietnamese forces would stop the enemy invasion.[11]

However, early decisions at the national level set in motion fresh deployments of American combat aircraft and naval ships into Southeast Asia. Thus, galvanized by the invasion, America's military reacted.

The Easter Offensive caught all the U.S. services off guard. In the Gulf of Tonkin only the aircraft carriers *Coral Sea* and *Hancock* were on station. The *Constellation* and *Kitty Hawk* were immediately ordered to join the expanding naval task force which was forming to thrust its power against the North Vietnamese formations in MR-1.[12]

Off the coast of Quang Tri Province additional squadrons of U.S. destroyers began arriving. On 5 April five destroyers were off the Cam Lo-Cua Viet delivering critically needed fire support on NVA targets. By the 17th the U.S. Navy had assembled over twenty destroyers and a cruiser, all available for duty on the gunline. Commander Thearle's USS *Buchanan*, DDG-14, was now steaming beside the cruiser *Oklahoma City*, CLG-5.[13]

During the first critical week, when weather precluded all but a few flights of high performance aircraft, these destroyers provided a vital backup to the 3d Division's depleted artillery assets. Since by 3 April the South Vietnamese forces had lost over sixty of their eighty artillery pieces, naval gunfire was the only certain supporting arm.

An air armada was also alerted for deployment back into Southeast Asian bases. Under the direction of President Nixon there was an immediate step-up in B-52 operations. U.S. Air Force and Marine tactical squadrons began a hurried return to Vietnam. On 1 April the Air Force 3d Tactical Fighter Wing, stationed in Korea, was alerted and on the evening of Easter Sunday, eighteen of its F-4 aircraft had completed their deployments from Korea and were positioned at airfields located at Danang or Ubon, Thailand. After a two-day indoctrination period, crewmen from the 35th Tactical Fighter Squadron began flying combat missions. Danang, just sixty miles away, was a mere ten minutes flight time from the battered Quang Tri defensive line.[14] On 5 April two Marine F-4 squadrons stationed in Japan, VMF 115 and 232, were ordered back to Vietnam. By 7 April, twenty-two aircraft and crews were on-station at Danang and flying combat missions by the 9th. On 13 April a third Marine F-4 Squadron arrived at Danang from Kaneohe, Hawaii.[15]

Also, on 5 April, General Abrams requested the urgent deployment of specialized aviation assets including aircraft, such as the F-105G—the so-called "Wild Weasels," designed to counter the surface-to-air missile threat. Next to deploy were eight EB-66s, configured with electronic countermeasure systems to jam the enemy's SAM missile radar. By 13 April the U.S. Air Force had deployed over eighty aircraft into the combat zone.

Increasing numbers of the ever-present B-52 bombers were also called upon to come to the aid of South Vietnamese forces. During April, three groups of B-52 aircraft were deployed to Guam, raising the B-52 strength in the Pacific to 138 bombers. At Anderson Field, Guam, eighty-five bombers were stationed while fifty-three were in U-Tapao, Thailand. Over 1,800 B-52 ARCLIGHT strikes were flown in April, all but 200 against targets in South Vietnam.

To support the B-52 bombers a fleet of KC-135 tankers was needed. Air refueling requirements rose from thirty-six sorties per day to a peak of 130 daily. Eventually, 136 KC-135 tankers and 285 crews would be committed to the U.S. air armada supporting South Vietnamese forces.

In addition to this direct combat support, the U.S. military began to replenish the vehicles, artillery pieces, supplies and equipment lost during the early days of the invasion. The first of this equipment arrived in Danang on 11 April. Eighteen 105MM and 155MM howitzers were flown to Vietnam on Air Force C-141 aircraft. In Washington, D.C., Marine Corps Headquarters received a telephone report from the logistics officer of the Marine Advisory Unit in Saigon regarding the loss of the Vietnamese Marine artillery batteries at Camp Carroll and Mai Loc combat base. The U.S. Marine commandant acted immediately and directed that howitzers be withdrawn from storage and also taken from gun batteries on Okinawa and in Hawaii.

Under the supervision of Major Pratt, the critically needed artillery pieces were off-loaded, hooked to the accompanying trucks and driven north to Quang Tri Province. Stan Pratt, a veteran of a previous tour near Danang, took matters into his own hands by personally forming a convoy to deliver the much needed weapons. At his insistence the reluctant convoy left Danang without escort, drove north over the infamous Hai Van pass at dusk, raced to Phu Bai, through Hue and, finally, to Quang Tri. It was a feat of bravery, skill, determination and madness. Before dawn arrived on the 13th these guns were firing against the NVA. This emergency replenishment was only the beginning as the U.S. government and its military leaders came to the aid of the South Vietnamese government and its armed forces.

Another, more special, type of support was provided by an American officer to the South Vietnamese military in MR-1. It was the unique leadership role thrust upon Colonel Dorsey. As the senior Marine advisor he properly co-located his advisory staff beside the Marine division headquarters in Hue—a combat headquarters that Lieutenant General Lam refused to recognize as being in his military region. While the Marine commandant, Lieutenant General Khang, impatiently waited to assume control of his three infantry brigades and undertake a division defensive role, Dorsey became the personal emissary between the two most senior generals in MR-1. He was seemingly ubiquitous as he moved back and forth between General

Kroesen's regional assistance command which was located adjacent to Lam's headquarters. In his laid-back, easy-going style Dorsey became the primary coordinator of the Vietnamese Marine divisions' activities and support requirements in MR-1. He skillfully effected an open channel of communication with the other U.S. advisory headquarters.

As General Khang's emissary, Dorsey became the catalyst in planning and coordinating all U.S. air and naval gunfire support for the 14,000 Vietnamese Marines in MR-1. As such, he methodically organized his own advisory staff to work smoothly with the U.S. Army advisory command, the U.S. Air Force 1 DASC, the commander, U.S. naval armada offshore as well as the MACV headquarters in Saigon. In this critical position of advising and coordination he won the respect and trust of both Generals Khang and Lam. It was a role like no other advisor had ever played before.

The test of Vietnamization had arrived; the South Vietnamese military would determine the outcome of this phase of the second Indo-China war. While the opposing Vietnamese armies were approximately equal in strength, each enjoyed certain exploitable advantages—the NVA had more armor and artillery while the South Vietnamese and U.S. airpower dominated the skies above the DMZ whenever weather permitted it to operate. The outcome of the pending battle would be decided by the leadership of field commanders and their resolve to fight. It was time for South Vietnam's combat leaders to draw together in the defense of their country and collectively beat back the poised enemy. Time would shortly reveal the tragic outcome of their inability or reluctance to do this.

# CHAPTER SIXTEEN

# LOSS OF QUANG TRI PROVINCE

General Lam's optimism was further buoyed by what he saw as a growing U.S. determination to support the South Vietnamese military fully, if not with troops at least with air and naval gunfire support. The successes enjoyed by the ARVN and Marine units under his command during the period of 9–11 April reaffirmed his personal conviction that the time had arrived for a counteroffensive. He directed that planning be started.

Initially, his MR-1 staff conceived a plan for an attack north across the Cam Lo-Cua Viet River to retake the district of Gio Linh and the fire bases along Highway 1 just below the DMZ. Although this counteroffensive plan was discussed thoroughly within his staff and considered at length, it was finally discarded because drawing together the amount of forces required to recross the river and attack northward would have seriously weakened the western flank.[1] Since the Cam Lo Bridge had not been destroyed, the NVA had continued to build up a sizeable infantry and armored force in the Camp Carroll and Cam Lo area.

With the bridge intact, the NVA was able to move without impediment to strike the flank exposed by the original plan. Under these circumstances, should the 3d Division's western flank fail to hold, Quang Tri City itself would be in serious jeopardy. Therefore, after presenting his plan and receiving much opposition from his field commanders, General Lam decided that, instead of to the north, his first counteroffensive effort would be better directed westward. The objective of this second plan was the reestablishment of the former western defensive line by launching an all-out attack to regain the village of Cam Lo, Camp Carroll and the Mai Loc combat base.

The code name for the proposed counteroffensive was Operation Quang Trung 729, which was an allusion to the same historical events that the NVA exploited in naming its Nguyen Hue Offensive. The imperial name of the ancient leader Nguyen Hue was Quang Trung.[2] The ARVN operation was scheduled to begin on 14 April.

During the planning period South Vietnamese intelligence sources and U.S. aerial observers continued to report the steady buildup of NVA forces west of Highway 1 as three large-scale attacks were conducted against the 3d Division on 10 April. Southwest of Pedro enemy tank and infantry forces again struck back at the 1st and 6th Battalions. Although both attacks were repulsed, Marine casualties continued to mount, and the NVA continued to build its strength around Pedro, while other forces had moved unopposed around the fire base, and further eastward toward FB Anne and Highway 1.

To the north toward the Cam Lo-Cua Viet River, two ranger battalions were also attacked by enemy tanks and infantry. The rangers held, fighting gallantly, but lost several of their attached APCs and one M-48 tank.

A more ominous sign for the South Vietnamese was the first artillery attack on Quang Tri City itself which indicated that the NVA had displaced its longer range 130MM guns forward out of the DMZ into new firing positions just north of the Cam Lo-Cua Viet River. This repositioning meant that enemy artillery could now strike targets five miles south of Quang Tri City. An ARVN ammunition dump in Hai Lang was struck and approximately 2,000 rounds of critical 90MM tank ammunition were destroyed.

Northeast of Quang Tri City, near the coastline, the 2d ARVN Regiment along with regional forces were engaged in heavy skirmishes designed to halt the enemy advances. Despite these efforts NVA forces crossed the river with amphibious

PT-76 tanks and advanced to within six miles of the provincial capital.

It seemed clear that the siege of Quang Tri City was beginning as NVA forces were reported approaching the provincial capital from three sides. Facing these advancing enemy forces, General Giai's 3d Division was further expanded as additional ARVN forces arrived as part of the buildup to halt the invasion. During this rapid buildup the division had nearly tripled in size and now consisted of nine brigades or groups containing thirty-six battalions in addition to the RF and PF forces. Further, Giai's extraordinary responsibilities also included supervising the positioning of, and protecting, the regional artillery and logistics units, as well as monitoring the status of the provincial and district governments in Quang Tri. It was from this rather extended posture that General Lam launched Operation Quang Trung 729.

Organized into five task forces, the 3d Division assigned the unstable 57th ARVN Regiment on its northern flank the important defensive mission of providing security along the south bank of the Cam Lo-Cua Viet River. On the first day of the counteroffensive there were only scattered contacts. In spite of Lam's exhortations to advance, the early hours of the ARVN attack saw no great surge forward by his infantry and armor units. On the contrary, the weary troops on the western front advanced cautiously. Their officers tacitly observed the deliberate nature of their movement and did nothing to hasten the tempo.[3] NVA artillery responded to the attack immediately, countering with devastating fire, inflicting heavy casualties on the exposed infantry. By 17 April, the fourth day of the counteroffensive, none of the five task forces of the 3d Division had advanced over 1,000 meters from their starting point.

With his limited command and control facilities, Giai was experiencing great difficulty in coordinating a strong, well-supported attack. To hamper his control problems further, every request for U.S. fire support effort had literally to be run back and forth by hand across the Citadel's Quang Tri compound to be coordinated, approved or disapproved. Thus, critical moments were lost and internal dissent again arose between the U.S. advisors and 3d Division staff. This situation was the result of the relocation of the division headquarters (and U.S. advisors) from Ai Tu to the Citadel where separate fire support coordination centers were established in two different buildings some fifty meters apart. No telephone lines were laid between these two vital coordination centers—a glaring error that violated one of the most basic principles in fire support coordination. However, neither the commanding general of the Vietnamese forces nor his American counterpart took corrective action to alleviate the problem even after it was recognized. The effect upon the ARVN attack plans was serious.

With so many dispersed units, Giai soon discovered that he was physically unable to exercise personal command over his five task forces. These disparate battle groups, composed of ARVN infantry, rangers, armor and a Marine brigade, repeatedly delayed their attacks by claiming logistical problems, unit attrition and troop fatigue and every other possible reason to procrastinate launching the offensive. In one situation the commander of the 1st Armored Brigade insisted that his brigade was not getting sufficient tactical air support or ARCLIGHT missions and as a result he would not attack until B-52s had bombed the area immediately forward of his front lines. When this request was found to violate the safety parameters because of the close proximity to troops, the strike was not approved. Although there was only light enemy contact at that time, the brigade refused to move forward.[4]

Thus, rather than being a bold counterattack to regain battlefield momentum, Operation Quang Trung 729 settled into a costly battle of attrition in which the ARVN forces were steadily reduced in strength and effectiveness by the enemy's deadly artillery fire. Morale deteriorated rapidly and General Giai appeared unable either to restore it or prod his forces out of their fighting holes and into the attack. The counteroffensive stalled while the NVA continued to maneuver armor, infantry artillery and antiaircraft units across the Cam Lo Bridge toward the ARVN defensive line.

During this period the "war of the generals" continued as Lam still refused to allow either the Marine commandant or the armor and ranger commanders to assume any responsibility over their own forces in Quang Tri Province. The opportunity to reorganize the South Vietnamese forces into a more cohesive regional army passed because of previous, petty differences between senior commanders. The needs of the ego were served over the pressing requirements of the military situation.

Giai's most serious problem continued to be command and control. The three Marine brigades and the four ranger groups gave their first loyalty to the commanders of their own headquarters as all new tactical orders issued by the 3d Division to these forces were in turn radioed back to Hue City or Danang to the idle commanders for approval before execution. Thus, endless hours were lost and the very fiber of effective command and control frayed.

The chain of command was further compromised as Lam began personally to intercede at all levels and on occasion even issued orders by telephone and radio to individual brigade commanders, especially to the 1st Armored Brigade.[5] The U.S. advisory effort, in turn, was severely handicapped by the duplicity of the Vietnamese general as the staff of the 3d Division

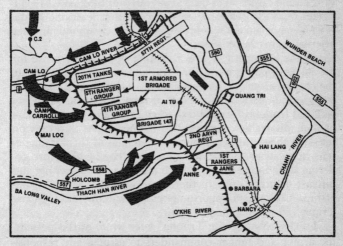

**OPERATION QUANG TRUNG 729**

and its Advisory Team 155 often learned of Lam's directives only after they had been implemented. With no unity of command, confusion and distrust gradually set in, further exacerbating the deteriorating defensive posture of the South Vietnamese forces in Quang Tri Province. As Giai's authority over his key subordinate units eroded, the situation could only end in ultimate disaster.

By 18 April, rather than being thrown back, NVA pressure actually increased all along the Quang Trung western battle line—a fragile "defensive" line only seven miles west of Highway 1. All ARVN and Marine units reported contact with enemy infantry and armored forces and as darkness set in the NVA launched a major attack. General Giai's units reported movements of enemy tanks as the 5th Ranger Group, with tanks of the 20th in support, was confronted by a regimental-sized NVA force and held in place. The ARVN armor was repeatedly fired upon by the enemy's antitank teams using B-40 rockets with good effect.

In Quang Tri City the 3d Division's TOC submitted emergency request for air support. The DASC, in Danang, coordinated the diversion of tactical aircraft and B-52 ARCLIGHT strikes onto the nearest enemy force and at least one of the NVA's major attacks was broken with the enemy falling back after suffering heavy losses.

In the aftermath of this a fleeting opportunity arose for the 3d Division's ground forces to advance and fully initiate the counteroffensive. Understandably, General Giai was beset by indecision because of the lack of reliable information being received from his forward task force commanders. As a result of their disloyalties, nothing had happened. At daybreak on the 19th the South Vietnamese forces, still in their static defensive positions, demanded saturation bombings before ordering their forces forward. Such inertia, petty bickering, and distrust of other units further permeated the ARVN's leadership. A battlefield opportunity passed and operation Quang Trung 729 was doomed to failure.

Lt. Gen. Ngo Quang Truong* later wrote of this period:

---

*Lt. Gen. Ngo Quang Truong later assumed command of MR-1 in May 1972.

The fact that another major effort by the enemy had been effectively stopped deluded General Lam into thinking once more the situation in Quang Tri was under control. But the inertia developing among ARVN units should have alerted him to the pressing requirement for reorganizing his positions and rotating weary combat units. This need totally escaped him. The enemy's demonstrated ability to conduct a sustained offensive, on the other hand, should also have stimulated a major ARVN effort to implement a coordinated defense plan if Quang Tri was to be held. But this effort was not made.[6]

Pressure was increasing on the outer edge of ARVN defenses which were little more than a thin shell. This resulted from General Lam's determination to conduct a counteroffensive and placing all available fighting forces on the forward battle lines. No ARVN units had been strategically placed to provide for a defense in depth or as strategic reserve. The 3d ARVN Division's only viable defensive posture was its outer shell. If the enemy attack penetrated anywhere along the line, the ARVN defenses could collapse.

Thwarted by the battle at Pedro, the invading NVA continued to push men, armor and supplies toward Quang Tri City, crossing the Cam Lo-Cua Viet River barrier over the Cam Lo Bridge. After more than two weeks of rain and monsoon cloud cover, the weather broke allowing a massive air effort to hit suspected enemy positions and staging areas. Taking advantage of the clearing weather, increasing numbers of B-52 ARCLIGHT strikes, as well as hundreds of tactical air strikes, were flown each day to support South Vietnamese forces.

Despite heavy casualties suffered from this concentrated air offensive, the enemy continued to move its units into position, readying for a new offensive which all expected momentarily.

Shortly before dusk on 18 April, the NVA ended the apprehension as it struck all along the western front. Marine Brigade 258 was the first unit to report that it was being attacked by enemy tanks and infantry advancing from the west. Colonel Dinh responded to these reports with artillery fire and coordinated with Jon Easley in requesting air support.

Almost simultaneous with the reports of the attack on the

Marines, the 1st Armored Brigade reported enemy tanks advancing toward the 4th Ranger Group which was located in the center of the 3d Division's western defense line. Elements of the 20th Tank Battalion that were deployed along Route 9 were also attacked. Soon the 3d Division's TOC was flooded with reports that the NVA were attacking or its units were being sighted along the full seven miles of the 3d Division's western defensive line.

As the momentum of the NVA attack increased, enemy artillery raked the South Vietnamese positions. However, the line held firm as ARVN artillery struck back at the exposed NVA infantry causing the attackers to break off the attack and withdraw to the west. After a full day of combat the NVA's first attacks were finally repulsed at 2100.

During this renewed offensive the NVA also made a secondary attack out of the Ba Long Valley, southwest of Pedro, aimed directly toward Quang Tri City. The 1st Ranger Group, in a blocking position three miles southwest of the city, was attacked by an NVA force estimated to be of battalion size. In fierce fighting the rangers held as the NVA's attempt to cut off elements of the 3d Division fighting along the Cam Lo-Cua Viet River and western defense line was also repulsed. The NVA withdrew in the growing darkness, but shortly thereafter were reported massing forces for another attack, which was expected the next day.

As the morning of the 19th dawned, numerous contacts were reported all along the trace of the front line. Enemy artillery resumed the shelling of ARVN positions, the Ai Tu combat base and Quang Tri City. Fire from the NVA's 130MM guns began to strike at major road junctions, especially along Highway 1 and around the two key bridges which crossed the Thach Han River into Quang Tri City. The Thach Han was not fordable so the highway and railroad bridges spanning the river were critically important as the 3d Division's primary supply line to the ARVN's units, Marines, rangers and armored brigade defending northern Quang Tri Province. General Giai, rightfully concerned about his only supply line north, directed that security be increased around both bridges.

On the morning of 22 April, Marine Brigade 147, which

had been in the Hue City since its difficult withdrawal from FSB Mai Loc, redeployed north to relieve Brigade 258. The 1st, 4th, and 8th Infantry Battalions and the 1st Artillery Battalion under Colonel Bao's command had all received replacements and new equipment, and were again considered at full strength and combat ready.

Upon relief of Colonel Dinh's brigade, the 4th Battalion assumed the responsibility for the perimeter security of the Ai Tu combat base. The 1st Battalion under command of Major Wong, with his two COVANs Maj. Bob Cockell and Capt. Larry Livingston, was deployed to the southwest of Ai Tu. The NVA had overrun the former ARVN position on Pedro several days earlier so its new line of defense was only a mile and a half from the TOC bunker at Ai Tu. The 8th Battalion, with Maj. Emmett Huff as the senior advisor, was deployed on a line about a mile to the northwest. Colonel Bao placed his artillery battalion with its eighteen 105MM and four 155MM howitzers inside the perimeter of the combat base itself. The Marine artillerymen were eager to employ their newly acquired weapons against the NVA. Many of these howitzers had recently been flown into Danang to replace the guns destroyed at FSB Mai Loc. The tactical markings of the U.S. Marine Corps units revealed that the guns and six-by-six trucks had arrived from Okinawa, Hawaii and California only days earlier.

When the two Marine brigades completed their changeover the 3d and 6th Battalions climbed aboard trucks and began the road trip back to Hue City. The 3d Battalion, heroic defenders of Dong Ha, and the tank-killing 6th Battalion were ordered out of the battle line and back to Hue City for rest, replacements and replenishment. On that Easter Sunday, when the 3d Battalion literally halted the NVA's three division attacks, few in the TOC bunker believed the offensive would be stopped. The cost was 500 of the 700 Marines in the battalion. The 200 remaining had continued fighting the battle around the perimeter at Ai Tu.

On its first morning in Hue, the 3d Battalion fell out on parade. General Khang, Marine commandant, desired to speak to his men and commend them on their heroic stand at Dong Ha. Exactly fifty-two Marines stood there on parade, including

Major Binh and Capt. John Ripley. Fifty-two men received the cheers, the gratitude and the respect of their brothers in arms. However, little was heard of their commandant's praise. Those too weak or wounded had circled their comrades and were too overcome with emotion to hold back their cries of joy and sadness. To those present it was readily apparent the thoughts of these Marines were on the 650 other Marines for whom they were standing. The gallant fifty-two were now South Vietnam's smallest, but proudest battalion.

"We will fight in Dong Ha and we will die; we will never give up." Major Binh's prophetic statement had become a reality.

A ranger battalion had assumed the responsibility for security of part of Dong Ha City and the areas around the bridges.

With the 3d and 6th Battalions also went their three COVANs: Capt. John Ripley, who had remained with the 3d Battalion until the last possible day before returning to Saigon and rotation, along with Maj. Bill Warren and Capt. Bill Wischmeyer who were also rotating and would leave the 6th Battalion after its arrival in Hue. Each of them had remained beside his counterpart and fulfilled the role of the COVAN as envisioned by Colonel Croizat almost two decades earlier.

Relentlessly maintaining pressure on General Lam's defensive line, the NVA continued to move its artillery batteries forward in order to strike deep into ARVN positions south of Quang Tri City. At 1925 on 22 April the enemy scored a major hit when its long-range artillery struck a large ammunition dump in La Vang, two miles south of the provincial capital. A major supply point was destroyed. The commander in charge of the dump reported that after the shelling 100 percent of the ammunition stocks and nearby gasoline supplies were destroyed along with about half the rice depot. In addition, large quantities of communications supplies, primarily batteries, were also lost in the explosions and fires.

By the morning of 23 April, the enemy activity increased substantially as units of the 1st Armored Brigade were attacked by infantry supported by at least twelve tanks. Later that morning the 4th Ranger Group and 17th Cavalry were attacked, with the fighting reported as being conducted at close quarters. Again, the ARVN's western defenses held.

Easily the most significant event of the 23rd, however, was when the enemy introduced a new tank-killing weapon onto the battlefield. At 0930 elements of the 20th Tanks began to engage NVA tanks and infantry on the high ground over-looking Route 9. While the attack was in progress three M-48 tanks were destroyed by wire-guided anti-tank missiles. The erratic flying missiles initially mesmerized the South Viet-namese tank and APC crewmen. Before the day ended eight ARVN vehicles had been destroyed by the Soviet-made AT-3 Sagger missile.[7]

Despite increased enemy activity along the western line General Giai ordered Brigade 147's 1st and 8th battalions to attack west. By nightfall both battalions were on their assigned objectives. As the Marines settled in for the night they discov-ered that the ARVN units, which were supposed to be on their flanks, had not yet come on line. Large gaps existed on both flanks leaving the Marines exposed and vulnerable to infiltra-tion and enemy attack. They remained at full alert. It was an uneasy night but there were only scattered enemy contacts.

The NVA commanders planned their attacks well, with the South Vietnamese soldiers given little opportunity to rest. The ever-present threat of incoming artillery caused the morale of the ARVN troops to continue to deteriorate. Unsure of when or where the next enemy attack would occur, the defenders were at the mercy of this intense tempo. The ranger groups and armored units along the battle line had to spend long, tense, and sleepless nights agonizing over the prospect of enemy infantry assaults which experience had shown could suddenly surge forward out of the darkness.

The inertia demonstrated by the ARVN's five task forces in Operation Quang Trung 729 a week earlier made it possible for the NVA to rest and recuperate at almost any time it chose. The short interludes experienced during the fighting were in-variably the times that the enemy chose to rest, while the ARVN forces were constantly on the alert, under tension day and night, their energy sapped by fear and uncertainty. Slowly but surely, as the NVA Nguyen Hue Offensive entered its fourth week, the resolve to fight was ebbing from the soldiers who made up the often bloodied 3d ARVN Division.

On 25 April, the Sagger missile reappeared as elements of

the 20th tanks suffered more tank and APC losses to hits from the wire-guided missiles. Just before sunset, 2d Troop of the 20th tanks reported observing thirty armored vehicles moving south from Charlie 2 to Cam Lo. Artillery fire was promptly called on the column, but because of the darkness no observations could be made as to the effectiveness of the fire mission.

At 1900 on the 26th, Maj. Jim Joy received a radio message over the secure voice net from Colonel Dorsey's advisory headquarters in Hue. This radio message was passed from the advisory team with Brigade 369 to the CP of Brigade 147 in the Ai Tu TOC bunker. It was a most alarming message declaring that "Quang Tri City would be attacked that night by a division-sized force from the southwest, supported by an artillery regiment." Obviously alarmed by this prospect, Joy radioed the unconfirmed report back to U.S. Advisory Team 155 in the Citadel TOC. As the word spread, once again the weary 3d ARVN units spent a long vigil anticipating a major enemy attack which did not materialize.

However, at 0400 on the morning of the 27th a second message was received by the advisors radioed to Brigade 147 from Dorsey's headquarters in Hue City. The message was even more explicit, indicating that "At 0700 the 304th North Vietnamese Division, supported by artillery, will attack the Ai Tu area." Again, Joy informed his counterpart, alerted his fellow COVANs and passed this latest intelligence information to the 3d Division advisory team. Major Sheridan at FB Nancy had again been asked to retransmit the message because of the thirty-five mile distance between Hue and Ai Tu combat base. In the process, Sheridan emphasized to Joy that the reason the message could only be passed by way of the advisors' radio equipment was that the South Vietnamese did not have the capability for an encrypted, secure voice radio system. As a security measure, the South Vietnamese commanders were requesting their advisors to relay the information in order to prevent the NVA monitoring the ARVN radio nets from intercepting the alert.

The second intelligence warning proved to be correct as the morning of the 27th signaled the beginning of the enemy's major drive toward Quang Tri City. In an ominous repetition of the first desperate days of the NVA offensive, hundreds of artillery rounds began to strike the western defense line and the 57th ARVN Regiment positioned in Dong Ha on the south side of the Cam Lo-Cua Viet River.

Ironically, the weather also turned against the South Vietnamese as the monsoon weather returned and a solid overcast blanketed the DMZ and Quang Tri Province, cutting off the aircraft support which was so vital. At 0615 the 4th Ranger Group, in the center of the ARVN defensive line, was attacked by a large infantry force. To the south, the Marines' 1st Battalion was attacked at 0630. During the first two hours the battalion took over 500 rounds of 82MM mortar fire and beat off two ground attacks.

While these attacks were underway, the 8th Battalion discovered enemy units in its rear, an area supposed to have been occupied by an ARVN battalion. With light contact on their western front, the battalion deployed its Bravo group and two infantry companies to attack the enemy elements, wiping out the enemy pocket with over eighty NVA killed, and capturing numerous AK-47s, machine guns, recoilless rifles and 82MM mortars.

On the division's most southern positions, fronting the Ba Long Valley, the 2d ARVN Regiment was attacked at 0645. The ARVN defense held. Artillery fire began once again to strike Quang Tri City, Hi Lang and the Ai Tu complex as the unbroken roar of distant guns firing and the explosions of impacting rounds caused the ground to shake. The intensity of the NVA's bombardments and its indiscriminate shelling of populated areas had the desired effect as more civilians were forced onto the roadways further complicating the movement of military vehicles, personnel and supplies.

Refugees from Cam Lo and Dong Ha, who had fled to their provincial capital, were once again frightened and thousands of them began to flee south toward Hue City along Highway 1. Taking advantage of this helpless mass of humanity, North Vietnamese forward observers methodically began to adjust the fire from their 130MM guns all along the lines of unprotected refugees and ARVN stragglers. As expected, the effect was devastating and created chaos. The confused masses crossed over the bridge marking the southern boundary of Quang Tri Province where Marines of Brigade 369 were digging in. Col. Phan Van Chung, the brigade commander, was establishing his CP on the southern bank of the My Chanh River. Located near a small, tree-covered hilltop, this position provided him an unobstructed view of Highway 1 for at least eight miles north toward Quang Tri City. The sight that confronted him—a road jammed with fleeing civilians and straggling soldiers—was not a pretty one.

In the northwestern area of the 3d Division's area of operations, the 1st Armored Brigade controlled the pivotal northern portion of the line. At 0600, the enemy's artillery began striking their positions with a withering bombardment from 122MM and 130MM guns. Later, at 0715, the 5th Ranger Group was attacked by tanks and infantry forces. At 0900 incoming NVA artillery rounds scored a direct hit on the command APC of 2d Troop, 20th Tank Battalion killing or wounding all the officers with it. To add to this confusion, three tanks in the troop were shortly thereafter destroyed by Sagger missiles.

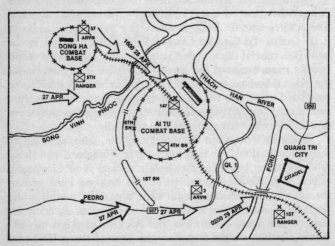

**NORTH VIETNAMESE ADVANCE ON QUANG TRI CITY**

Elements of the 3d Troop, 20th Tanks observed as the burning M-48 tanks broke without their leaders and drove their tanks east toward Highway 1. The ARVN infantry and ranger units who watched their armor suddenly bolt from the battle line also began to withdraw, lending to the confusion and disintegration of the battle line.

The NVA were now attacking all along the western line. In the area of responsibility assigned to the 5th Rangers, fighting continued at a heavy pace as the NVA infantry massed and assaulted the Ranger's 30th and 38th Battalions. By 0915, the 38th Ranger Battalion's position was overrun, and the 5th Ranger Group, finding itself exposed, began to withdraw to the east. The pressure continued and the NVA advanced eastward, leaving no time for the wounded or dead rangers to be evacuated. It was obvious that the outer shell of the 3d Division's defensive line was becoming critically thin and cracking.

All of these events were happening so quickly the 3d Division's TOC could not remain current on the tactical situation. No guidance from divisional headquarters was sent to the forward commanders other than "Hold at all costs." In this chaotic condition, ARVN units became fragmented, commanders were separated from their units (some by their own choice), and confusion reigned.

In the center of the defensive line, the 4th Ranger Group continued to hold as NVA tanks and infantry attacked their positions. The rangers reported destroying two tanks shortly before noon. However, at 1400 a Sagger missile struck one of the 4th's few remaining M-48 tanks. By 1615 an enemy force, estimated as at least two infantry battalions, assaulted into the 4th Ranger's fighting holes. At 1640 the 43d Ranger Battalion broke under the stress and began fleeing to the east.

The fragile outer shell of the 3d ARVN Division's defenses was broken. The "ripple effect" was felt immediately as the ARVN rangers began to withdraw without notifying their adjacent units. Colonel Luat, commander of the 1st Armored Brigade, concerned that one of his elements from 20th Tanks positioned along Route 9 was about to be cut off, ordered the tanks to fall back. On his own initiative, he directed his 20th Tank Battalion on the Cau Viet line west of Dong Ha to fall back toward Highway 1. As soon as the ARVN troops saw this second group of its supporting tanks move, they were gripped with panic, broke ranks and streamed alongside the tanks screaming and grasping at handholds without any sense of discrimination or shame. Before General Giai or his staff detected what was happening, many of his infantry troops had already arrived back at the Quang Tri combat base. Luat's decision to save his tanks by initiating a major withdrawal without reporting to his superior had ultimately caused the final collapse of the northern flank defenses.[8]

When Giai learned of the unplanned withdrawal, he and Colonel Murdock were flown by helicopter to a location just south of Dong Ha City. The general's courage was again demonstrated as he personally succeeded in reestablishing order. However, by the time he had succeeded in doing this and taking charge of the situation he was compelled to regroup his disorganized forces along a new defense line north of the Thach Han River. His hastily drawn new defense line surrounded only the Ai Tu complex.

On the western front, the Marine battalions held their positions as the ranger units broke to the east. However, late in the afternoon the 1st and 8th Battalions were attacked by fifteen tanks and a large infantry force. Eight of the NVA tanks confronting the Marines were destroyed as their artillery and ARVN M-48 tanks worked first to destroy the armor threat and then to halt the infantry assaults. Just before dusk the enemy troops and remaining tanks retreated in the face of a well-coordinated and devastating artillery barrage from the guns at Ai Tu.

The flanks of both the 1st and 8th Battalions, which had been exposed by the withdrawal of rangers, were in turn ordered to fall back. Shortly after darkness they would pull back to within 1,500 meters of the Ai Tu combat base perimeter.

The 2d ARVN Regiment, defending the natural approaches from the Ba Long Valley into Quang Tri City, also experienced a day-long series of probing attacks as the enemy units moved along the north side of the Thach Han River advancing to within two miles of the Quang Tri bridges. Had the NVA advanced unchecked along this route, the thousands of South Vietnamese fighting around Dong Ha and Ai Tu combat base would have been encircled. The 2d ARVN Regiment rose to the occasion.

In making his preparation, Colonel Tung had dispersed the CP of his 2d ARVN Regiment among several buildings at the Ai Tu combat base. Later that afternoon the enemy artillery intensified as Col. Bill Camper and Maj. Joe Brown discussed the worsening situation with their counterpart. Camper realized the critical need to keep the Quang Tri Bridge secure but information on the developing situation, particularly from the 2d and 3d Battalions, was sketchy at best. He became concerned upon hearing small arms fire along the river and decided he was going to check out the cause of the fire fight. He entered the regimental CP to look over the tactical map and found that his counterpart wasn't sure what was occurring or exactly where their infantry battalions were located. The situation was confusing in the regiment's AO.

Leaving the CP, Camper and Brown started checking out the tree lines along the river. Enemy artillery was impacting all around them with the largest concentrations striking around the highway and railroad bridges. As they approached the Thach Han bridges, an incoming artillery round hit a tree above them and the shrapnel sprayed the group, striking Bill Camper. He had just become the latest American casualty of the Nguyen Hue Offensive. He later recalled:

> I was hit in the face and neck with fragments from this artillery round and I immediately knew I was in pretty bad shape, with blood coming out. I tried to tell Joe Brown what had happened to me but I was unable to speak coherently; one of the fragments had damaged my vocal cords and blood inside my face and skull was choking me. Joe laid me down so that I could drain. The last thing I remembered vividly was lying in the dirt, in some kind of potato patch, so that my mouth, nose and face would drain.[9]

Brown radioed the 2d Regiment's CP to send emergency assistance. He was aware that Camper was seriously wounded and required immediate evacuation so he sought assistance from other ARVN units straggling toward the Quang Tri bridges, but to no avail. In desperation he radioed the advisor's TOC located in the Citadel. Two Americans, a soldier and a Navy corpsman, immediately volunteered to attempt a rescue. One of them, Sgt. Roger Shoemaker, located an ARVN APC driver while HM1 Thomas Williamson assembled his medical kit. Disregarding enemy artillery and intense small arms fire, they crossed the Thach Han River from the city and proceeded on foot to the injured officer. Reaching him, Corpsman Williamson rendered immediate aid to Camper. The two enlisted men placed the now-unconscious colonel on a canvas stretcher and transported him into the APC for movement back to Quang Tri City.* Joe Brown remained with him until he was evacuated by helicopter at 1840. Thus, unknown to thousands of South Vietnamese soldiers, an exceptional American officer had given his all for their country. To a man we advisors knew, once we learned that Bill Camper had been struck down, that one of the Army's finest, certainly one of its bravest, had paid the price.

---

*HM1 Williamson and Sergeant Shoemaker were both awarded the Silver Star medal for their heroic action.

# CHAPTER SEVENTEEN

# LOSS OF AI TU COMBAT BASE

As the demoralized ARVN units filtered away, the NVA advanced to fill the void. Thus, as darkness closed on Quang Tri Province, the 3d Division's commander was not certain where his forces were located, or indeed which units remained effective. In the meantime, hundreds of ARVN soldiers, rangers and others were straggling down Highway 1 toward Quang Tri.

At 1730 Colonel Luat, his U.S. Army Advisor Lt. Col. Louis C. Wagner, Jr., and the 32d Ranger Battalion commander were, by extraordinary efforts, finally able to stop the elements of the 43d Ranger Battalion which were attempting to flee the northern battlefield. It was a tense moment as the three officers lowered their weapons and at gunpoint turned the frightened groups around and headed them back to defensive positions.

The 2d Troop of the 20th Tanks and the 18th Cavalry Troop were ordered by Colonel Luat to make a night withdrawal back to the Dong Ha combat base. They were to link up with elements of the 57th ARVN Regiment. However, during the withdrawal three M-48 tanks were lost to enemy fire. Further, when these units finally arrived at the Dong Ha combat base they did not find friendly troops, but instead were attacked by enemy units. They were later to learn the 57th had already abandoned Dong Ha and moved south. Under heavy fire the units of the 20th Tank Battalion withdrew from the city, fought their way to Highway 1, and moved south only to run into heavy small arms fire. They were confronted by the overly frightened rearguard elements of the 57th who believed they were enemy forces. Chaos reigned once again. Fortunately, there were no casualties from the engagements.

The situation throughout Quang Tri Province was becoming ever more critical. However, one more event would occur to close out the tragic day as enemy artillery struck the ammunition dump near Ai Tu. With a horrendous blast, the last stocks of critically needed artillery ammunitions, powder and fuses were destroyed. The huge pall of fire and smoke could be seen from the walls of the Citadel within the city.

The 1st Armored Brigade spent the night desperately trying to locate its assigned units and getting an assessment of the combat effectiveness of each. At 0300 Colonel Wagner recorded in his log the following:

| | |
|---|---|
| 20th Tanks: | Eighteen M-48A3 tanks operational. 1st Troop with Marines at Ai Tu. |
| 57th Regiment: | Approximately 1,400 men. |
| 4th Rangers: | Approximately eighty men, one battalion ineffective. |
| 5th Rangers: | Approximately 600 men, two battalions ineffective. |
| 13th and 17th Cavalry Regiments: | Two-thirds of combat vehicles still operational.[1] |

At 0630 heavy incoming artillery began striking units of the armored brigade as Colonel Luat and Colonel Wagner moved north of the Vinh Phuoc River where NVA tanks had been sighted moving toward the strong point.

Following a short artillery barrage three T-54 tanks began firing at the few remaining ARVN tanks holding the line and a tank battle ensued which resulted in the destruction of the NVA armor. At 0930 an enemy infantry force of about 100 men launched an attack down Highway 1 against the strong point but was driven back by machine gun fire. The ARVN's northernmost, hastily established defensive position held momentarily.

Colonel Luat ordered his 5th Ranger Group and 2d Troop, 20th Tanks to establish a new defense line south of the Vinh Phuoc River as it was the last river barrier north of Ai Tu combat base. The new line was to extend approximately 1,000 meters to the east and west of the highway bridge. This was supposed to be accomplished while the strong point at 1,000 meters north was fighting the enemy tanks. At 1030 it was discovered that the units had not established the new defensive line along the Vinh Phuoc, but were fleeing south.

To prevent the tank and APC forces in the strong point from being cut off, Luat ordered them to withdraw. Approximately half the elements had crossed over the Vinh Phuoc Bridge when it was struck by two rounds of 130MM artillery, blowing out a portion of one span. Before the span collapsed two APCs from Luat's command group were able to jump the gap but six APCs and one M-48 tank were prevented from crossing and were abandoned by their crews without being disabled or destroyed.

Just as Luat had crossed over the damaged bridge he was seriously wounded by anti-tank rocket fire and evacuated to Quang Tri, leaving the 1st Armored Brigade for a time without a leader.

While Colonel Wagner sought out the new acting commander he requested that U.S. aircraft destroy the vehicles north of the bridge to prevent them from falling into enemy hands. Although low clouds continued to hang over the battlefield, shortly after 1200 several aircraft penetrated the cloud cover, came in low and destroyed the vehicles.

While the air strike was occurring, the Brigade CP, attached artillery and 4th Ranger Group started moving south. Highway 1 became clogged with vehicles and a massive traffic jam developed north of the Ai Tu combat base when Marines from Brigade 147 refused to let vehicles or personnel through a roadblock.

Earlier that morning Colonel Bao and Major Joy had driven into the Citadel to attend a conference with General Giai. While at the Division CP, Joy received a radio message from his advisors at Ai Tu that friendly units to the north were leaving their positions and retreating south through the Ai Tu combat base. Bao and his COVAN hurriedly returned to Ai Tu and observed the massive traffic jam. After a conference between the Marine brigade commander and the commanders of the retreating units it was agreed to let them pass as opposed to retaining a milling mob to the north of Ai Tu combat base.

By nightfall on the 28th, the 4th Ranger Group was located on the north end of the Quang Tri airstrip; the 5th Rangers were south of Ai Tu, to the east of the bridges leading into Quang Tri City. Elements of the 2d Regiment had established blocking positions around the highway bridge. The unreliable 57th Regiment and most elements of the 1st Armored Brigade had withdrawn into Quang Tri City.

Reinforcements were needed if the Marines were to hold. The 7th Battalion was ordered north from the My Chanh line to assist Brigade 147. The battalion was attacked by an enemy force south of Quang Tri City and only two companies succeeded in reaching Ai Tu.

At 0200 on 29 April the NVA launched a tank and infantry attack on the two bridges on Highway 1 across the Thach Han River leading into Quang Tri City. The attack originated from the southwest and quickly rolled up the 2d Regiment's two infantry battalions. The 18th Cavalry's APCs fought hard and contained the attack. Jim Joy later reported:

> Then, in one of the most timely and most devastating air shows I've ever witnessed, TAC Air, guided by a forward air controller with a flare light, put air strike after air strike on the enemy. The attack was beaten off and resulted in three out of five enemy tanks destroyed.[2]

General Giai recognized that the Quang Tri combat base was a bad choice for defense from a tactical point of view. A new defense plan was undertaken which Lieutenant General Truong later recorded:

> The 3d Division commander decided to evacuate Ai Tu and withdraw south of the river. He worked on the withdrawal plan by himself; he consulted only his division senior advisor. General Giai feared if his subordinate commanders learned of his

plan, they were apt to wreck it through hasty actions. He also deliberately withheld this plan from the MR-1 commander (General Lam).

He simply wanted to be cautious, to get things done. But it was this action that alienated him from the MR-1 commander and created the growing distrust that developed between them . . .[3]

While the collapse of the 3d ARVN Division's northern defenses received the highest immediate concern during the day other events of equal significance were happening in Quang Tri Province. The North Vietnamese forces attacking southward along the coastline had advanced to within three miles of the provincial capital. Infantry units, supported by light PT-76 amphibious tanks, had overrun the RF and PF forces north and east of the city and were steadily advancing, almost unopposed.

South of Quang Tri City enemy units were interdicting Highway 1 at a number of locations along the flat eight-mile stretch of road to the My Chanh Bridge. On several occasions this vital supply line was physically severed. General Giai was repeatedly ordered by General Lam to reopen the highway. The enemy artillery and small arms attacks upon civilian refugees and any military vehicle traffic along the roadway increased. Giai was finally compelled to divert an armored cavalry squadron from a front line role to conduct the necessary road-clearing operations. In their efforts to sustain the growing supply needs of the division, ARVN logistics units frequently found themselves in heated fire fights before their convoys could break through the enemy roadblocks. All too often other truck convoys with less dedicated officers simply refused to drive north beyond the My Chanh River and turned back.

To aggravate the confusion, the enemy artillery continued to strike the masses of confused, frightened ARVN soldiers and civilian refugees moving down Highway 1 from north of Quang Tri City. Under the best of conditions there was no way for the military to maintain unit integrity as individuals continued to move around destroyed or abandoned vehicles. From the air it must have taken on the appearance of an ant colony, with its thousands of workers skirting around each obstacle to keep pace in the move forward toward some distant and unknown destination.

With no semblance of order and no ability to manage the growing traffic, all control was rapidly lost as the growing sense of panic was about to foster another rout. At 1820 Lt. Col. Joseph Devins, U.S. Army,* the senior advisor with the 57th ARVN Regiment, radioed the division TOC that the regiment was ineffective and disintegrating around him as its commander had no knowledge of the status of two of his battalions that had been assigned to defend Dong Ha. Indeed, the only troops under his immediate physical control consisted of a reconnaissance platoon.[4]

Throughout the night men stranded on the north side of the Vinh Phuoc River continued to infiltrate south without their equipment and vehicles. The only effective unit still defending the Ai Tu combat base was Marine Brigade 147 and it was under heavy and nearly continuous artillery fire. Earlier in the day Major Huff, with the 8th Battalion, reported that what was left of the old 3d Division TOC bunker had taken twenty-five direct hits. Under such fire, the southwest corner had finally collapsed and the unit's radio antennas had been shot away on several occasions. He reported it was doubtful the bunker could withstand many more hits.

West of Ai Tu the enemy had continued its day-long attacks as large numbers of enemy tanks and infantry had forced the 1st Marine Battalion to pull its western defense line back to within a mile of Highway 1. Brigade 147's defenses were under attack on three sides and being steadily forced back against the unfordable Thach Han River.

By dawn on 29 April the situation in Quang Tri Province had further deteriorated. The 2d Regimental headquarters, which earlier had reported two of its battalions as being to the west and south of the Quang Tri Highway Bridge, could not be located. The U.S. advisor, Maj. Thomas MacKenzie, USA, with the 2d Troop of the 18th Cavalry, reported that his unit

---

*Replaced Lieutenant Colonel Twichell in the 57th Regiment on 17 April.

had succeeded in holding through the night despite taking heavy casualties. At 0520 the troop, operating without infantry support, repulsed an enemy attack which was directed at the bridges spanning the river.

The North Vietnamese exploited their tactical advantage over the withdrawing ARVN forces and intensified the artillery bombardments along Highway 1, both north and south of the city. Enemy units were reported to be 3,000 meters northeast of the capital, and again 4,000 meters to the east, indicating a slow but steady NVA effort aimed at encirclement of the ARVN positions. The RF and PF forces in the coastal area reported PT-76 tanks and infantry advancing toward Hai Lang from the east. To the southwest, all traffic on Highway 1 continued to be interrupted by artillery fire and enemy infantry forces moving in from the Ba Long Valley and FB Anne. Quang Tri City was slowly being surrounded and laid under siege from an endless shelling by artillery and rockets.[5] The North Vietnamese Army's encirclement of the provincial capital was almost identical to its systematic attacks to isolate and then overrun the French at Dien Bien Phu.

At 0800 Colonel Bao received a radio message at his Ai Tu TOC that no friendly forces remained on the west side of the Quang Tri bridges to his south. This was grim news because unless the highway remained open there would be no way to resupply his units on the northwest side of the river. Two infantry companies from the 7th Battalion, located on the Ai Tu southern perimeter, were assigned the mission of keeping the highway open. By 0930 the Marine unit, accompanied by 18th Cavalry's M-41 light tanks, cleared the roadway, deploying around the western approaches to the bridges. Twelve NVA were routed out of the highway bridge's concrete bunkers on the west bank. Two prisoners were taken, one of whom was carrying a U.S. 1:50,000 tactical map and the other a small radio. Their map showed ARVN positions and also targeting information for NVA artillery.

At that time it could not be determined if the routed NVA had mined the bridges, so traffic across the bridge was halted until engineers verified whether or not it was safe. However, the investigation also determined that the main highway bridge had been damaged by hits from the enemy's artillery fire and would no longer support heavy vehicular traffic. This left only the rail bridge available for crossing the river into the city.

Within the ever-diminishing enclave which the South Vietnamese held on the north bank, the friendly forces were suffering steady casualties from the incessant enemy fire. The 1st Armored Brigade reported that the 20th Tanks had only nineteen of its M-48 tanks and twelve APCs still operational. The 2d Troop of the 11th Cavalry reported that four of its M-41 tanks and twelve APCs were still operating and able to fight.

At the Ai Tu combat base, Brigade 147 continued to hold the perimeter under heavy enemy pressure which was expected to increase as enemy tanks were reported approaching from the north. Other T-54s were advancing from the west to within their main guns' range of the two bridges, raising the threat of direct fire interdiction or destruction of the vital river crossing.

Late in the afternoon the Ai Tu ammunition dump was again hit and the remaining ammunition, much of which had just arrived from the South, was destroyed. This was a crushing blow as ARVN commanders had already reported critical shortages of ammunition and fuel. Artillery batteries were standing idle because they were without fuses or powder bags.

At 1550 an M-48 tank stalled on the western end of the single lane railroad bridge into Quang Tri causing all vehicle traffic to stop. This delay caused further confusion, generating fear within the masses of soldiers and civilians still trying to flee into the city. Elements of the 4th Ranger Group attempted to move the tank out of the way. After several attempts to push the fifty-ton tank physically, the rangers moved around it on foot. Finally, at 1850 the rail bridge was cleared and vehicle traffic began crossing into the city.

To the south of the city, 29 April was also a day of great confusion. Units that had previously been defending the northern defense line had passed through Quang Tri City but had still not been assigned specific defensive missions. The 3d ARVN Division was not certain where most of its units were, because so many had reported false locations. Most units simply pulled back to positions near Highway 1 on their own initiative.

ARVN efforts to reopen its only escape route to the south were progressing at an extremely slow pace because of the lack of coordination and positive leadership at the command level. Individual units did from time to time attempt to break through the small enemy force that had overrun Highway 1. However, these efforts were severely hampered by civilian and military traffic. Adding to the already confusing situation, other ARVN APCs and tanks which were moving south would not cooperate or assist in the attacks on the NVA roadblocks. When questioned by American advisors as to why they were moving south the senior officer stated, "They were ordered to go south for maintenance." Lack of coordination between the various commanders drifting through that area and the sight of the departing ARVN armor heightened the fear and panic among the units positioned along Highway 1.

In the face of the impending disaster, General Giai developed a plan to attempt to hold Quang Tri City with his Marine brigade and to establish a defensive line on the southern bank of the Thach Han River with infantry and ranger troops. If successful, he hoped that this would release enough tank and cavalry units to conduct the now critical task of reopening Highway 1. To coordinate the plan his Marine, ARVN, ranger and armored commanders were all requested to be present at a conference in the Citadel at 0900 the next morning, 30 April.

The CP at Ai Tu had been under such heavy fire during the day of the 29th that Colonel Bao decided to split his command group into two sections. Shortly after dark he moved his "light" or forward CP group to the southern edge of the Ai Tu perimeter. Accompanying Bao at the Alpha group was his S-3 operations officer, the commander of the 11th Cavalry Squadron, his artillery commander (who served as the fire support coordinator) and two U.S. advisors: Lieutenant Colonel Wagner, USA, from 20th Tanks, and Major Joy.

Joy had earlier divided his detachment of brigade advisors into two groups, and on the 28th he sent three COVANs into Quang Tri City to establish a rear CP. This group consisted of Capt. Marshall Wells who had earlier been slightly wounded and was still ill from an attack of heat exhaustion, along with Majs. Charles Goode and Tom Gnibus. Arriving in the city, Major Goode, the senior officer, established their CP near the advisors' TOC in the Citadel.*

At 0448 on 30 April, Ai Tu combat base and the city began receiving another onslaught of heavy artillery and rocket fire. The South Vietnamese cannoneers could do little by way of counterfire to suppress the enemy guns. For example, the 33rd Artillery Battalion had 4,000 rounds of 105MM artillery at its position but only 400 fuses. The situation throughout the area was similarly serious, as the Marine artillery battalion at Ai Tu had less than 1,000 rounds of 105MM remaining. North of the Thach Han River the situation was deteriorating rapidly even as Colonel Bao, Jim Joy and the other commanders climbed aboard two APCs for the drive back into Quang Tri for a meeting with the division commander to discuss a plan to stabilize the battle and conduct an orderly withdrawal.

When all subordinate commanders had assembled, General Giai explained his new plan to save Quang Tri City and reopen the Highway south. The conference was tense, charged with emotion as the commander candidly, often excitedly, reviewed the critical situation. There was open criticism of General Giai's plans. Throughout the conference the division commander stressed that the new defense line he intended to

---

*Captain Wells had previously been with the 5th Battalion fighting around FB Jane. On one occasion, while with the Bravo group, their lead company found itself within the perimeter of an NVA battalion command post. The NVA were taken by surprise and initially the Marines inflicted heavy casualties on the enemy. The enemy force was well trained and quickly reorganized to overwhelm the Bravo group and one infantry company.

Captain Wells narrowly escaped with his life during the attack. His counterpart was seriously wounded and later confirmed to have been captured. Wells organized the surviving Marines and led them on a four-hour march to link up with the Alpha group. The action took place in extreme weather conditions that reached over 100° F. While they evaded the enemy, Wells, in coordination with Major Price, repeatedly called in artillery and air strikes on the enemy units attempting to intercept his group.

The action was at extremely close range and very intense. Wells's small tape antenna was shot off the radio on his back. Two Vietnamese Marines were seriously wounded and could no longer keep up with the column. Skip Wells, who had long been known for his brute strength, picked up both Marines and besides his rifle and radio carried the wounded the last half mile to safety. When they finally reached the battalion CP, Wells collapsed from heat exhaustion.

establish would have to hold or all Quang Tri Province would be lost to the communists. As General Giai ended the meeting he emphasized that individual units were not to withdraw or move until specific orders were received from his headquarters on the morning of 1 May.

While the meeting was being held, another enemy force was reported building up southwest of Ai Tu. The source of this information was an ARVN officer who had been captured at Camp Carroll on 1 April, and, having escaped, made his way through the lines to the 8th Battalion area. The officer, nearing exhaustion, reported having observed twenty tanks and a regimental-sized infantry force in an attack position southwest of Ai Tu. Because the massed enemy force was too far inland for U.S. naval gunfire to attack the target, it was necessary to rely on TAC Air as the primary supporting arm to bring the NVA's attack position under fire. Working with airborne controllers, Major Huff brought flight after flight of close air support down on the enemy. The attacking jet aircraft were bombing so close to the 8th Marine Battalion's front lines that NVA soldiers were fleeing from the bombs and napalm into the Marines' outer wire and their small arms fire.

At noon on the 30th, Colonel Bao advised Jim Joy that General Giai had made the decision to withdraw from the Ai Tu combat base and that Brigade 147's new mission would be to defend Quang Tri City. Immediately, the two officers began to develop a withdrawal plan. Colonel Bao placed his executive officer in charge of the withdrawal itself as he and Major Joy proceeded into the city to conduct a reconnaissance.

During the reconnaissance Colonel Bao selected the abandoned U.S. Army Team 19 "tiger pad" for his new CP. Even as Colonel Bao and his deputy were in Quang Tri City the battle around Ai Tu itself reached a new level of intensity. Enemy pressure had caused the 1st and 8th Battalions to pull back inside the perimeter wire.

Colonel Bao decided to remain in Quang Tri and directed his deputy to return to Ai Tu to commence preparations for the move back into the city. Jim Joy, however, felt it was imperative that the commander and he both return to Ai Tu personally to supervise the brigades' withdrawal. Colonel Bao listened to his recommendation but decided that he could best control the withdrawal from his new CP.

Radioing to Maj. Emmett Huff in the Ai Tu TOC bunker, Major Joy informed him of the plan and that the brigade's deputy commander, rather than Colonel Bao, was returning to brief the four battalion commanders on the withdrawal plan. Major Joy later noted, "The brigade staff at this time was in fact functioning under Major Huff's direction. The brigade commander, deputy commander and S-3 operations officer were all absent from the TOC."

While en route to Ai Tu, the brigade deputy's jeep was hit by enemy artillery fire and his driver was killed. The deputy was lucky and survived the explosion without injury. Now, without transportation, he radioed his infantry battalion commanders and the executive officer of the artillery battalion to meet him at the eastern entrance of the combat base where his jeep had been destroyed.

After the brigade deputy had departed Quang Tri, Colonel Bao was called back to the 3d Division CP and ordered Brigade 147 to begin its withdrawal immediately. A new intelligence report indicated that a division-sized attack on Quang Tri City was expected during the night. Using the advisors' secure voice radios, Colonel Bao passed this new information to Major Huff who was in turn to inform the deputy commander of the new urgency added to the brigade's withdrawal.

The sudden change in withdrawal plans was too much for the South Vietnamese officers and men in the TOC. It was almost a repeat of the 3d ARVN Division relocation back to the Citadel. A Captain Xuon began demanding that the advisors leave their radios and equipment and immediately join in moving to the deputy's location. Major Huff refused, saying, "I will not leave until the secure radio equipment and classified material is destroyed." The captain, perplexed by Huff's firmness, reentered the bunker several more times requesting that the advisors join him. With artillery pounding the area, the Texas-born tenacity of Emmett Huff came to the fore as he methodically and meticulously located and accounted for all the sensitive materials and then saw to their being stacked in one corner of the bunker. This done, he, Capt. Skip Kruger, and Army Captain Guernsey began pulling the pins on incendiary grenades, then placing them in and among the stacked materials. When they were certain that the fire had started burning the sensitive materials and that the bunker's heavy timbers were in flames, they shouldered their rucksacks and left. Huff was the last to leave. He took one last look around the burning bunker to ascertain that nothing of value was left for the enemy. Dark smoke billowed out the east entrance. The burning bunker had been a safe haven for many of the U.S. advisors during the first month of the NVA offensive. It had served its purpose well.

Outside the burning bunker, Huff put the final touch on his destruction plan as he requested naval gunfire from all available guns to commence on the Ai Tu base, its bunker and the few remaining fuel tanks nearby. Again, the American ships offshore responded, placing a nearly solid wall of steel from the five-inch guns between the advancing NVA and the advisors.

By the time Huff and Kruger had completed their task and were assured the fire would envelop the bunker, the deputy commander and the brigade staff had already departed. The three advisors joined up with the 4th Battalion on the southeast corner of the Ai Tu perimeter.

Colonel Bao's plan for withdrawal and repositioning called for the brigade headquarters and artillery battalion to depart first, followed by the 1st and 8th Battalions, with the 4th Battalion serving as rearguard. The withdrawal was executed smoothly under incoming artillery fire. As the lead elements of the brigade approached within sight of the city, ARVN engineers, who had fallen back into the city, prematurely destroyed the last useable bridge. In disbelief the Marines continued the march to the west bank, only to see the few remaining twisted iron girders of the bridge causing ripples in the fast-flowing Thach Han River below.

In desperation the commander of the artillery battalion attempted to ford the river with his trucks but failed. With no way to get his trucks and the eighteen howitzers across, the artillery men began spiking their guns, removing the firing mechanism, shooting the tires and setting the vehicles on fire.

As the withdrawing infantry battalions closed in, on the destroyed bridges, over a hundred vehicles had been set ablaze.[6]

Moving down to the old vehicle fording site, almost 2,000 Marines began crossing the river. Most attempted to walk out in the shallowest area, then would swim about fifty yards before they could again touch bottom. Stray sampans and every other possible flotation device were scrounged up and put into service. What few air mattresses remained quickly became rafts for wounded or radios. Many rucksacks were left on the north bank but most of the Marines managed to hold onto their rifles while fighting the river's current. A few drowned; it was unavoidable.

The 4th Battalion's rearguard held the west bank perimeter until the brigade completed its crossing then proceeded to make its own way across the river. Major Huff continued to coordinate air strikes and naval gunfire until his own time came to cross. The three advisors were all over six feet, so by moving slowly and remaining on the submerged fording roadway, the water was only neck-high as they slowly crossed the river.

They had placed their radio and weapons on an air mattress and were in the deepest part of the river when a floundering Vietnamese Marine suddenly grabbed Captain Kruger and climbed upon his shoulders. Kruger, wearing his helmet and flak jacket and carrying a belt load of rifle ammunition, lost his footing and went under. Fortunately, he had his hand around the radio handset and held it as the cable extended its full length without breaking. Emmett Huff, holding firmly to the radio, was able to pull the two Marines back on to the safe footing by pulling on the cable of the handset. Thus, the three advisors were the last to emerge on the east bank.

The brigade's desperate decision to swim the Thach Han was but another instance of confusion and needless loss of life and equipment because the 3d ARVN Division failed to provide coordination among its units. Through all this, the work pattern of the 3d Division remained unchanged and out of touch with reality as orders were routinely issued, often immediately countermanded and always assumed to have been instantly implemented by the subordinate units. There had never been a sincere effort made within the division staff to venture out into the forward battle positions to supervise and assist in the difficult execution of the division's tactical orders.

I recognized this on one of my more memorable flights into the Quang Tri Citadel on 26 or 27 April. I toured the 3d Division TOC and then walked across the compound to the advisor's TOC, Fire Support Coordination Center. Tragically, these two critical coordination centers remained separated. At a time when mere seconds determined when artillery, naval gunfire missions or an aircraft's load of bombs could be released, officers were still required to dash back and forth between centers to authorize the firing of all U.S. supporting weapons on enemy targets. More often than not, either the artillery, naval gunfire or the orbiting aircraft were "on-hold" which resulted in no one firing at the massing North Vietnamese. After a month of exceptionally intense combat, the

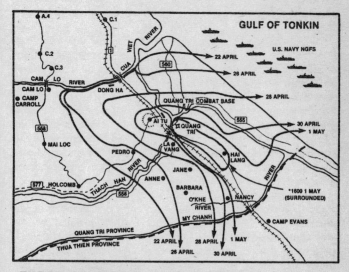

**THE ENCIRCLEMENT OF QUANG TRI CITY, MAY 1972**
**\* SURROUNDED, 1600 1 MAY 1972.**

two coordination centers were still inefficient. There was a feeling of total frustration amongst the U.S. Army, Air Force and Marine naval gunfire personnel. They wanted to provide better support, but because of a flaw in the team's leadership it would never come about.

By dusk of the 30th, the North Vietnamese invaders controlled all of Quang Tri Province north of the Capital. All intelligence indicators signalled that another big attack was imminent.

# CHAPTER EIGHTEEN

# EVACUATION OF THE PROVINCIAL CAPITAL

During the night of 30 April the situation around the provincial capital deteriorated further as the enemy increased its artillery shelling, indiscriminately striking both civilian and military targets. With North Vietnamese soldiers a mere 500 meters away on the west bank of the Thach Han River, the 8,000 to 10,000 civilians remaining in the capital were in a state of mass panic as there seemed to be no secure place to hide from the war.

The U.S. advisors at the headquarters of the 3d Division continued to request and orchestrate their supporting arms on enemy positions around the city. Maj. Jimmy Davis, Jr., USA, the G-3 advisor to Team 155, skillfully performed his operational duties, welding together the vast array of U.S. air and naval gunfire assets. Major Dave Brookbank remained fervent in his desire to provide the South Vietnamese all possible air support. Dave and his air liaison team had been managing over 200 sorties of TAC Air each day.

As the ARVN defensive perimeter continued to shrink, all fire support coordination problems increased as the ARVN artillery positions were constantly changing. It was never certain when or in what direction their guns were firing. The high trajectory of these artillery shells often endangered U.S. pilots as more than once aircraft flew through a salvo of "friendly" artillery projectiles.

The efforts of the massive armada of ships providing naval gunfire support was being coordinated by Maj. Glen Golden, USMC, who belonged to ANGLICO's Sub Unit 1. In mid-April, he had been sent to Quang Tri because of his demonstrated expertise in the coordination of all types of supporting arms. Immediately, Glen and Dave had become invaluable to Advisory Team 155 and, unknowingly, these two Americans were about to play yet another critical role in the Easter offensive.

Throughout the night Quang Tri City was bathed in light from flares. The ships offshore, artillery batteries and aircraft overhead dispensed hundreds of parachute flares. On the ancient walls of the Citadel eerie shadows flickered and danced as the sky above was filled with artificial illumination to reveal the advancing enemy.

Shortly before dawn on 1 May, General Lam called General Giai and told him he did not approve of the latest withdrawal plan. He issued orders to Giai that all units were to hold their present positions "at all costs" and not withdraw unless he personally approved. "The capital must be held at all costs."

General Lam's countermanding order was little more than a reiteration of instructions he had just received from President Thieu in Saigon and not the sober reflections of a commander who had analyzed the tactical situation.[1] Acknowledging the order, Giai vainly tried to countermand his earlier orders and issue new ones on the division command radio channels but it was too late. Some units had already moved out to clear the enemy from along Highway 1. Others simply refused to comply with the new orders; one by one the ARVN units withdrew from their positions along the Thach Han River, to the east of the city, and began moving south.

Having crossed the river and regrouped, Marine Brigade 147 remained in its new defensive positions around the city while ARVN units to the east and west of the capital were in full retreat to the south. This left the Marine brigade, the headquarters elements of the 3d Division, and the members of the U.S. Advisory Team 155 as the only effective front line units. With these few forces, the U.S. advisors continued to coordinate TAC Air and naval gunfire on enemy positions in defense of the city but with so little ground combat support their position was fast becoming untenable.

The advisors in the Citadel began to make their final plans for evacuation. Around 1000 Colonel Murdock met with the team's deputy senior advisor, Lt. Col. William E. Lozier. He and Majors Davis and Golden discussed the situation with Murdock as Lozier took the lead in coordinating the plan for the evacuation. It was decided to attempt a U.S. Air Force (SAR) helicopter mission because of the deteriorating situation on Highway 1.[2] He organized the Americans into three teams and also formulated an alternate evasion plan if the SAR mission was not successful.

Throughout the Citadel, rumors were rampant as word spread that the NVA was about to unleash a massive artillery attack on Quang Tri City. Colonel Bao and Jim Joy returned to the division headquarters for a conference with General Giai. While there, Giai indicated that intelligence sources had revealed that the NVA would begin a 10,000-round artillery attack on Quang Tri City at 1700. Departing the dismal scene, the two Marines returned to the brigade's positions and began to make what arrangements they could.

At 1200 Giai declared the situation hopeless; the city could not be held under the circumstances. Shortly thereafter two ARVN APCs entered the Citadel. Immediately, Giai and approximately twenty-five of his more senior staff officers climbed into and on top of the vehicles to begin their attempt to escape toward the My Chanh River. This sudden departure left about eighty Americans alone in the Citadel hoping desperately for evacuation by helicopter. Dave Brookbank and Glen Golden skillfully planned their supporting fires around the Citadel to "box themselves in."

At 1400 the two APCs carrying General Giai and his staff reentered the Citadel. It turned out that after leaving the city, their two vehicles had been discovered and attacked by an NVA unit about a mile south. With their escape route blocked, they were forced to return north to the immediate safety of the Citadel. Upon arrival, Giai requested additional helicopters be sent to save his staff.[3]

At 1420 the I DASC in Hue passed a coded message to

Dave Brookbank containing a set of coordinates for its SAR pick up. The intended landing zone was 1,000 meters south of the Citadel. However, to reach that position the Americans would have been required to fight their way out of the Citadel to the pick-up point. Murdock directed that the SAR landing site be changed to the heli-pad inside the Citadel.

With the stage set for their evacuation, Brookbank contacted the three airborne controllers (FACs) around the city to cover Brigade 147's movement south. At 1500 each FAC was given four flights of aircraft to use as they saw fit to strike enemy targets as the U.S. Air Force Jolly Green rescue helicopters began their final approaches into the Citadel. This air cover commenced at 1530 with F-4s on-station and capable of delivering every type of ordnance.

Within the Citadel preparations for the evacuation continued at a rapid rate as advisors continued to burn classified material and destroy as much equipment as possible. At 1520 the power station was blown. Still not certain of their rescue, the advisors began to hear increasing amounts of small arms fire outside the Citadel walls. All around them the ancient city was in flames. There was nothing to do but wait and stay alert.

At 1600 Brookbank's radio came alive with a radio message that the Jolly Greens were on the way. At 1615 the first helicopter was seen coming in at a low altitude. A-1 aircraft were flying their usual clover leaf fire suppression patterns around him.

Finally, at 1630 the lead helicopter, callsign Jolly Green 71, landed. General Giai, some of his staff and a few advisors rushed on board. At 1632 the helicopter lifted off with thirty-seven passengers. The second rescue aircraft, Jolly Green 65, landed, picked up forty-seven passengers and lifted off after only two or three minutes. The third Jolly Green followed to evacuate the remaining forty-five personnel. Colonel Murdock and Major Golden were the last to enter the aircraft. A fourth helicopter landed, but took off in thirty seconds when the pilot discovered everyone had been evacuated.[4]

The Air Force SAR mission had successfully evacuated 129 people. In a matter of moments they had been rescued and flown to safety in Danang. Brookbank best summed up the experience of the advisors who were surrounded in the Citadel:

> The city became cut off and isolated. The intense NVA heavy artillery and tanks created maximum havoc by splitting some ARVN forces and inducing panic in others. NGF and U.S. TAC Air were more effectively used while ARVN artillery gradually lost all value. Many ARVN forces held while others broke and ran. The ARVN Marines never lost fighting effectiveness and had to be ordered to withdraw many times to plug gaps in the line. In the end, the 147th Marine Brigade, 258th Marine Brigade, and the 20th Tank Squadron, because they never stopped fighting and remained effective, enabled the U.S. advisors, cut off at the Citadel, to evacuate.[5]

As the smoke of the burning city billowed around them and the helicopters disappeared southward, the NVA had achieved its first objective, the capture of the provincial capital of Quang Tri. Before dusk of that day North Vietnamese flags were seen flying over the ancient Citadel.

Brigade 369 had not been idle along the My Chanh line. Col. Phan Van Chung's force of over 3,000 Marines had initially been assigned an area of responsibility (AO) that extended deep into the western Annamite mountains and north of the My Chanh River to tie in with a ranger group south of La Vang. Within the brigade's AO were fire bases Jane, Nancy and Barbara and the multi-canopied Hai Lang forest in the western mountains, a rugged area which had been a staging area for Viet Cong and NVA troops. National Highway 1 passed through the center of his brigade's AO and served as the 3d Division's main supply line into Quang Tri Province.

Like many of the other senior Marine officers, Colonel Chung had been born in North Vietnam and elected to emigrate to South Vietnam when the French withdrew. Being from the north, he was of larger frame and heavier than most of his South Vietnamese counterparts. Chung was not only the most senior Marine commander, but he also had the most combat experience. A firm disciplinarian, he was also known for his sensitivity to the plight of helpless civilians caught up in the Indo-China wars.

During early April, his 2d, 5th, and 9th Battalions had fought a series of battles while the focus of fighting remained on those units defending the Dong Ha-Cam Lo areas. At that time, Chung's senior U.S. advisor was Marine Maj. Robert Sheridan. They had become an inseparable team. Later recalling Chung's cautionary tactics to elude the enemy's long-range artillery during April, Bob Sheridan said:

> No unit was allowed to remain in one location for over thirty-six hours. During April we displaced our command post twenty-one times. Our artillery batteries, which were the main target of enemy fires, displaced more frequently. During one twenty-four-hour period near the end of April our artillery battalion displaced four times and one of its batteries had to move six times. In spite of these many displacements our infantry battalions were never without the fires of the guns when they were needed.[6]

By mid-April the war in Brigade 369's AO increased in tempo as the NVA began launching battalion-sized attacks aimed at severing Highway 1. On FB Barbara the 2d Marine Battalion had been subjected to extremely heavy artillery fires. During one twelve-hour period the battalion's position had been cut in half during an NVA "human wave" assault. However, in spite of such heavy enemy pressure the 2d Battalion, with its COVANs Maj. Bill Sweeney and Capt. Merl Sexton, successfully held the hills that dominated and overlooked Highway 1 and the My Chanh Bridge. Thus, Chung's Marine brigade had been in continuous contact with NVA forces since their arrival on 3 April.

Around mid-morning on 29 April, Capts. George Philips and Bob Redlin drove their jeep into Brigade 369's CP perimeter and located Major Sheridan. Philips' first remarks were, "My God, have you seen the road? There are thousands of people coming down the highway from Quang Tri. As far as you can see north and south the road is covered with refugees."

Chung had also just been made aware of what was happening to the east of their CP and moved to see the situation himself. Sheridan and the other advisors followed Chung to a clearing on the edge of the village where they could view the road. Sheridan later recorded:

> George Philips had not overestimated. There were literally thousands of people moving southward.
>
> There were not any soldiers in this group; only the very old, very young, the sick, the blind, the wounded. Women were toting their few possessions in one basket which was balanced on the other end of a carrying stick by their babies.
>
> The Marines gave them food, water, money. The generosity could not alleviate the suffering of the people as their numbers were too great.[7]

The column continued for hours. Around mid-day, the NVA artillery again unleashed their guns on the column. On into the night, the refugees moved past the Marines' position. Around 2100 the refugee column, except for a few stragglers, abruptly ended. Chung soon learned that the reason for this sudden change was due to the success of the North Vietnamese in severing Highway 1 south of Quang Tri City. Apparently the bridge over the Song Nhung had been captured from an ARVN ranger unit. Elements of the 3d Division were thus isolated five miles north of the My Chanh River.

Just after midnight, Brigade 369 was given the mission to move north to link up with the rangers and attempt the reopening of the main highway. Chung assigned this task and another to attack north at dawn to his 5th Battalion, commanded by Major Lick. Maj. Don Price, the senior advisor with the battalion, moved with the Alpha command group. Initially the movement of the battalion's infantry companies met only light resistance, consisting mostly of snipers on the west side of the road. However, after crossing the O-Khe River the lead elements came under heavy fire from an old triangular-style fort originally built by the French in the 1950s. The Marines did not return this fire because they believed the entrenched force was a regional force unit and the column halted.

Both Majors Lick and Price reported the situation through

their radio channels back to the brigade. When Chung finished talking on the radio, he walked over to Sheridan and asked "Do you have any TAC Air available?" Sheridan had just received Price's radio report and wasn't certain if his counterpart had been informed that RFs could be mistakenly firing on the Marines.

Chung's response was short and clear. "Regional forces don't shoot at Marines. They are VC. Please get air." Sheridan thereupon made a radio request for U.S. TAC Air. A FAC was assigned and Price was directed to take control of the flight and destroy the fort. He quickly briefed the FAC on the situation and locations of the Marines. Thereafter ten sorties of fixed-wing aircraft and an attack with a USAF C-130 Specter gunship were run on the fort with devastating effect. Then, 5th Battalion assaulted the position and later counted 234 bodies—all in NVA uniforms, part of the elite 27th Regiment. Wounded prisoners later recounted how their regiment had taken the fort the night before, after it had been abandoned by the regional force unit assigned to it.

This action by the 5th Battalion cleared most of the opposition at that section of Highway 1 and the unit pressed onward to the scheduled link-up with the rangers and tanks that had been directed to move down the highway from the north. Arriving at another bridge, the Marines met and overcame a platoon-sized NVA force, and set in a 360° security perimeter while they waited for the arrival of the rangers. Eight hours later, as the sun was setting, no link-up had been effected. With its lines overextended, in need of resupply and concerned for its dead and wounded, the 5th Battalion reluctantly withdrew to positions along the O-Khe River. This left the two South Vietnamese columns on the highway separated by approximately three miles, with the NVA between them.

On the morning of 30 April the 1st Armored Brigade made an attempt to reopen Highway 1 to the My Chanh but met heavy resistance and achieved only limited success. The brigade sought first to destroy the enemy's major roadblock by recapturing the bridge spanning the Song Nhung River. Flowing out of the Annamite Mountains, the river was too deep to ford, hence the Song Nhung bridge became critical to the survival of the 3d Division's remaining units.

By mid-afternoon the highway had still not been opened and other ARVN units fleeing south were immobilized as the enemy road block held. The 18th Cavalry Regiment was ordered to lead the attack and reopen the highway. This attack was met with heavy resistance as the NVA responded with RPG recoilless rifle, mortar and small arms fire. Finally, the enemy position was overrun and the command group of the 1st Armored Brigade moved forward to assess the situation. It discovered that the bridge was blocked by burning vehicles at both entrances and by several vehicles on the bridge itself. While recovery vehicles were being brought forward to clear the bridge, the NVA began firing AT-3 Sagger anti-tank missiles at the ARVN vehicles silhouetted on the raised roadway. Enemy artillery began to strike the men and vehicles that had been assembled in an attempt to clear this critical point south of the provincial capital.

The situation became even more critical as attempts to suppress the enemy fire were not effective and the enemy artillery intensified, striking the stalled masses of people and vehicles. With no place of safety to be found in the sandy salt flats that flanked both sides of the highway, confusion and panic set in. The exodus had been stopped. In some cases artillery crews in the column abandoned their weapons while large numbers of refugees and soldiers ran north, then south along the highway, attempting to avoid the enemy artillery.

Hundreds of ARVN stragglers filled the roadway. Hundreds more simply drifted aimlessly across the salt flats and sand dunes. As the tide of disorganized people sought to flee and was halted by the enemy roadblocks, they struck out in all directions to escape the impacting artillery and mortar rounds. Those in the rear of the column, which at that point was miles long, did not understand why their escape efforts had been halted and continued to push forward. For a hundred yards on each side of the Street Without Joy hysterical refugees and deserters fled between the burning vehicles, climbing over huddled families, the dead and dying, and piles of discarded personal effects and weapons.

Author Arnold R. Isaacs was to travel by jeep over this section of the highway of horrors during June. He was overwhelmed by the scope of the tragedy and wrote:

At the start of counteroffensive the South Vietnamese para-troopers met one of the most appalling scenes of the entire war: the burned, blasted remains of a huge convoy of soldiers and refugees that had been trapped on the wrong side of the blown bridge and destroyed during the flight out of the province. For miles, smashed vehicles lay in an almost unbroken line on both sides of the road. Driving north with a jeepload of other cor-respondents a couple of days after the paratroopers recrossed the river, I counted more than 400 wrecks in the first two miles, and I stopped counting long before we reached the end of the destruction. Army trucks, their canvas burned or shot away, lay with their ribs sticking up like the skeletons of dinosaurs. Slewed among them were scores of civilian vehicles: buses with their side panels shredded by shrapnel and bullet holes; bent, broken motorbikes; shattered scooter-buses; burned, blackened cars with shot-out headlights staring like the eye sockets of a skull.

Although government soldiers had already removed hundreds of bodies, many wrecked vehicles still contained a grisly cargo of corpses, shriveled, blackened mummies after two months under the beating Vietnamese sun. No one ever reliably counted the dead; casualties ranged into the thousands.[8]

Major Sheridan also recorded what he observed of the ever-growing scene of tragedy and devastation:

The column continued for hours and I thought it would be impossible to witness a worse sight when just after noon the North Vietnamese gunners, for reasons I'll never know, opened fire with their large artillery guns on the column. Hundreds were killed and maimed, yet the masses continued to flow southward.

We could not return artillery fire as the enemy's guns were well out of range of our guns. Any respect I had for the North Viet-namese military, I lost that day. His forward observers, who were directing this withering hail of fire were close enough to determine that these were mostly civilians and not a military force.[9]

At 1600, NVA forces still blocked the road south. Around 1700 an order was passed over the 3d Division's ARVN radios "to execute a night withdrawal to the south along the highway and to destroy all equipment without an amphibious capability." Before this order could be clarified and the advisors could stop the action, twelve of the 17th Cavalry's M-41 light tanks and eighteen 105MM howitzers of the 33d Artillery Battalion were destroyed. Although the order was rescinded around 1800, this vital equipment was already irretrievably lost as the armored brigade was ordered by the 3d Division to continue attempts to secure the Song Nhung Bridge.

Although enemy forces had been identified only 500 meters northeast of the Brigade's CP there was no harassment during the night. Thus at first light on the morning of 1 May the armored brigade's loose conglomeration of units began another attack to the south. An urgent request had been sent by the 3d Division for B-52 strikes east and west of the bridge but at 0500 Lieutenant Colonel Wagner was notified that no B-52 ARCLIGHT strikes would be allocated to assist in the attacks southward.

At 0600 a FAC flying over the armored brigade reported the Song Nhung Bridge had been destroyed. Elements of the brigade then turned east toward the village of Hai Lang in another desperate maneuver to break out of their impending encirclement. The 17th Cavalry, now minus twelve of its M-41 tanks, led off and after several hours found a site where the Song Nhung could be forded. Once the APCs from the 17th's troop were across the river, the 18th and the brigade headquarters broke contact along the highway and moved across the ford. By 1230 these units were reassembled on the other side of the river. From this point the brigade column once again turned south and proceeded toward the My Chanh River.

With the headquarters of the 3d Division no longer in the area and incapable of controlling its forces, there was much confusion as to which units were friendly or enemy. Thus, when the column of the armored brigade approached the My Chanh, Colonel Chung ordered it to halt as he wanted to ascertain that it was not an NVA unit or that enemy troops were not intermixed with friendly units or riding on the few remaining APCs.

Everywhere, the U.S. Army advisors encouraged the senior officers of the ARVN units to attempt to organize the stragglers into some kind of cohesive units. Nothing was done or even attempted; all semblance of ARVN military leadership was gone.

When dawn broke on 2 May, vehicles of the armored brigade and thousands of ARVN infantry who had joined the column once again began to move southwest toward the O-Khe Bridge and the My Chanh line. The lead APCs were within a mile of the Marine lines when the NVA struck the column with a heavy artillery barrage.

With this sudden onslaught the last semblance of ARVN leadership in the beleaguered column simply collapsed. Vehicle commanders became excited and leaders lost control of their units. There was mass confusion as dozens of vehicles drove into one another as they attempted to flee the enemy fire in every possible direction. A number of their own infantry troops were run over in the process and left behind.

An American FAC orbiting over Hai Lang assisted Colonel Wagner in trying to find an opening through the enemy's positions. Finally, at 1200, what was left of the 1st Armored Brigade moved through the Marines' forward positions and crossed over the My Chanh River Bridge into Thua Thien Province and straggled to safety at Camp Evans. There had been times when the brigade was heroic in its stand against the North Vietnamese divisions, but after thirty-three days of conventional warfare it had lost ninety percent of its tanks and APCs and was no longer an effective combat force.

Thus, by 1400 on 2 May, only Marine Brigade 147 and its small cluster of assorted units remained north of the My Chanh River and capable of any organized resistance to the NVA offensive.

On 1 May, when General Giai had precipitously decided to evacuate Quang Tri City, Marine Brigade 147 had been ordered to escort the remaining elements of the 3d ARVN Division staff south to the My Chanh. To execute this order Colonel Bao, on that afternoon, positioned his 8th Battalion to lead the column, the 4th Battalion on the left flank, the 1st Battalion on the right flank and the two companies from the

7th Battalion to guard the rear of the column. His tanks and APCs were to move to the center of the column with the division staff, brigade headquarters and artillery headquarters. Major Joy reassembled his advisors as Major Goode and Captains Wells and Kruger joined the brigade formation for the march south.

Shortly after 1430 the Marines had begun their withdrawal, with their route initially to the east for approximately 2,000 meters and then the column turned south. The column made good progress for several hours until 1600 when the lead elements encountered a steeply banked stream where three tanks were lost during the crossing. The advisors watched as Marines and cavalrymen dropped hand grenades into the hatches to disable the vehicles.

Continuing southward, the column stopped at 1730 to watch the four Air Force helicopters fly into the Citadel to extract the Americans and 3d Division staff. As the rescue helicopters passed over carrying the last survivors out of Quang Tri City, no one spoke or needed to. The impact of that action on their own situation spoke for itself.

By 1900 the column had reached the Hai Lang area, five miles southeast of the city where it halted west of Hai Lang district headquarters. ARVN stragglers were encountered everywhere. Radio contact was made with the staff of Brigade 369 and its advisors as the My Chanh defensive line was only 5,000 meters south.

Colonel Bao and the other commanders decided not to risk a nighttime encounter with the enemy, partly because of the uncontrolled movement of large numbers of civilians and troops throughout the area. Thus, an attempt to break through to the Marines of Brigade 369 would be delayed until morning. A route for the morning move was selected and Brigade 147 set up a tight night perimeter. Colonel Bao and Jim Joy met with the battalion commanders and it was determined the units were still well-organized and effective. Like the 1st Armored Brigade, located a 1,000 meters to the south, the Marines planned to move at first light.

As the units settled in for the night, Emmett Huff and the

brigade operations officer planned the coordination of the night's defensive fires and provisions were made to assure that an airborne FAC would remain on-station all night.

During that night Major Goode, one of the advisors with Brigade 147, remembered:

> We had lost contact with the rest of the advisors. I was lying on a sand dune and had a radio. I just kept switching from one channel to another to see if I could contact anybody.
>
> I made contact with an FAC and he told us about everything that had happened that day.
>
> Later I made contact with Don Price, with the 5th Battalion. The reception was really bad, but I was able to get the message to him that we were all together, the advisors were all right. God, it was comforting that they now knew we were alive.[10]

The night passed quietly for the tired troops, with no activity being reported until about 0500 the next morning when the 1st Battalion reported tank noises coming from the west. Shortly thereafter a couple of PT-76s were sighted, both fired their main tank guns in the direction of Hai Lang. At the head of the column the 8th Battalion broke to the south, having been surprised by the appearance of the enemy armor. Jim Joy later wrote of this as follows:

> It seemed to spook the whole column. The headquarters elements and stragglers started to climb on top of the tracked vehicles. The advisors tried to settle down the brigade staff. I advised Colonel Bao he must get all the headquarters elements off the tanks and APCs so they could engage the enemy.[11]

Calling a hurried meeting of his commanders, Colonel Bao regained control of the brigade and directed his 8th Battalion to move with the tanks and APCs as opposed to being positioned ahead of them. Just as the meeting broke up, the brigade's perimeter was attacked from the east by enemy recoilless rifle fire, emanating from Hai Lang Village. Major Joy recorded:

It was the most inopportune moment possible; the tanks and APCs broke without returning a single shot at the enemy. The headquarters elements were still embarked on the tracked vehicles and the unit commanders were on their way back to their units. When the armored vehicles broke it fragmented the whole column.[12]

Majors Joy and Huff were at the rear of the brigade's command APC when its driver also panicked and began to move away. When he did so, Majors Goode and Gnibus, two Army advisors and an American civilian, Gerry Dunn, were sitting on top of the vehicle. When they saw that Joy and Huff had been left standing on the ground, Goode, Gnibus and Dunn all jumped off as the vehicle sped away with the Army advisors still aboard. Captains Kruger and Wells on the other command vehicle also jumped off. In doing so the advisors soon found themselves at the end of the column as it continued to move toward the My Chanh River. For three hours they could do little but follow along in the rear. Major Joy formed the six Marine advisors and one civilian, a former Marine pilot, into a group and together they began to move south. Major Goode later recorded:

We wandered around quite a bit that morning. I remember we went south, then east, then west. Every time we would look over a sand dune some place we would see naked or semi-naked Vietnamese, former soldiers who had stripped off all their clothing. They carried no weapons. There were a lot of deserters and refugees around us.[13]

Moving toward the My Chanh, the brigade column was attacked first from the east and then the south. As their APCs retreated north, this further disorganized the column. Throughout the chaotic situation Major Huff stayed on the radio calling air strikes on Hai Lang from where the first NVA attack of the day had come. An FAC was orbiting over the area. When it became apparent that Joy's group of advisors had become completely separated from the staff of Brigade 147, Joy directed Huff to contact the FAC and request an emergency helicopter evacuation. Immediately Huff radioed the FAC to the effect that "there are NVA on all sides and it appears we have about five minutes before the enemy is on top of us."

As fate would have it, the only helicopter that could immediately respond to the rescue call was Brigadier General Bowen's command Huey, an aircraft designed to carry a maximum of eleven passengers. Recognizing the gravity of the situation, the general instantly ordered his pilot to fly directly to the encircled Americans.

In the interim, one of the advisors located a depression and picked out a small landing zone. It was in a little, dried up rice paddy with dunes on all sides. As the helicopter began its approach Major Joy ignited a colored smoke grenade. The helicopter, which already had six people on it, landed in an inferno. The on-rushing NVA opened up with fifty-one caliber machine guns, mortars and small arms before the helicopter dropped out of sight of the enemy.

Once the helicopter was on the ground it couldn't be seen by the enemy. As the advisors and Gerry Dunn scrambled aboard, ARVN stragglers also grabbed at holds on the sides and skids of the Huey. With so many on-board, the helicopter could not lift off. On one side of the aircraft General Bowen and Joy fought off the Vietnamese while Huff and Kruger physically beat others off their side. The aircraft finally lifted off with Huff astraddle the landing skid, holding onto the aircraft with one hand and Kruger with the other. Kruger was dangling below the aircraft, desperately holding on to Huff. The pilot, Capt. Stanley A. Dougherty, U.S. Army, had climbed up about fifty feet when he was told of the American hanging below the aircraft. He immediately set back down to permit Kruger to be pulled into the aircraft.

Once again, the helicopter lifted off as more Vietnamese were beaten off the skids. Seriously overloaded by this time with seventeen people inside or hanging onto the Huey, the aircraft gained some altitude as its red RPM limit light came on, while enemy tanks were seen less than 100 yards away. The North Vietnamese gunners turned every available weapon toward the straining aircraft.

With desperate measures called for, Captain Dougherty

pushed his aircraft into a deep dive at about 120 knots, correcting its threatening course just above treetop level, as more enemy bullets struck the helicopter. Gerry Dunn was wounded as a bullet grazed his scalp. The pilot, fighting against impossible odds in terms of strain on the helicopter and the heavy enemy fire, flew across the My Chanh River toward Camp Evans. As it passed over Don Price's position he radioed the pilot that the aircraft was streaming fuel and an individual was clinging to a landing skid.[14]

Thus, the last helicopter evacuation from Quang Tri Province had been successfully completed. The helicopter had to be left where it skidded to an emergency landing. It was no longer flyable because of the multiple hits from enemy guns. The U.S. Army general's decision and the subsequent heroic actions of his pilot had saved seven Americans from certain capture or even death.

The final battle for Quang Tri Province shifted to the area where Highway 1 crossed over the O-Khe and My Chanh rivers. Early in the afternoon on 2 May, Colonel Chung, his small executive staff and members of his Marine advisory team stood along the southern bank of the My Chanh and watched with sadness and disbelief as the remnants of the 3d ARVN Division, four ranger groups, an armored brigade, two cavalry squadrons and a Marine brigade and many other RF, PF and logistical support troops simply disintegrated as military units and fled south toward the city of Hue.

Only twenty-four hours earlier Quang Tri City had fallen to the attacking North Vietnamese, with little or no resistance. Ten thousand South Vietnamese had fled southward, the victims of sustained enemy artillery barrages and their own poor leadership. Some walked, some carried their wounded and fallen comrades, some rode atop the few remaining trucks and APCs. Most were disciplined enough to retain their individual weapons and equipment.

The My Chanh Bridge was like a radiating beacon light promising safe passage into Thua Thien Province. There was no order or attempt at control as the masses of humanity edged toward the positions of Brigade 369 deployed around the 100-

yard-long bridge. From the northwest, north and east, refugees and soldiers picked their individual routes toward the black steel girders of the bridge as the badly beaten South Vietnamese Army sought refuge from the guns of their brothers from the north.

After watching the bedraggled forces drift by for over an hour, Bob Sheridan remembered that at one point he turned to Colonel Chung and said, "Well, sir, it looks as if everyone else is heading south. What are we going to do?" Colonel Chung looked at his COVAN and stated, "No, No, we will not go south. We are a good brigade and with your help we will kill all the VC along this river. No VC will ever cross the My Chanh River and remain alive."[15]

The previous night, when Charlie Goode made radio contact with Major Price, he had related to the advisors at Brigade 369's headquarters Brigade 146's positions and predicament near Hai Lang. Major Sheridan ran to inform Colonel Chung of his unexpected radio contact. Chung did not know the city had fallen and at that time Colonel Bao's brigade was still located to the north of Quang Tri City. Together they hurried over to the advisor's radio where the two Vietnamese commanders talked for about fifteen minutes. When they finished talking, Colonel Chung looked at Sheridan and said, "Very bad, very bad. Quang Tri has fallen. Very little fighting. Army advisors and 3d Division officers left by helicopter. Marine advisors are with the Brigade. VC will try to take our bridges. Tomorrow we will have a big battle. Now we must prepare and plan."

The third and last of the Marine division's brigades prepared for battle the remainder of the night. The alert was sounded by Major Sheridan as he marshalled every destroyer and cruiser in the vicinity of MR-1, as they no longer had anyone north of the O-Khe River to support. Airborne controllers, as well as TAC Air, were scheduled to be on-station at first light.

Colonel Chung took the daring chance of placing some of his 105MM artillery batteries directly behind the 5th Infantry Battalion which could then support the front lines with direct fire. He then demonstrated his fine personal leadership when he visited each of his commanders and impressed on them the magnitude of the task ahead. Throughout the night he closely supervised the brigade's preparation for battle.

The 9th Battalion, commanded by Major De with Maj. Jim Beans as his senior COVAN, was deployed along the O-Khe River. Major Lick's 5th Battalion, with Don Price, was positioned 3,000 meters south along the My Chanh River.

During the month of April, Brigade 369 had operated in the same area. Colonel Chung and his advisors had learned the terrain well and had identified the avenues of approach that the NVA would most likely use. Commencing at midnight, the advisors began firing naval gunfire and artillery on these routes.

Throughout the night the Marines positioned furthest north along the O-Khe River heard the sound of approaching tanks. Parachute flares illuminated the area as the advisors struck the suspected enemy areas with artillery and naval guns. The NVA struck back about an hour before first light. Major Sheridan recalled:

> The enemy opened the most devastating artillery barrage that the brigade had ever received. We thought the whole world was falling apart around us. Our vehicles, bunkers, villages and guns were being demolished. We wondered if anyone would live to fight. All we could do was dig deeper—and pray.[16]

The enemy's opening fires lifted at dawn as eighteen of its tanks assaulted the positions of the 9th Battalion. Major Beans was in radio contact with an airborne observer and TAC Air was on station but because of the early morning haze and the smoke created by both friendly and enemy supporting arms fire, the observer could not positively identify the 9th Battalion's position. Initially, TAC Air could not be used near the Marine front lines.

Of the eighteen T-54 and T-55 tanks sighted as advancing on the Marines, five were able to penetrate into the battalion's CP area. However, almost as fast as each tank reached the perimeter wire, Colonel Chung's Marines attacked and destroyed them with M-72 LAAWs. For thirty minutes there was complete havoc as the enemy armor drove into and around the Marine positions.

Disregarding his own safety, Major Beans climbed to the best vantage point he could find from which he guided successive sorties of air strikes on the then clearly visible enemy armor. Using the burning enemy tanks as reference points for the fast flying jets, he directed the aircraft at the NVA armor. TAC Air was credited with at least three tank kills during the fight. The artillery pieces, which had been positioned forward under the cover of darkness, accounted for five additional tank kills. One tank escaped the Marines.

The battle was not over. Next came a human wave attack by NVA infantrymen which assaulted across the open piedmont. Hundreds died as the U.S. aircraft and naval gunfire supplemented the Marine artillery and soon gave the battle area the appearance of a cratered moonscape. The enemy's attack ground to a halt; within an hour the battle was over. As the smoke cleared, Jim Beans reported the fields littered with burning tanks and the dead and dying remnants of two North Vietnamese regiments. The NVA survivors were observed fleeing westward to their sanctuaries in the Hai Lang Forest.

The successful defense by the 9th Battalion against a numerically superior force had prevented the North Vietnamese from closing off the last escape route south to Hue. The enemy had suffered a major defeat in its first assault on the My Chanh line, and Highway 1 remained open for another twenty-four hours as over 10,000 ARVN soldiers and Marines crossed the bridge into Thua Thien Province. The carnage and confusion was temporarily over.

Later that afternoon Colonel Bao led Marine Brigade 147 over the My Chanh Bridge. All his battalions were accounted for and were the last organized force to leave Quang Tri Province. These Marines were the weary but hardened veterans of Nui Ba Ho, Sarge, Holcomb, Mai Loc, Pedro and Ai Tu combat base. There was no cheering or adulation as the tiger-striped Marines of two brigades came together. The hurt and losses had been too much. Rather, it was a silent but emotional meeting of comrades in arms, recalling their fallen brothers. Only the sounds of men walking and the rattle of their equipment were heard.

Just before dusk, on 3 May 1972, the 5th and 9th Battalions pulled back across the My Chanh and took up their final defensive positions along the southern bank. Majors Beans and Price assisted in destroying the bridges over the O-Khe and My Chanh Rivers; not as dramatically as Capt. John Ripley on the Cam Lo-Cau Viet, but with the same effect. These two COVANs were the last Americans to leave Quang Tri Province and they did so with pride in their units and themselves.

Thus, some thirty-five days after the Nguyen Hue Offensive had begun, the entire province of Quang Tri was under North Vietnamese control. The victorious NVA divisions quickly moved past the ancient Citadel and repositioned their forces to launch another offensive to capture the old imperial capital of Hue.

Later, the North Vietnamese would fail in bloody battles, often hand-to-hand, at the My Chanh. However, Colonel Chung's earlier prophesy that "The VC will not cross this river" held true. The river itself would flow red with the blood of NVA soldiers but while the My Chanh line bent, it never broke. Rather, it became the line of departure for the South Vietnamese Marine division and the ARVN airborne division who just two weeks later would launch their counteroffensive which eventually led to the recapture of Quang Tri City. But that's another story. . . .

# EPILOGUE

Military history is full of examples which demonstrate that in every major battle unforeseen circumstances have arisen which have affected the ultimate outcome of the fray. So it was with the Nguyen Hue Easter Offensive which forms the center of this account. Elements over which the combatants had little control, such as monsoon weather, created conditions which had great impact upon the early chaotic days of the battle. Adverse weather conditions favored the North Vietnamese attack.

Involved also were human factors which saw highly creditable intelligence information on the North Vietnamese Army's buildup disregarded. The obvious growing threat was either ignored or certainly misread. When the crisis arose, South Vietnamese military leadership failed.

Although this narrative was not intended as a discourse on leadership in battle, the story nevertheless provides an insight into the important role of the commander during times of military crisis. During the hectic days of the offensive one saw the full array of leadership traits. Heroic, traitorous, skilled and nearly incompetent leaders all passed in review. Unresponsive leadership from the highest levels of command within the South Vietnamese government accounted for much of the tragedy which resulted from the early encounters.

Conversely, effective leadership, such as that exhibited in MR-1 by Lieutenant General Truong, succeeded where others failed. Small unit leadership, as demonstrated by Sergeant Loum, halted a communist armored column. Throughout, the

U.S. advisors played a pivotal leadership role in bringing order out of what otherwise was, and would have remained, mass confusion. It was a time of great challenge.

As the victorious North Vietnamese divisions repositioned troops and armor south of Quang Tri City for the announced offensive to capture Hue, President Thieu acted to restore confidence in the battered South Vietnamese forces. He fully recognized that he had only a critically short period of time to prepare for the battles he knew would be immediately forthcoming. On May 3 he ordered General Lam removed from command of MR-1 and reassigned to an unimportant post in Saigon. Admittedly, it was a "face-saving" gesture by the JGS, but it avoided, at a critical period, a harsher military review of General Lam's actions during the first month of the Easter offensive.

Lt. Gen. Ngo Quang Truong, commander of MR-4, was reassigned to Danang and directed to reorganize his forces and halt the communist invasion. This was a psychological, as well as a tactical, move because, in addition to General Truong's acknowledged military competence, he also brought to the battered forces in MR-1 a reputation as the commander of the 1st ARVN Division which had successfully beaten the NVA during Tet in 1968, recapturing Hue City.

Finally, President Thieu emphasized his personal concern for the defense of Hue City by visiting Phu Bai and the ancient capital on 4 May. This trip raised the president's prestige and gave renewed hope to the defenders of MR-1. On the same day, the *Pacific Stars and Stripes* published an emotional letter from Brigadier General Giai in which he was quoted as saying:

> I bear full responsibility for history and the law for the withdrawal. The capital of Quang Tri Province is in ruins. Our food, our ammunition, all our fuel supplies are gone. Our force is exhausted. I see no further reason why we should stay on in this ruined situation. I ordered you to withdraw in order to fortify our units again from a new front to annihilate remaining communist forces if they still engage in this wrongful war.*

*On October 2nd, 1973, Brigadier General Giai was sentenced by Court Martial to five years hard labor with loss of rank and decorations, being charged with disobeying an order and abandoning a position in the face of the enemy.

Because of his conduct, General Giai was also removed from his command of the 3d ARVN Division, returned to Saigon and placed under house arrest, for a short period of time leaving the division without a commanding general. In reality the general's absence made little or no difference because, on 6 May, the 3d Division could account for less than 2,700 of its officers and men. Of these, over 1,100 were assigned to the newly reconstituted, and now infamous, 56th Regiment which was undergoing basic training and not yet declared combat ready. The division's combat support and service support elements were depleted and badly drawn down, having lost most of its tanks, artillery pieces, vehicles and supplies. The 3d Division was relieved of all combat action and relegated to a retraining status.

As such, a herculean task faced General Truong, and he took swift, drastic action which helped calm and restore confidence as he entered the area in MR-1. Initiating a new defense plan and, during the counteroffensive which followed, spearheaded by the airborne and Marine divisions, he was personally credited with several tactical plans and moves which overcame the chaotic situation in MR-1.

By mid-May the offensive turned into a situation of stalemate and attrition for both sides. The massive buildup of U.S. military support sustained the South Vietnamese forces, ultimately turning the hotly contested battles in their favor. The invaders' momentum was lost without the North Vietnamese Army achieving the major objectives desired by General Giap.

In general terms, the test of Vietnamization had been met when the South Vietnamese forces overcome the enemy in MR-1, while also defeating him in MR-2 and MR-3. By mid-June the RVNAF had wrestled the initiative from the NVA and the threat to Saigon had dissipated. In the central highlands, around Kontum, the enemy was pushed into the jungles as ARVN troops retook two lost districts.

In June, Lieutenant General Khang was elevated to the JGS as the J-3 director of operations. Under the leadership of a new commandant, Brig. Gen. Bui The Lan South Vietnamese Marines recaptured Quang Tri City on 15 September. In the house-to-house struggle which ensued, his Marines suffered over 5,000 casualties before raising their national colors over the Citadel's destroyed walls. The only provincial capital to fall to the North Vietnamese during the offensive was thus restored to South Vietnamese control.

The battle for MR-1 continued until 27 January, 1973 when the North Vietnamese Le Duc Tho and Dr. Kissinger signed the cease-fire agreement. A short fifteen minutes before the 0800 cease-fire deadline, the USS *Turner Joy*, steaming off the Cam Lo-Cua Viet River outlet, fired the last salvo of naval gunfire directed at a North Vietnamese target area near Dong Ha.

The American COVANS, still with their Vietnamese counterparts, were ordered out of the now silent battle areas as the special role of the COVAN ended not in victory but in a diplomatic impasse. U.S. Army Advisory Team 155 was deactivated shortly thereafter. In March 1973 the Marine advisory unit was also deactivated, its colors folded and returned to headquarters, Marine Corps. An era of camaraderie had thus ended between our two Corps of Marines.

When the final collapse of the South Vietnamese government came in April 1975, the Vietnamese Marine division was split with part being deployed in MR-1 and around Saigon. In the final hours VN Marines were reported fighting off North Vietnamese forces west of Danang around their headquarters at the Bo Tu Linh and near the presidential palace.

Less than 250 Marines ultimately escaped to the U.S. Of these, their two commandants, approximately twenty officers and 180 enlisted men arrived in stateside refugee camps. Hastily erected cardboard signs, printed in Vietnamese, alerted VN Marines that their former COVANs were prepared to assist them in the task of beginning their new lives. Capt. Ray Smith and his family directly aided over thirty Marines and their families who were fortunate enough to escape the enemy, while my family shared our home with my counterpart, Lt. Col. Tran Van Hien and his family during their resettlement process.

Seldom in a military career does an officer have the opportunity to experience two periods of intense professional challenge. Yet several of the COVANS were faced with this. When the U.S. Marines landed on the island of Grenada in 1981, the 2d Battalion, 8th Marines, was commanded by Lt. Col. Ray Smith. His Marines secured the island and then redeployed to Lebanon where they fulfilled their peacekeeping mission until rotating back to Camp Lejeune, North Carolina in April 1984. As fate would have it, while in Lebanon Smith's battalion was placed under the operational control of his former COVAN senior. Now a brigadier general, Jim Joy was serving as the Commander, U.S. Joint Task Force, Lebanon.

Time has placed many other COVANs in significant positions of service. Jim Beans is a brigadier general and serves as the Assistant Division Commander, 3d Division, Okinawa, Japan. When Col. Josh Dorsey, USMC, rotated home from Vietnam he was assigned to HQMC where in 1981 he retired to live in Upper Marlboro, Maryland. This superb leader of Marines lost a battle to cancer in August 1984. Both Jon Easley and Bob Sheridan were promoted to lieutenant colonels before each retired in the Washington, D.C. area; while Walt Boomer, now a colonel, currently serves as Director, 4th Marine Corps District, headquartered in Philadelphia, Pennsylvania. Col. Bill Warren is assigned at the Marine Corps Logistic Support Base, Albany, Georgia, while Lt. Col. Bill Wischmeyer serves with the 8th Marine Corps District in Overland Park, Kansas.

In July 1984 Colonel John Ripley began serving in a position of special leadership as the Senior Marine Officer at the U.S. Naval Academy. Colonel Don Price is assigned to the staff of the Secretary of the Navy.

Before retiring in the Seattle, Washington area, David Brookbank was promoted to lieutenant colonel, USAF. When Lt. Col. William (Bill) Camper was medically retired as the result of his wounds, he and his wife Peggy settled in Peachtree City, Georgia. Louis C. Wagner, USA, has advanced to the rank of major general and serves with the Army staff in the Pentagon.

There are many other Army, Air Force and Navy officers who aided the South Vietnamese military in 1972, but the Privacy Act prevented my tracing their careers and identifying their whereabouts. This does not diminish the quality of their service in those desperate times in 1972.

After thirty-two years of service, the author retired from the Marine Corps and settled in northern Virginia.

Appendix A

# ORDER OF BATTLE FOR THE NORTH VIETNAMESE NGUYEN-HUE OFFENSIVE IN MR-1

## GENERAL BACKGROUND ON NVA FORCES

In preparing for their Nguyen-Hue Invasion, the North Vietnamese undertook a massive buildup of forces near the DMZ. Allied pilots reported that the intensity of antiaircraft fire in the DMZ was equal to that encountered during earlier raids in the Hanoi area. In addition to the 23 MM, 37 MM, and 57 MM antiaircraft weapons used in the past, the North Vietnamese introduced 85 MM and 100 MM guns into the DMZ. Also, in the final weeks before the offensive, SA-2 surface-to-air missiles were emplaced and on occasion were fired, in volleys, from multiple locations. This progressive buildup of an air defense system, which conformed to Soviet doctrine, placed in formidable threat an umbrella over the North Vietnamese assemblying invasion forces.

The North Vietnamese deployed the equivalent of 17 infantry regiments, supported by 3 regiments of artillery and rocket launchers, and at least 2 regiments of tanks. This force consisted of 400 armored vehicles, several hundred artillery pieces, heavy and medium mortars, in addition to several thousand crew-served antiaircraft weapons. Over two divisions were staged to attack across the DMZ into Quang Tri Province. Another NVA division, the much experienced 324B, was poised west of Hue City, and scheduled to attack from out of the A Shau Valley.

The two mainline NVA divisions staged along the DMZ were also augmented by forces from the B-5 Front. These independent units were used to complement, protect, and preserve the unit integrity of regular Army divisions. Actions by these independent units are summarized by the following categories:

(1) Leading attacks
(2) Diversionary attacks
(3) Replacement of divisional units during temporary detachments
(4) Covering movements/retrograde operations of divisions, and,
(5) Interdiction of key lines of communications.

The combat missions assigned to the B-5 Fronts' independent regiments dramatically demonstrated the NVA's desire to preserve the integrity of their regular forces to the maximum extent possible. The sustained continuity of regular units appears to be the basis for much of the tactical planning evidence during the offensive. Another dimension of this reasoning may have been the desire to have independent units absorb most of the casualties in subordination to the psychological effect of division-associated victories. This reasoning is consistent with NVA thinking in allowing traditionally elite units the honor of executing final assaults of major objectives.

*December 1971–20 March 1972*

## NVA FORCES IN OR ALONG THE DMZ

| 304th DIVISION | 308th DIVISION | INDEPENDENT B-5 FRONT FORCES |
|---|---|---|
| 9th Regt | 36th Regt | 126th Sapper Regt |
| 24th Regt | 88th Regt | 31st Infantry Regt |
| 66th Regt | 102nd Regt | 270th Infantry Regt |
| 68th Artillery Regt | | 246th Infantry Regt |
| | | 84th Artillery Regt (Rocket) |
| | | 38th Artillery Regt |

Two (possibly three) armored regiments. (203rd, 204th and 205th (?))

## NVA FORCES IN ASHAU VALLEY (WEST OF HUE CITY)

| 324 DIVISION | INDEPENDENT FORCES |
|---|---|
| 29th Regt | 5th Infantry Regt |
| 803rd Regt | 6th Infantry Regt |
| 812nd Regt | |

*April–May 1972*

| 320th DIVISION | This Division arrived in Quang Tri Province after the offensive began, then infiltrated and fought against South Vietnamese forces at Cam Lo, La Vang and in Hai Lang |
|---|---|
| 48B Regt | |
| 64B Regt | |

| 325th DIVISION | Elements of this Division participated in the attack on Quang Tri City during late April 1972 |
|---|---|
| 18th Regt | |
| 995th Regt | (Infiltrated on 1–20 July) |
| 101st Regt | (Arrived in Quang Tri City, during late July and defended the capital against South Vietnam's counteroffensive (July–September 1972) |

Primary Sources:

MACV Historical Study: "The Nguyen-Hue Offensive: 1972"

CNA Study–#1035, *Defense of Hue and Quang Tri City: The 1972 NVN Invasion of MR-1*

USAF Southeast Asia Monograph Series: Vol II, 3: "Air Power and the 1972 Spring Invasion."

# Appendix B

# Appendix C

## Commanding Officer, 56th Regiment, 3D ARVN Division, Message of Surrender

On 3 April 1972 Lt. Col. Pham Van Dinh made the following broadcast over Radio Hanoi, less than twenty-four hours after he surrendered the 56th Regiment at Camp Carroll, Quang Tri Province to the North Vietnamese forces. His radio message was recorded at that time and subsequently translated into English.

I, Lieutenant Colonel Pham Van Dinh, 56th ARVN Infantry regiment commander have returned to the National Liberation Front forces. My regiment was stationed at Tan Lam (CARROLL) fire base. On 30 March 1972 my unit was receiving a heavy shelling from NLF forces. All of the other friendly forces which were operating around our area or were stationed near our fire base were destroyed one after another. If we continued to fight we would be without all of our logistical and combat support as well as medical evacuation. I was sure that my unit was going to have many casualties. Meanwhile most of the friendly forces and the rest of the 3rd ARVN Division were evacuated to places which were safer. They left us alone under strong pressure of the NLF forces.

Most of the troops of my unit in all ranks refused to fight anymore. I and Lt. Col. Vinh Phoy, who is my executive officer, also decided to refuse to fight anymore. In order to prevent further loss of life of my soldiers, I called for a meeting attended by all of my unit commanders. At the meeting we decided to surrender to all of the NLF forces. We communicated this decision to the NLF at 1430 hours 2 April 1972 via PRC-25 radio.

After we left the fire base we were well treated by the NLF forces. The relationship between us and the NLF forces was getting closer and closer.

On this occasion, I advise you ARVN troops that you better return to the NLF, because the NLF fighting spirit is getting higher and higher than ever, and of course, the American-Thieu gang is going to lose the war; the war the Americans called the

Vietnamization war. They have been trying to use us against part of our own people's patriots.

The South Vietnam government is also using us to continue the war that they feel can benefit them as individuals.

I think that your continued sacrifice at this time means nothing. Again, I ask you to not let the Thieu-American regime take advantage of your fighting potential. If they send you out to the field you must refuse the combat order. If they force you to go, then you must not fight the NLF. Instead, find out how to get in touch with the NLF forces in order for your to return to the people. Your action will effectively assist in ending the war quickly and also save your life.

My personal feeling is that the NLF forces are going to win the war. The NLF is ready all the time to welcome you back. The NLF is expecting you to return very soon.

# Appendix D

**THE SECRETARY OF THE NAVY**
WASHINGTON

      The President of the United States takes pleasure in presenting the NAVY CROSS to

**CAPTAIN RAY L. SMITH**
**UNITED STATES MARINE CORPS**

for service as set forth in the following

CITATION:

      For extraordinary heroism during the period 30 March to 1 April 1972 while serving as advisor to a Vietnamese Command Group numbering approximately 250 Vietnamese Marines located on a small hilltop outpost in the Republic of Vietnam. With the Command Group repulsing several savage enemy assaults, and subjected to a continuing hail of fire from an attacking force estimated to be of two-battalion strength, Captain Smith repeatedly exposed himself to the heavy fire while directing friendly air support. When adverse weather conditions precluded further close air support, he attempted to lead the group, now reduced to only 28 Vietnamese Marines, to the safety of friendly lines. An enemy soldier opened fire upon the Marines at the precise moment that they had balked when encountering an outer defensive ring of barbed wire. Captain Smith returned accurate fire, disposing of the attacker, and then threw himself backwards on top of the booby-trap-infested wire barrier. Swiftly, the remaining Marines moved over the crushed wire, stepping on Captain Smith's prostrate body, until all had passed safely through the barrier. Although suffering severe cuts and bruises, Captain Smith succeeded in leading the Marines to the safety of friendly lines. His great personal valor and unrelenting devotion to duty reflected the highest credit upon himself, the Marine Corps, and the United States Naval Service.

      For the President,

*John W. Warner*

Secretary of the Navy

# Appendix E

The President of the United States takes pleasure in presenting the NAVY CROSS to

CAPTAIN JOHN W. RIPLEY
UNITED STATES MARINE CORPS

for service as set forth in the following

CITATION:

For extraordinary heroism on 2 April 1972 while serving as the Senior Marine Advisor to the THIRD Vietnamese Marine Corps Infantry Battalion in the Republic of Vietnam. Upon receipt of a report that a rapidly moving, mechanized, North Vietnamese army force, estimated at reinforced divisional strength, was attacking south along Route #1, the THIRD Vietnamese Marine Infantry Battalion was positioned to defend a key village and the surrounding area. It became imperative that a vital river bridge be destroyed if the overall security of the northern provinces of Military Region ONE was to be maintained. Advancing to the bridge to personally supervise this most dangerous but vitally important assignment, Captain Ripley located a large amount of explosives which had been prepositioned there earlier, access to which was blocked by a chain-link fence. In order to reposition the approximately 500 pounds of explosives, Captain Ripley was obliged to reach up and hand-walk along the beams while his body dangled beneath the bridge. On five separate occasions, in the face of constant enemy fire, he moved to points along the bridge and, with the aid of another advisor who pushed the explosives to him, securely emplaced them. He then detonated the charges and destroyed the bridge, thereby stopping the enemy assault. By his heroic actions and extraordinary courage, Captain Ripley undoubtedly was instrumental in saving an untold number of lives. His inspiring efforts reflected great credit upon himself, the Marine Corps, and the United States Naval Service.

For the President,

*John W. Warner*

Secretary of the Navy

# Notes

It is the sincere hope of the author that these notes and unpublished sources will assist in filling a literary gap on a very important period of American involvement in the Vietnam War. The years 1971 and 1972 were a time of dynamic change. Vietnamization had removed American ground combat forces from the war as the South Vietnamese military expanded their forces to fill the void. American politics had shifted the national focus away from an unpopular war to internal issues. Interest in a distant war had diminished as fewer Americans were fighting or there to report or write about this critical battle between oriental brothers.

## Chapter One

1. Wheatcroft, Andrew. *The World Atlas of Revolutions.* P.138. Also, Karnow, Stanley. *Vietnam: A History.* P.639–640.
2. Harrison, James P. *The Endless War: Vietnam's Struggle for Independence.* P.29. Also, Lung. "Intelligence." (Indochina Series) P.6–9.

## Chapter Two

1. Turley, G. H. and Wells, M. R. "Easter Invasion 1972." *Marine Corps Gazette,* March 1973. (This article was written at the Vietnamese Marine Division Headquarters, Huong Dien, RVN.)
2. Smith, R. L. "Leatherneck Square." *Marine Corps Gazette,* Quantico, Va.: August, 1969. Vol 53. No. 8. The "Square" itself was a six by eight mile piece of a flat piedmont area about five miles from the east coast of Vietnam which abutted the DMZ.
3. Hinh, Nguyen Duy. "Vietnamization and the Ceasefire." Indochina Monograph Series, Washington, D.C.: U.S. Army Center of Military History, 1980. P.1. The Indochina Monographs are a series of papers written after the war by high-ranking Vietnamese, Cambodian, and Laotian officers who succeeded in reaching the U.S. The papers were commissioned by the U.S. Army, and the authors were given access to U.S. military records while preparing them.
4. Ibid. P.1.

5. Ibid. P.13.
6. Truong, Ngo Quang. "The Easter Offensive of 1972." Indochina Monograph Series. Washington, D.C.: U.S. Army Center of Military History, 1980. P.10.
7. Hinh. "Vietnamization and Ceasefire." P.17. Lt. Gen. Ngo Quang Truong, who assumed command of MR-1 in June 1972, was later to evaluate General Lam's MR-1 headquarters in its response to the NVA offensive:

   His MR-1 headquarters had been located in Danang since 1966. It was primarily a non-tactical headquarters. Although his staff excelled in procedural and administrative work and was effective in the operation and control of routine territorial security activities, it lacked the experience, professionalism and initiative required of a field staff during critical times.

8. Ibid. P.18.
9. Ibid. P.22.
10. Tho, Tran Dinh. "Pacification." Indochina Monograph Series. Washington, D.C.: U.S. Army Center of Military History, 1979. P.26, 46.
11. Command Chronology, 1st Marine Division and III Marine Amphibious Force (MAF) Memoranda of Historical Record of Events: Historical Division, Headquarters Marine Corps: September 1971. Navy Yard, Washington, D.C. P.6:1.
12. U.S. Marine Corps. "U.S. Marine Corps Combat Actions in Vietnam, 1971–1972." (Draft) P.2,4.
13. Ibid.
14. Eisenstein, Joel B. After-Action Report (30 March–10 April 1972, P.1) and Oral History tape, transcript and interviews, 1983. (senior naval gunfire officer in Quang Tri Province on 30 March 1972).
15. Truong. "Easter Offensive" P.8.
16. Brookbank, David A. Special Report, Air Liaison Officer: Subject: VNAF TACs and the Fall of Quang Tri (U) July 31, 1972. USAF Advisory Group, MACV. P.5 and Interviews, 1982, 1983.
17. Truong. "Easter Offensive" P.16.
18. The 3d ARVN Division's strength for April and May 1972

was cited in a U.S. Army Advisory Team 155 Personnel Report on file at the National Federal Records Center, Suitland, Md.

19. Hinh, Nguyen Duy. "Lam Son 719." Indochina Monograph Series. Washington, D.C.: U.S. Army Center of Military History, 1979. P.31–33.

20. Truong. "Easter Offensive" P.10 and *A Short History of the Vietnam War*. Edited by Allen R. Millet. P.35.

21. U.S. Navy Defense of Hue and Quang Tri City. The 1972 NVN Invasion of MR-1, Center of Naval Analysis. Arlington, Va., 1972 (CNA Study 1035). Appendix A presents the Order of Battle of both the North and South Vietnamese forces on 30 March 1972. Also, Truong ("Easter Offensive") P.9. (There are a multitude of sources which referenced the NVA's pre-invasion buildup. Most writings are found to be inaccurate as to the NVA order of battle.)

22. MACV, Historical Study. "The Nguyen-Hue Offensive" (declassified). January 1973. P.1.

23. Ibid. P.2.

24. Truong. "Easter Offensive." P.12.

25. MACV, Nguyen Hue Offensive Study. P.3.

26. CNA Study 1035. P.19 and Appendix A.P.A.4.

27. Truong. "Easter Offensive" P.18.

28. Mann, David K. "The NVA 1972 Invasion of Military Region 1: Fall of Quang Tri and Defense of Hue." (Man, Project CHECO Report) 1973. P.9.

29. Truong. "Easter Offensive" P.18.

30. Ibid. P.22–23.

31. Ibid. P.29.

32. Ibid. P.22.

33. Mann. CHECO Report. P.9. Second source, USAF, Pacific Air Force "Intelligence Review" (AIR), PACAIR 272, 7 April 1972.

34. Ibid. P.9.

35. Truong. "Easter Offensive" P.22–23.

36. Lung, Hoang Ngoc. "Intelligence." Indochina Monograph Series. Washington, D.C., U.S. Army Center of Military History: 1981, P.155. Also, both General Truong and General Vien refer to the South Vietnamese, JGS alert that

29 March was to be the D-Day for the NVA general offensive.

## Chapter Three

1. Nolan, Keith. *The Battle for Hue: Tet* 1968 P.55–71, 81–111.

2. Boomer, Walter. Oral History Transcript and interviews, 1983, 1984 and his field diary notes during March 1972.

3. Ibid. Field diary entry.

4. Camper, William. Oral History Transcripts and Interviews. 1983, 1984.

## Chapter Four

1. Camper, William C. Transcripts and Interviews. 1983–84.

2. Ibid. Transcripts.

3. Ibid. Transcripts.

4. Ibid. Transcripts.

5. Twichell, Heath, Jr. After-Action Report: Activities of 57th ARVN Regiment: 28 March–17 April 1972. P.1.

6. Truong. "Easter Offensive." P.20.

7. Truong. "Easter Offensive." P.21. Lieutenant General Ngo Quang Truong, who assumed command of MR-1 in June 1972, was later to evaluate General Lam's MR-1 headquarters in its response to the NVA offensive:

   His Military Region 1 headquarters had been located in Danang since 1966. It was primarily a non-tactical headquarters. Although his staff excelled in procedural and administrative work and was effective in the operation and control of routine territorial security activities, it lacked the experience, professionalism and initiative required of a field staff during critical times.

8. Battreall, Raymond R. U.S. Army Oral History Transcript #2034. Military History Branch, MACV (Maj. Scott Dillard, Interviewer. January 73). Military History Library, Carlisle, Pa. (Battreall Transcript).

9. Easley, Jon. Interview notes, 1982, 1983.

10. DeBona, Andrew. U.S. Marine Corps Oral History Tape Transcripts (March-April 1972) and interview notes, 1983.

11. Eisenstein. Transcripts.

12. Thearle, W. Jones. Letter of 19 September 1972 to Maj. J. W. Ripley: (Commanding Officer USS *Buchanan* DDG-

14) and Marine Advisory Unit, Monthly Historical Summary of Vietnamese Marine Corps Operations for period 31 March–6 April 1972. USMC History and Museum Dept., Navy Yard, Washington, D.C.

13. Smith, Ray. After-Action Report (30 March–1 April 1972). USMC History and Museum Dept., Navy Yard, Washington, D.C.

14. Ibid. P.2.

15. CNA Study 1035. P.A-9. Boomer. Transcripts. Mann. CHECO Report. P.10–12.

16. Brookbank, David. ALO, 3d Infantry Division (ARVN) Progress Report on VNAF Activities in 3d ARVN Division dtd 31 March 1972.

17. DeBona. Transcripts.

18. MACV Command Chronology, March 1972 and newspaper articles citing his presence in Bangkok, Thailand.

19. MACV, Headquarters, Daily Operational Summary Message (OPSUM) to the JCS, Pentagon, Washington, D.C. (Secret message declassified *302200Z* on microfilm). Military History Library, Carlisle Barracks, Pa.

**Chapter Five**

1. Smith. After-Action Report, P.3.

2. Ibid. P.2.

3. Joy, Jim R. After-Action Report, 30 March–2 April 1972. (Hereafter cited as Joy AA Report), P.3–4, and Smith AA Report P.2,3.

4. Smith. AA Report; and in his Navy Cross Citation (See Appendix D).

5. Turley, Gerald H. Special Combat Situation Report to Commander, U.S. Naval Forces Vietnam; for period 30 March–2 April 1972. (Declassified) P.2,5.

6. MACV, Daily OPSUM message *302200Z*, (declassified). Military History Library. Carlisle Barracks, Pa.

**Chapter Six**

1. Camper. Transcripts.

2. Lung, Hoang Ngoc. "Intelligence." Indochina Monograph Service. U.S. Army Center of Military History, Washington, D.C. 1981. P.155.

3. Brookbank. Report. P.6.

4. Smith. AA Report and interviews, 1983 and 1984.
5. Ibid. And Boomer interviews.
6. Eisenstein. Transcripts.

**Chapter Seven**

1. Advisory Team 155, G-3 Journal entry, 1 April 1972 and
   Turley Special Situation Report.
2. Ripley, John W. Oral History Tapes #5090, 5091, 6032
   and a series of interviews, 1982, 1983, 1984. Marine Corps
   Oral History Tapes, Museum and History Div. Navy Yard,
   Washington, D.C.
3. O'Toole, Thomas. After-Action Report: Easter Offensive:
   Personal Evaluation. April 1972. P.2,3.
4. Camper. Transcripts.
5. Randall, David S. U.S. Marine Corps Oral History Tape
   #5093.

**Chapter Eight**

1. Advisory Team 155, G-3 Journal of 1 April 1972.
2. Advisory Team 155, Equipment Expenditure Forms and
   Supply Records Dated April 1972: Archives, National
   Federal Records Center. Suitland, Md.
3. MACV Daily OPSUM (Declassified) 011400Z April 72.
4. Ibid.
5. O'Toole. AA Report. P.4.
6. Brookbank. Report. P.5. Mann. CHECO Report. P.17.
7. Twichell. AA Report. P.2.
8. Wright, Regan. Oral History Transcripts #5089/5090:
   Easter Offensive and Interview Transcript of June 1983.
9. Eisenstein. Transcripts and Interviews, 1983.

**Chapter Nine**

1. Boomer. Transcript, 1983.
2. Ibid.
3. DeBona. Transcript.
4. Twichell. AA Report. P.2.
5. Nettleingham, Allen. U.S. Marine Corps, Oral History Tape,
   Transcript #5085. USMC, Corps History and Museum
   Division, Navy Yard, Washington, D.C.
6. U.S. Marine Corps (Draft) Combat Action in Vietnam,
   1971–1972. P.76.
7. Brookbank. Report. P.6.

## Chapter Ten

1. Ripley. Transcripts and After-Action Report. Evaluation of the NVA Invasion 72. USMC, History and Museum Division, Navy Yard, Washington, D.C.
2. Ripley. Transcripts.
3. Ibid.
4. Ripley. Transcripts.
5. Twichell. AA Report. P.3.
6. Ripley. Transcripts and draft copy of proposed Bronze Star award for Sgt. Luom. Ripley. Personal papers.
7. Ripley. Transcripts.
8. Smock, James E. Letter of 23 March 1976, (to Lt. Col. Gene Arnold), U.S. Marine Corps Historical Division, Washington, D.C.
9. Ripley. Transcripts and interview notes with Lt. Col. Gene Arnold (a Marine Corps historian) and with author.
10. Ripley. Transcripts.
11. Starry, Donn A. "Mounted Combat in Vietnam," Vietnam Studies: Department of the Army, 1978. P.207–208. Also, Battreall Transcripts.

## Chapter Eleven

1. Camper. Transcripts and interviews.
2. Joy. AA Report. P.7.
3. Camper. Transcripts.
4. Gnibus, Thomas. Oral History Tapes #5086/5087. Also, Randall, Dave C., Jr. After-Action Report: Counterbattery Fire, Fire Support Base Mai Loc. P.2.
5. Camper. Transcripts.
6. Ibid.
7. Ibid.
8. Ibid.
9. Ibid.
10. Ibid.

## Chapter Twelve

1. Ripley. Transcripts.
2. Ibid.
3. Ibid.
4. Ibid.
5. Both Smock and Ripley refer to this interchange as a nat-

ural release of their pent-up emotions. The USMC History and Museum Division's draft on the Marine Corps combat activities in Vietnam during the 1971–1972 period also references this oral interchange.

6. Smock. 1976 letter to USMC Historical Division.
7. Ibid. P.3; USMC (Museum and History Department) Draft of 1971–72 combat actions in Vietnam. Chapt. 4, P.15–17.
8. Ripley. Transcripts.
9. Ibid.
10. Advisory Team 155, G-3 Journal of 2 April 1972; Brookbank Report; and Turley Special Situation Report, Enclosure (1).
11. Regan, Wright. After-Action Report: 30 March–14 April 1972. P.1.
12. MACV, Daily OPSUM *031000Z*. April 1972 (Declassified). Military History Library, Carlisle Barracks, Pa.
13. Vien, Gao Van. "Leadership." Indochina Series. P.137–138.

**Chapter Thirteen**
1. Joy. AA Report. P.8.
2. Ibid. P.10.
3. DeBona. Transcripts.
4. Ibid.
5. Ibid.
6. Anderson, William C. *BAT 21*. P.3
7. USAF, SEA Monograph Series: "Air Power and the 1972 Spring Offensive." P.36.
8. Mann. CHECO Report. P.19–20.
9. Brookbank. Report. P.7. Also Mann. CHECO Report. P.19.
10. Ibid.
11. Mann. CHECO Report. P.19–20.
12. Ripley. Transcripts and interviews.

**Chapter Fourteen**
1. DeBona. Transcripts.
2. Ibid.
3. Fall, Bernard. *Street Without Joy*. Pages 137–157 describe in detail the French-Viet Minh fights over this segment of National Highway 1.
4. Dorsey, Joshua, III wrote these two questions on a copy

of the 2 April 1972 Navy message while at the MACV headquarters.

5. U.S. naval message of 2 April 1972 (See Appendix B).
6. MACV, Report. "The Nguyen Hue Offensive" (declassified 31 December '76).
7. Cockell, Robert. Oral History Tape #5090 and After-Action Report 1st Bn. VNMC: Evaluation on Easter Offensive and Oral History Tape #5092.
8. Truong. "Easter Offensive." P.32–33.
9. Ibid. P.36–37.
10. Ibid. P. 38.

**Chapter Fifteen**

1. Ripley. Transcripts and interviews.
2. Warren, William, USMC. Oral History Tape Transcript #5094, 5095 and Interviews, 1983-1984 and Special Report: Personal Evaluation and comments on Easter '72 Offensive, 22 April 1972. P.2–4.
3. Warren. Transcripts.
4. Wischmeyer, William, USMC. Oral History Tape #5094, 5095 and series of interviews 1972–1984.
5. Warren. Transcript.
6. Wischmeyer. Transcript.
7. Nettleingham. Transcript.
8. Warren. Transcript.
9. Cockell. Transcript.
10. Warren. Transcript.
11. Department of Defense, Newspaper files. *Early Bird*, Issues for April 1972, cites Presidential News Secretary Ron Ziegler and his Deputy Gerald Warren as stating "we are confident that South Vietnamese can cope with the enemy."
12. CNA Report 1035. Mersky and Polmar P.195.
13. Mersky, Peter B. and Polmar, Norman. *The Naval Air War in Vietnam*. Chapter 9, P.185–205 has a detailed summary of the U.S. Navy's responses to assemble their largest concentration of aircraft carriers and naval gunfire ships in the U.S. involvement in the Vietnam War.
14. USAF, SEA, Monograph Series, Vol. 11, Monograph 3. P.16.
15. Mersky, Peter B. *U.S. Marine Aviation: 1912 to Present.*

Chapter 12. P. 256–277 very accurately chronicles the Marine Corps aviation units' redeployment back to RVN and their progressive return to combat missions.

Also, the Marine Corps conducted the following study: Analysis of Marine Corps Readiness in Action (MCOAG Report). Headquarters, Fleet Marine Force, Pacific. 1972.

**Chapter Sixteen**

1. Truong. "Easter Offensive." P.33.
2. Ibid. P.36.
3. Ibid. P.36.
4. Ibid. P.37.
5. Ibid. P.38.
6. Ibid.
7. Dunstan, Simon. *Vietnam Tracks: Armor in Battle 1945-1975*. P.187. Also Starry, P.210.
8. Vien. "Leadership." P.138. Truong. "Easter Offensive." P.39.
9. Camper. Transcripts and interviews. 1983.

**Chapter Seventeen**

1. Wagner, Louis C., USA. After-Action Report, 1st Armored Brigade (1 April–2 May 1972) Advisory Team 155 G-3 Journal, 28 April 1972.
2. USAF, SEA, Monograph Series, Vol. II, Monograph 3. P.49.
3. Truong. "Easter Offensive." P.40–41.
4. Devins, Joseph, USA. Input for After-Action Report, 57th ARVN Regiment: April 18–2 May 1972. P.7.
5. Giap, Vo Nguyen. *People's War, Peoples Army*. P. 206–217 vividly record the NVA's systematic encirclement and isolation of the French strongpoints at Dien Bien Phu during April and May 1954.
6. Joy. A.A. Report. P.6. Interview with Major Emmett Huff, USMC, 1983.

**Chapter Eighteen**

1. Vien. "Leadership." P.132.
2. Golden, Glen, USMC. Oral History Tape #6216: Debrief/ Fall of Quang Tri City (18 April–1 Sept. 1972). Goode, Charles J., Jr. and Wells, M. R. Oral History Tape Transcript: Brigade 147's Withdrawal from Quang Tri City: 27 April–2 May. Interview notes 1983, 1984. Also, Oral His-

tory Tape Transcript provided to author and interviews, 1983, 1984.

3. Brookbank. Report. P.18. Also, Truong. "Easter Offensive." P.45, 46. Also, Golden Transcript.

4. This is a well-documented SAR mission: Mann CHECO Report. P.33–36: Brookbank. Spl. Report. P.17, 18. Golden Transcript and USAF, SEA Monograph Series Vol. III, 3. P.349–51.

5. Brookbank. Special Report. P.19.

6. Sheridan, Robert. "Personal Memoranda: Easter Offensive." Outline for proposed article (written in 1975). P.19.

7. Ibid. P.26,27.

8. Isaacs, Arnold. R. *Without Honor.* P.24,25.

9. Sheridan. P.28.

10. Goode and Wells. Transcripts.

11. Joy. AA Report. P.7.

12. Ibid. P.8,9.

13. Goode and Wells. Transcripts.

14. Price, Donald, USMC. Interviews, 1983.

15. Sheridan. P.2.

16. Ibid. P.34,35.

# Abbreviations

| | |
|---|---|
| AAA | Antiaircraft Artillery |
| ALO | Air Liaison Officer |
| ANGLICO | Air Naval Gunfire Liaison Company |
| ARVN | Army of the Republic of Vietnam |
| CINCPAC | Commander In Chief Pacific |
| CINCPACFLT | Commander In Chief Pacific Fleet |
| COMUSMACV | Commander, U.S. Military Assistance Command, Vietnam |
| COVAN | U.S. Advisor to Vietnamese Armed Forces |
| DASC | Direct Air Support Center |
| DMZ | Demilitarized Zone |
| FAC | Forward Air Controller |
| FB | Fire Base |
| FSB | Fire Support Base |
| JGS | Joint General Staff (VN) |
| JCS | Joint Chiefs of Staff (US) |
| KIA | Killed in Action |
| LAAW | Light Anti Armor Weapon |
| MACV | Military Assistance Command, Vietnam |
| MIA | Missing in Action |
| MR-1 | Military Region One |
| NVA | North Vietnamese Army |
| NGF | Naval Gunfire |
| PF | Popular Forces |
| POW | Prisoner of War |
| POL | Petroleum, Oil, Lubricants |
| RF | Regional Forces |
| RVN | Republic of Vietnam |
| RVNAF | Republic of Vietnam Armed Forces |
| SAM | Surface-to-Air Missile |
| SAR | Search and Rescue Mission |
| TAC AIR | Tactical Air Support |
| USAF | US Air Force |
| USA | US Army |
| USMC | US Marine Corps |
| USN | US Navy |

| VC | Viet Cong |
| VN | South Vietnam |
| VNAF | South Vietnamese Air Force |
| VNMC | South Vietnamese Marine Corps |
| WIA | Wounded in Action |

# Bibliography

Anderson, William C. *BAT-Twenty-one*. Englewood Cliffs, NJ, Prentice-Hall, 1980.

Baker, Mark. *NAM*. New York: William Morrow & Company, Inc., 1981.

Braestrup, Peter. *Big Story: How the American Press & Television Reported and Interpreted the Crisis of Tet in Vietnam and Washington*. Garden City, New York: Anchor Press/Doubleday, 1978.

Browne, Malcolm. *The New Face of War*. Indianapolis, New York: Bobbs-Merrill, 1968.

Bunting, Josiah. *The Lionheads*. New York: George Braziller, Inc., 1972.

Del Vecchio, John M. *The 13th Valley*. New York: Bantam Books, 1982.

Doyle, Edward and Samuel Lipsman, Ed. *Vietnam Experience*, 3 vols. Boston Publishing Company, 1983.

Dunstan, Simon. *Vietnam Tasks: Armor in Battle, 1945–1975*.

Fall, Bernard B. *Street Without Joy*. Harrisburg, Pa.: The Stackpole Company, 1961–64.

Fall, Bernard B. *Hell in a Very Small Place: The Siege of Dien Bien Phu*. New York: Vintage Books, 1968.

Fanning, Louis A. *Betrayal in Vietnam*. New Rochelle, N.Y. Arlington House. 1976.

Giap, Vo Nguyen. *People's War, People's Army*. Hanoi: Foreign Languages Publishing House, 1974.

Giap, Vo Nguyen. *Big Victory, Great Task*. New York: Frederick A. Praeger, 1968.

Henderson, William Darryl. *Why The Viet Cong Fought*. Westport, Connecticut: Greenwood Press, 1979.

Herbert, Anthony B. (with James T. Wooten). *Soldier*. New York: Dell Publishing Co., 1973.

Herr, Michael. *Dispatches*. New York: Alfred A. Knopf, 1977.

Isaacs, Arnold, R. *Without Honor: Defeat in Vietnam and Cambodia*. Baltimore: The Johns Hopkins University Press, 1983.

Kalb, Martin and Bernard Kalb. *Kissinger*. Boston-Toronto: Little, Brown & Company, 1974.

Knappman, Edward W. *South Vietnam, Vol. 7. U.S.-Communist Confrontation in Southeast Asia, 1972–1973*. New York: Facts on File, Inc., 1973.

Knoebl, Kuno. *Victor Charlie*. London, England: Pall Mall Press, 1967.

Lewy, Guenter. *America in Vietnam*. Oxford-New York-Toronto-Melbourne: Oxford University Press, 1978.

Manchester, William. *Goodbye Darkness*. Boston, Mass: Little, Brown & Company, 1979.

Mersky, Peter B. and Polmar, Norman. *The Naval Air War in Vietnam*. Annapolis, Md: The Nautical and Aviation Publishing Company of America, 1981.

Mersky, Peter B. *U.S. Marine Corps Aviation: 1912 to the Present*. Annapolis, Md: The Nautical and Aviation Publishing Company of America, 1983.

Millet, Allen Reed. *A Short History of The Vietnam War*. Bloomington, Ind: Indiana University Press, 1979.

Nolan, Keith. *Battle For Hue: Tet 1968*. Novato, Calif.: Presidio Press, 1983.

O'Ballance, Edgar. *The Wars in Vietnam: 1954–1980*. New York: Hippocrene Books, Inc. 1981.

Oberdorfer, Don. *Tet*. Garden City, NY: Doubleday & Co., 1971.

Pan, Stephen & Lyons, Daniel. *Vietnam Crisis*. New York: East Asian Research Institute, 1966.

Pearson, Willard, Lt. Gen., USA. *The War in the Northern Provinces, 1966–1968*. Washington, D.C.: Department of the Army, 1975.

Pisor, Robert. *The End of the Line: The Siege of Khe Sanh*. New York: W. W. Norton & Company, 1982.

Schemmer, Benjamin F. *The Raid*. New York: Harper & Row, 1976.

Simmons, Edwin H. Brig. Gen., USMC. *The United States Marines, 1775–1975*. New York: The Viking Press, 1976.

Starry, Donn A., Gen., USA. *Armored Combat in Vietnam*. New York: Arno Press, 1980.

Tran Van Don. *Our Endless War*. San Rafael, Calif.: Presidio Press, 1978.

Vandegrift, A.A. Gen. as told by Robert A. Asprey. *Once a Marine*. New York: W. W. Norton & Company, Inc., 1964.

Webb, James. *Fields of Fire*. Englewood Cliffs, NJ: Prentice-Hall, 1978.

Westmoreland, William C., Gen. USA. *A Soldier Reports*. Garden City, NJ: Doubleday & Company, Inc., 1976.

Wheatcroft, Andrew. *The World Atlas of Revolutions*. New York: Simon & Schuster, 1983.

# Unpublished U.S. Documents

Brookbank, David, Maj., USAF. *March 1972 Progress Report: Air Liaison Officer 3d Infantry Division (ARVN).* (31 March 1972).

Brookbank, David, Maj., USAF. *Special Report VNAF Tacs and the Fall of Quang Tri.* (31 July 1972).

Camper, William C., Lt. Col., USA and Brown, Joseph, Jr., Maj., USA. *Special Report: Surrender at Camp Carroll.* (13 April 1972).

Dorsey, J. W., III, Col., USMC. *Vietnamese Marine Corps/Marine Advisory Unit Historical Summary.* 1954–1973 (22 March 1973).

Eisenstein, Joel, B., 1st Lt., USMCR. *Naval Gunfire Liaison Officers' After-Action Report.* (30 March–10 April 1972) (30 April 1972).

Joy, Jim R., Maj., USMC. *After-Action Reports, Marine Brigade 147, VNMC.* (30 March–2 April 1972) (22 April–3 May 1972).

Kroesen, Frederick J., Maj. Gen., USA (as referenced in) *"1972 Vietnam Counteroffensive,"* BB 100-2 Command & General Staff Course 1974, Ft. Leavenworth, Kansas. Selected Readings & Tactics.

O'Toole, Thomas, Capt., USMC. *After-Action Report: Easter Offensive; Personal Evaluation* (April 1972).

Oldhan, R., Lt. Comdr., USN, Medical Officer, Marine Advisory Unit, VNMC. *Special Report: Medical Support in the Vietnamese Marine Corps Between 30 March 1972–14 April 1972* (19 April 1972).

Pratt, Stanley G., Maj., USMC. *Special Report on Movement of VNMC Division Headquarters and Brigade 369 from Saigon to Hue; 3–4 April 1972.* (18 April 1972).

Mann, David K., Capt., USAF. *The NVA 1972 Invasion of Military Region I: Fall of Quang Tri and Defense of Hue.* (7th AF CHECO Report).

Randall, D. C., Jr., Capt., USMC. *After-Action Report: Counter-Battery Fire FB Mai Loc.* (18 April 1972).

Ripley, John W., Capt., USMC. *After-Action Report Evaluation of the NVA Easter '72 Offensive.* (14 Jan. 1973).

331

Sheridan, Robert F., Maj., USMC. *Personal Memoranda: Easter Offensive.*

Smith, Raymond L., Capt., USMC. *After-Action Report.* (30 March–1 April 1972).

Smock, James E., Maj., USA. *Letter to U.S. Marine Corps Historical Division, Navy Yard.* Washington, D.C. (23 March 1976).

Sweeney, William T., Maj., USMC. *After-Action Report on 2d Bn. VNMC.* (8 May 1972).

Turley, Gerald H., Lt. Col., USMC. *Special Report to Commander, U.S. Naval Forces, Vietnam: Combat Situation/Actions for Period 30 March–2 April 1972.*

Wagner, Louis C., Lt. Col., USA. *After-Action Report, 1st Armor 14 April 1972.*

Wright, Regan, Maj., USMC. *After-Action Statement: 30 March–14 April 1972.*

Warren, William, Maj., USMC. *Special Report: Personal Evaluation and Comments on Easter '72 Offensive.* (22 April 1972).

U.S. Army Advisory Team 155, 3d ARVN Division, First Regional Assistance Command, MACV. *Combat Operations After-Action Report.* (30 March–1 May 1972). Archives Files, National Federal Records Center (NFRC), Suitland, Md.

U.S. Army Advisory Team 155, 3d ARVN Division, First Regional Assistance Command, MACV. *Combat Operations Report, Quang Trung 729.* NFRC, Suitland, Md.

U.S. Army Advisory Team 155, 3d ARVN Division, First Regional Assistance Command, MACV. *Daily Staff Journal, G-3 Operations, Quang Tri Province.* (28 March–15 May 1972).

U.S. Army Advisory Team 155, 3d ARVN Division, First Regional Assistance Command, MACV. *After-Action Reports, Senior Advisor 57th Infantry Regiment.* (28 March–17 April and 18 April–2 May 1972).

MACV. *Special Intelligence Report (declassified): The Nguyen Hue Offensive.* MACV. *Historical Study of Lessons Learned.* January 1973.

MACV, First Regional Assistance Command, 20th Tank Squadron (ARVN). *Fact Sheet; Operations 1 April–2 May 1972.* (undated).

U.S. Marine Corps, Marine Advisory Unit, Naval Forces, Vietnam. *Historical Summary*. April 1972.

U.S. Marine Corps, Marine Advisory Unit, Naval Forces, Vietnam. *Historical Summary*. May 1972.

U.S. Army, Commander, U.S. Military Assistance Command, Vietnam (COMUSMACV). *Daily Operational Summary (OPSUM)—Reports to JCS*. March, April, May 1972. Military History Library. Carlisle Barracks, Pa.

U.S. Army Advisory Team 155, 3d ARVN Division, First Regional Assistance Command, MACV. *Recommendations for Decoration For Merit*. (MACV Form 200). Narratives and proposed citations of over twenty U.S. advisory personnel cited during period (30 March–5 May 1972).

# U.S. Government Documents

Hinh, Nguyen Duy, Maj. Gen., ARVN. *Lam Son 719;* Indochina Monograph Series. Washington, D.C. U.S. Army Center of Military History, 1979.

Hinh, Nguyen Duy, Maj. Gen., ARVN. *Vietnamization and the Cease-Fire,* Indochina Monograph Series. Washington, D.C. U.S. Army Center of Military History, 1979.

Le Gro, William E., Col., USA. *Vietnam From Cease-Fire to Capitulation.* Washington, D.C. U.S. Army Center of Military History, 1980.

Lung, Hoang Ngoc, Col., ARVN. *Intelligence:* Indochina Monograph Series. Washington, D.C. U.S. Army Center of Military History, 1981.

Mann, David K., Capt., USAF, 7th AF CHECO Report. *The NVA 1972 Invasion of Military Region I: Fall of Quang Tri and Defense of Hue.* 1973.

Starry, Donn A., Gen., USA. *Mounted Combat in Vietnam.* Department of the Army, Washington, D.C., 1978.

Tho, Tran Dinh, Brig. Gen., ARVN. *Pacification:* Indochina Monograph Series. Washington, D.C. U.S. Army Center of Military History, 1979.

Truong, Ngo Quang, Lt. Gen., ARVN. *The Easter Offensive of 1972.* Indochina Monograph Series. Washington, D.C.: U.S. Army Center of Military History, 1980.

Truong, Ngo Quang, Lt. Gen., ARVN. *RVNAF and U.S. Operational Cooperation and Coordination.* Indochina Monograph Series. Washington, D.C. U.S. Army Center of Military History, 1980.

Vien, Cao Van, Gen. et al. *The U.S. Advisor,* Indochina Monograph Series. Washington, D.C., U.S. Army Center of Military History, 1980.

Vien, Cao Van, Gen., ARVN and Khuyen Dong Van, Lt. Gen., ARVN. *Reflections on the Vietnam War:* Indochina Monograph Series. Washington, D.C. U.S. Army Center of Military History, 1980.

Vien, Cao Van, Gen., ARVN and Khuyen Dong Van, Lt. Gen.,

ARVN. *Leadership:* Indochina Monograph Series. Washington, D.C. U.S. Army Center of Military History, 1981.

U.S. Air Force. *Airpower and the 1972 Spring Invasion.* USAF Southeast Asia Monograph Services, Vol. II, Mono 3. U.S. Government Printing Office, 1976.

U.S. Marine Corps. *An Analysis of Marine Corps Readiness in Action.* MCOAG Report. Headquarters, Fleet Marine Force Pacific, Camp Smith, Hawaii, 1972.

U.S. Marine Corps. *The Marines in Vietnam 1954–1973.* An Anthology and Annotated Bibliography. History and Museum Division, USMC, Navy Yard, Washington, D.C., 1974.

U.S. Marine Corps. *The Marine in Vietnam, The Advisory & Combat Assistance Era.* Capt. Robert H. Whitlow, USMC. History and Museum Division, Navy Yard, Washington, D.C., 1977.

U.S. Navy. *Documentation and Analysis of U.S. Marine Activity in Southeast Asia:* 1 April–31 July 1972. Center of Naval Analysis Study 1016. Arlington, Va., 1976.

U.S. Navy. *Defense of Hue and Quang Tri City.* The 1972 NVN Invasion of MR-1: Prepared for Office of the Chief of Naval Operations (OP-03). (CNS 1035) Center of Naval Analysis. Arlington, Va., 1974.

# Articles

Braestrup, Peter, "Destruction of Bridge Halted Communist Push at Dong Ha." *Washington·Post,* 26 April 1972.

Newspaper files. Thousands of newspaper clippings on the Vietnam War, organized roughly by date and stored at Wilson Center for Scholars, Smithsonian, Washington, D.C. This twice-daily digest of morning and afternoon papers (it often included transcripts of television, radio, and wire service reports) was prepared to keep Pentagon officials aware of every detail of American media coverage of the Vietnam War.

Stacey, K. N., Lt., Royal Australian Armor Corps. "North Vietnam Armor Operations: The Lessons of 1972 and 1975." *Armor Magazine,* July–August 1981.

Duncan, Donald. "Khe Sanh," *Life,* Vol. 64, No. 8, February 23, 1968.

Tran, Pham. "The Red 1972 Spring-Summer Offensive." Magazine published by Asian Peoples Anti-Communist League, Saigon (May 1972).

Turley, G. H., Lt. Col., USMC, and M. R. Wells, Capt., USMC. "Easter Invasion 1972," *Marine Corps Gazette* Vol. 57, No. 3, March 1973.

"A Conference Report: Some Lessons and Non-Lessons of Vietnam: Ten Years After the Paris Peace Accords. Woodrow Wilson International Center For Scholars, Smithsonian, Washington, D.C. 1983.

# Oral History Tapes and Interviews

Arnold, Gene, Lt. Col., USMC. Personal notes in preparation of official U.S. Marine Corps History on U.S. Marine Corps Actions, Vietnam, 1971 and 1972.

Battreall, Raymond R., Col., USA. (U.S. Army Advisory Group). Oral History Tape #2034, Military History Branch, MACV, Headquarters. (Maj. Walter Scott Dillard, Interviewer) (January 1973). Military History Library, Carlisle Barracks, Pa.

Boomer, Walter E., Col., USMC. U.S. Marine Corps Oral History Tape. Loss of FB Sarge. (March–April 1972) and interview notes of 1983.

Camper, William C., Lt. Col., USA. Oral History Tape (U.S. Advisor to 2d ARVN and 56th ARVN Infantry Regiments, 3d Division). Quang Tri Province (March–April 1972) and interview notes of 1983.

Cockell, Robert, Maj., USMC. U.S. Marine Corps Oral History Tape #5090.

DeBona, Andrew, Maj., USMC. U.S. Marine Corps Oral History Tape (March–April 1972) and interview notes of 1983.

Eisenstein, Joel B., 1st Lt., USMC. U.S. Marine Corps Oral History Tape. (1 April 1972 Evacuation from Alpha 2) and interview notes of 1983.

Gnibus, Thomas, Maj., USMC. U.S. Marine Corps Oral History Tapes #5086/5087.

Golden, Glen, Maj., USMC. Debrief/The Fall of Quang Tri City. (18 April–1 Sept. 1972). U.S. Marine Corps Oral History Tape #6216, and interview notes of 1983.

Goode, Charles J., Jr., Col., USMC. Wells, M. R., Lt. Col., USMC. Oral History Tape. Brigade 147's Withdrawal From Quang Tri City: (27 April–2 May 1972) and interview notes during 1983–84.

Marine Advisors Conference, U.S. Naval Academy (February 28, 1973). U.S. Marine Corps Oral History Tape #1030.

Metcalf, Donald J., Col., USA. Oral History Tape, Military History Branch, MACV Headquarters (September 1972). Military History Library, Carlisle Barracks, Pa.

Nettleingham, Allen, Capt., USMC. U.S. Marine Corps Oral History Tape #5085. (March–April 1972).

Phillip, George, Capt., USMC. U.S. Marine Corps Oral History Tapes #5086/5087. (March–April 1972).

Randall, David S., Capt., USMC. U.S. Marine Corps Oral History Tape #5093. (March–May 1972).

Ripley, John W., Capt., USMC. U.S. Marine Corps Oral History Tapes #5090, 5091, 6032. (March–April 1972) and series of interviews 1982, 1983, 1984.

Warren, William, Maj., USMC. U.S. Marine Corps Oral History Tapes #5094, 5095 and interview notes of 1983.

Wischmeyer, William, Capt., USMC. U.S. Marine Corps Oral History Tapes #5094, 5095 and series of interviews 1981, 1982, 1983.

Wright, Regan, Maj., USMC. U.S. Marine Corps Oral History Tapes #5089/5090. (March–May 1972) and series of interview notes during 1982, 1983.

Wright, Regan, Maj., USMC. *Oral History Tape: Easter Offensive.* (June 1983).

# INDEX